Not Dark

A Celebration of John Herdman

NOT DARK YET

A CELEBRATION OF JOHN HERDMAN

LEAMINGTON BOOKS

Contents

Foreword

As fervent readers and supporters of John Herdman's work we decided in late 2020 to compile an anthology to mark John's eightieth birthday, in July 2021. We were bowled over when our call for submissions elicited such a vibrant range of responses in the form of essays, poems, fiction, criticism, memoirs and interviews. The contributions that make up this book reflect the ways in which John, through his writing and as an individual, has reached and moved many people.

Some of the cast of this book are John's contemporaries and friends, others are his students and readers. Being witness to the strength of admiration that exists for John's work has been encouraging, especially when — as at least one contributor here has pointed out — that work extends now over a period of seven decades. And seven decades is impressive — especially for a man who is only just turning 80 years old.

John, let us wish you many happy returns. We hope this book reaffirms within yourself the many literary, academic, political and personal contributions you have made over a working life which has been dedicated to excellence, in all your endeavours. We additionally hope that in time this book adds to the growing body of work on the Edinburgh and Scottish literary scenes of the second half of the 20th century. Our last and most important hope is that with this volume you enjoy the belated recognition your writing richly deserves.

Peter Burnett and Richie McCaffery, editors
July, 2021

The Background of a Friendship

D. M. Black

In this *festschrift* for John Herdman's eightieth birthday, I thought I would write something about the background of what has grown over the years into a deeply precious friendship. Dante in Purgatory writes about the pleasure of seeing a friend's face — paradoxically, on the terrace of gluttony, where souls are so starved that their faces have become unrecognisable — and that apparently simple pleasure is, I think, close to the heart of the matter. (It's ironic to be writing this essay after a year in which 'lockdown' to do with the Covid-19 pandemic has forbidden most of us to see our friends' faces.)

In a quite factual sense, John Herdman is my oldest friend. Aside from my brother, there is no one else alive whom I have known and been known by for so long and so (relatively!) consistently. We must have met first when we were both aged ten or eleven, and both disoriented. I had recently moved to Scotland from what was then Tanganyika, now Tanzania, and was gradually coming to terms with a world in which roads were lined with something called pavements, trees lost their leaves in something called autumn, and in something called winter ice formed in fern-like patterns on the inside of one's bedroom window. John had made a less theatrical transition but still a very unsettling one. He had been expelled from the safe setting of a prosperous middle class home in Wester Coates, Edinburgh, to the scary uncertainties of a single-sex boarding school in St Andrews, where frightening bullying went on behind the bike-sheds and there was little sense of anyone around who was 'in loco parentis'. (When I write this I still catch myself thinking: why on earth did he have to make this transition? Were there not at least equally good schools in Edinburgh?)

I was a 'dayboy' at the same school, and though I heard rumours of these fears it was only much later, talking with John in adult life, that I learnt more about them specifically. The time was the early 1950s: Britain was impoverished, still recovering from World War II, still not entirely free of rationing; several children at the school had no fathers (they had been killed in the war); corporal punishment was taken for granted; emotional education was largely limited to contempt for anyone who 'made a fuss'. Dutiful children, we learnt not to make a fuss, even about bullying, even about neglect, often at great cost in later life.

John and I got to know each other well a year or two later, when we were both in the top form, a small group of 'clever boys' — seven, I think — who were being groomed for scholarships to the next phase, 'public school', in this academically privileged, emotionally witless education system. This small group, however, was a good experience for both of us: important relationships were forged, and for John and me it gave what became the basis of a lifelong friendship.

John went on to Merchiston Castle School in Edinburgh, I to Trinity College, Glenalmond, in Perthshire. We didn't meet again for many years but, unusually for teenage boys, we wrote letters to each other for two or three years — about what, I have no idea! We were both precociously 'literary' in our interests. I heard at some point that John had gone on from Merchiston to Magdalene College, Cambridge, where he graduated impressively with a double first in English. I have no picture of what else was happening to him during these years. Superficially, my path was less straightforward: I became depressed, left school a year early, spent a year teaching in France, went to Edinburgh university for a year and then dropped out and spent two years working in London. By the time I returned to Edinburgh to study philosophy, John had already graduated from Cambridge.

The apparent straightforwardness of his path, however, was clearly misleading: he might well have gone on into an academic career, for which he had obvious talent — and he did indeed start on postgraduate work in Cambridge — but he then made a momentous decision: he returned to Edinburgh, determined to commit himself to Scotland and Scottish culture. He too came back to Edinburgh therefore, in the early 1960s, disappointing his father, who had looked forward to his gifted son pursuing a conventional career. But John was now marching to at least two very different drummers.

One was nationalism. While at Cambridge, despite his academic success, he had become intensely aware of his 'difference', as a Scot, from his English contemporaries. I was interested, while meditating this piece, to see a letter in *The Guardian* from a Scottish woman who was at Cambridge in the later 1960s. She described how, even at that date, she was ridiculed for her accent, told 'jokes' about the meanness of the Scots, and 'invited to fuck off back to Scotland'; she attributed it to the persistent 'othering' tendency of the British class system, by which I suspect she meant in particular the world of private education. Presumably such miserable experiences were standard fare for outsiders in this domain of privileged Englishness. More encouragingly, while at Cambridge John discovered the modern Irish writers, above all Joyce, though also Yeats and Beckett, and recognised that there were hugely different and more serious ways in which the English language could be used and the world of English-Englishness regarded. By the time I re-met him in the 1960s, his nationalist views (already intensely strong) were closely modelled on those of Ireland and recent Irish history.

The second drummer was continental Romanticism. Rimbaud has a lot to answer for! The image of the marvellously gifted adolescent, contemptuously rejecting all adult expectations of him, going his own way, mocking all respectable good sense about sexuality, drugs, education, or career — and yet producing compellingly and intoxicatingly communicative writing — that was an image whose appeal was very hard to withstand. (The young Joyce of course had something of the same quality.) When John came to write his first independently published booklet, *Descent,* at the age of twenty-three, his models were the Rimbaud of *Une Saison en Enfer,* and also Rilke's *Notebooks of Malte Laurids Brigge,* another product of no-holds-barred late romanticism.

I call these two different drummers, but of course in the 1920s and 1930s the youthful Hugh MacDiarmid had marched to a rather similar pair. I don't know exactly when John became aware of MacDiarmid, but in the 1950s MacDiarmid and Scottish nationalism were virtually synonymous; by the time John and I started to re-meet, occasionally, in the middle 1960s, Joyce and MacDiarmid are the two writers I remember him as most frequently quoting. (He has always had a most impressive memory, and an ability to quote fluently large chunks of the writers he loved.)

Mentioning MacDiarmid reminds me of John's gift for mimicry. If he spoke of MacDiarmid, he might suddenly fall into mimicking MacDiarmid's very distinctive accent and manner with hallucinating precision. Many people are good mimics, but John had a quite exceptional talent. Later, he could be more like Sorley MacLean than Sorley himself; he could take off many figures on the Scottish scene in a way that seemed to go beyond superficial mannerism, and to actually re-enact characteristic movements of thought or feeling. Whether the intention was homage or parody was not always clear: perhaps it was sometimes neither, but more a recognition of the unalterable fact of otherness. The effect could be hilarious, but sometimes also surprising, and in a way disconcerting. John has always been very emphatically himself; he has always had strong moods and strong views, held passionately and very articulately; his sudden transformation into a totally different persona could be startling.

This talent must have had something in it that was disturbing for him too. I remember at one point his comic identification with an anarchic, alcoholic character whom he called 'wee Davie' became so extreme that he said (how seriously I am not sure) that he felt at risk of being taken over; he deleted wee Davie from his menu of alternative personalities. The acute observation that mimicry of this sort involves must also have contributed to his novelist's capacity to create character; it links too with his interest in the idea of 'doubles'" and multiple personalities — said to be a Scottish preoccupation, and certainly a preoccupation for John. (He later wrote an entire book on the subject, a work of academic criticism, *The Double in Nineteenth-Century Fiction* (Macmillan, 1990), in which he discussed its history in the work of Hoffman, James Hogg, Poe, Dostoevsky, Robert Louis Stevenson, and others.)

John in adult life has always been a nationalist. For a time in the 1960s his nationalism became close to fanaticism. He was involved with *Catalyst,* a strongly nationalist magazine (he was its editor for two issues), and he spoke of a willingness to die for Scotland. His moral seriousness was very impressive, and sometimes had an almost religious quality. And so it was, once again, surprising, when he started to publish his own work, to discover how intensely personal it was, and how remote, apparently, from the banal world of practical politics. It was clear that his literary trajectory was going to take him in a very different direction, towards much more imaginative, more 'confessional' and more self-interrogating work.

In my recollection, we didn't see much of each other in the later 1960s, but we were both by then publishing in the same circles, those around Duncan Glen's magazine *Akros* and Bob Tait's *Scottish International.* John wrote a generous piece about my own early work in *Scottish International* for February 1971. And when Alan Jackson published his splendidly satirical essay on Scottish nationalism, 'The Knitted Claymore' (*Lines Review*, June 1971), John and I were both among the people who responded to it. Gradually in the mid-1970s, as we both emerged into more adult personalities, we re-established our friendship on a much more definite basis. But before coming to that, I would like to comment briefly on John's earliest self-standing publication, *Descent*.

This twenty-five-page, self-published pamphlet (written at the age of twenty-three though not published until four years later in 1968) is a most extraordinary document — not obviously fiction, not a short story, but a sustained account of an agonisingly tormented state of mind. I am still surprised and rather distressed by it when I reread it. Macdonald Daly, in his excellent Introduction to John's *Four Tales* (Zoilus Press, 2000), describes it as a series of 'prose poems', and that may well be a good way to think of it. And I am inclined to agree with Daly that, for all its limitations, *Descent* is a key to many of John's preoccupations, which were then 'narrativised' in the early novels (those written in the 1970s). John tells me that, when he wrote it, he hadn't yet discovered Dostoevsky (later a major influence); he relates it directly to the Rimbaud and Rilke pieces I have already mentioned. And in some ways it reads like a nineteenth-century production. It's written in an extravagantly mannered, high-Romantic style, recklessly willing to go to extremes, but at the same time, it contains in concentrated form the themes that would unroll in John's work (from then on unmistakably 'fiction') over the next fifteen years. These include: religious yearning and fear of damnation, fascination with the past, an extreme sense of isolation and corresponding longing to belong, and profoundly ambivalent feelings about the body and sexuality. What is not present is the humour of the later work, and the ability to stand outside the emotions described and present them in a perspective, linked perhaps with the gift for mimicry, that perceives them (usually) in exaggeration or caricature.

The age of twenty-three, which I think of as approximately the end of adolescence, must have been a difficult time in John's life. In an interview in *Southfields*, also with Daly, John described himself as at that time 'a distinctly dysfunctional individual', though I doubt if he ever appeared like that to anyone except himself. His decision to stay in Scotland, and pursue a literary career, was opposed by his father, who wanted him to become a lawyer; there could well be a connection between that rift and the painful sense of isolation conveyed by *Descent*. In his much later memoir of the 1960s, *Another Country* (2013), John speaks intriguingly of his father as 'in a modest way a specimen of the 'Deacon Brodie' type, the double personality, which bourgeois Edinburgh repeatedly throws up'. This of course is the theme of the double again. This sort of double personality, severe and rule-setting at home, relaxed and permissive (even, in the case of Deacon Brodie, criminal) elsewhere, is hardly peculiar to Scotland — I think of Naguib Mahfouz's wonderful Cairo Trilogy, in which the patriarch 'Abd al-Jawad plays this role — and presumably it's common in societies in which there is acute anxiety, perhaps inflamed by a censorious religion, about ethics and sexuality. Typically, the rule-governed children of these divided parents are likely to be at sea when they encounter the actual world of adulthood for themselves; typically as well, in Edinburgh as in Mahfouz's supposedly teetotal Cairo, alcohol often provides the lubricant between the two parts of the 'double personality'. John's memoir is full of extraordinary characters, often expressing themselves with startling arrogance or contempt for one another — it's worth remembering that most of the Scottish writers of the 1960s spent an inordinate amount of time in pubs, and those who didn't — many of the best of them, in my view, including Robert Garioch, Ian Hamilton Finlay, and Edwin Morgan — tended to be regarded rather patronisingly. For someone like John, with austerely high academic standards, and yet passionately committed to the vehement world of Scottish writing, the 1960s must have been fascinating but his sense of isolation is also understandable.

One might make a comparison with Sydney Goodsir Smith, another product of the British private education system, who disappointed his father's conventional expectations for him, and committed himself with a passion equal to John's to the world of Scotland and Scottish poetry. It is tempting to say that 'wee Davie' got the better of Goodsir Smith: his best work was done before the age of forty and he drifted on into ever-less-productive alcoholism. John had the balance and determination to avoid such a fate, and in the 1970s he began to find a recognisable and original voice. He published *A Truth Lover* in 1973, *Memoirs of My Aunt Minnie/Clapperton* in 1974, and *Pagan's Pilgrimage* in 1978 — all now quite clearly fiction, and increasingly with the resources to reflect with more perspective on the sorts of mental states that had dominated *Descent*.

This was also the time when our friendship was renewed. It was partly on the basis of shared memories of schooldays — always very vivid in John — and our shared feeling for Modernist writing in general, and Scottish writing in particular. But a third element was also important: we were both becoming increasingly interested in religion. I had spent a year at the start of the 1970s with the Findhorn community on the Moray Firth, in those days still run by its founders, Peter and Eileen Caddy; nearby was the Benedictine Abbey of Pluscarden, which I had visited a number of times. I knew several of the monks there, and discovered to my surprise that John too had spent time at Pluscarden; he knew several of the monks, and was profoundly drawn to the simplicity and beauty of the Latin 'office' — the daily schedule of religious services that marks out the Benedictine day. At the beginning of the 1980s he officially converted to Catholicism, and for a long time he felt a strong attraction to the monastic life — much later he was even, briefly, to 'test his vocation' at Pluscarden. Initially, however, he was more strongly drawn in another direction, and in 1983 he married the well-known actress and singer Dolina MacLennan. They moved from Edinburgh to Blair Atholl and John's life entered a very new phase.

The person with whom my friendship now deepened had very different characteristics from those of the author of *Descent*. What I discovered or (to be more accurate I think) rediscovered was a person of extraordinary warmth, kindness, and loyalty. When Dante speaks of the pleasure of seeing the face of his friend, Forese Donati, my spontaneous association is to the pleasure of re-meeting John and of feeling safe in the warmth of his greeting and his company. The author of *Descent* is undoubtedly there, somewhere, but writing has been for John a path to self-knowledge and self-development; moreover, whatever difficult emotions he has had to wrestle with, in friendship he has always been able to emerge into generosity and genuine kindness. He can be very funny. He knew the Scottish writing scene very well, and loved many people in it, including Thomas MacDonald (Fionn Mac Colla), Duncan Glen, Sorley MacLean, Willie Neill, Stuart MacGregor, Rory Watson, Walter Perrie, Donald Campbell, Trevor Royle … the list is a long one, and I'm sure I should add many more names.

When Freud tried to understand the mystery of his own 'Jewishness', so powerful even though he believed neither in the religion nor in Zionism, he spoke of *die Heimlichkeit der inneren Konstruktion* (the comforting familiarity of their inner construction): he was at home among Jews because there was some way in which he and they were similarly 'inwardly constructed'. If I were to try to speak of this feeling of friendship psychologically, I would want to use some similar phrase. It must describe the real ground of the emotion that takes political form as nationalism.

Much more recently, in a 'conversation' with Walter Perrie and Richie McCaffery (Fras Publications, 2020), John said that he had found it very difficult to find his own voice, and didn't feel he had really done so until, after the writing of the 1970s had been followed by some ten years of silence, he began to write the series of novels that began with *Imelda* (published by Polygon in 1993) and which includes *Ghostwriting* (1995), *The Sinister Cabaret* (2001), and *My Wife's Lovers* (2007). It's probably on these novels, together with his non-fiction work and his criticism, that his reputation will primarily rest. In them, he goes well beyond the 'narrativisation' of the moods in *Descent* and creates a much wider range of characters, set in a much more fully imagined social context. Rory Watson has described their style as 'Scottish Gothic', and they certainly belong in a Scottish tradition that includes Hogg, Stevenson and David Lindsay. But they belong too in the larger European tradition referenced in John's book on *The Double* (which he wrote shortly before embarking on *Imelda*), and it's not an accident that French and Italian translations of these novels have recently started to appear.

But I want here only to describe something of the background and context of a faithful and steady friendship for which I am deeply grateful. A lifetime involves many changes of direction, assimilations of new influences, 'developments' which may or may not prove to be 'wrong turnings', and so forth, and there is something magical about a friendship that is able to persist and survive all such events, and has a continuity over many decades and, in this case, even back into childhood, and into such very different epochs as that of Scotland in the 1950s and 1960s. I am writing this in early 2021, as the Covid lockdown still grips the country, and one of the things I most look forward to, when we are free once again to visit our friends, is re-meeting John, and feeling once again the security of that warm and reciprocated interest in 'how life is going'.

For John Herdman

They say you are living in the highlands,
close to places you have always loved,

in the same way you loved poetry and people
on those nights with The Heretics in Edinburgh.

You would enter the room along with your friends.
Cordial, a benign presence encouraging everyone,

you brought the depth of your listening powers
by dusk or dawn, happed in your tweed jacket,

to hear stories or rhymes or flyting between poets.
Now old friends are meeting again, they recognise

your keen eye, the gaze that sees and smiles upon
Scotland's far horizon shimmering into view.

Valerie Gillies

Pluscarden Abbey

Hugh Gilbert

There was a time when Pluscarden Abbey, a monastery in Moray, brushed the life of John Herdman and he brushed its. I was fortunate to be there at the time. One literary consequence of John's monastic connection was pp.126ff of *Ghostwriting*, when Torquil Tod heading north in appropriate torment unexpectedly comes across a living Benedictine community. The description of the place, the rituals, some of the actual personalities is accurate; even the fictional Donald Kerr, turned a novice in the story, is more than plausible. I can name the 'very tall and gentle-looking' monk and his 'small and down to earth' companion returning to the monastery from the garden and I can name the 'delightful', practical, unworldly guestmaster — all of them now with their names on crosses in the monastery graveyard. It is a kind of blessing John has left the monastic community by including them in his novella.

I enjoyed his visits which were not infrequent. If guests wonder what passes through the minds of monks, monks of course can wonder what passes through the minds of visiting writers. Stooped and redolently Scottish as he was — he said it was constant walking into wind that fashioned the Scottish face — he was good to have around. He added to the place just by being himself, as surely he has in the world of literature. He seemed to prowl the environs benignly, sometimes with a poet friend from north London. He was often at the liturgical offices that punctuate the monastic day, and the prefatory quotation that heads *Ghostwriting* is a Latin Psalm-verse he would have heard there. He was ever the gracious guest, whatever it was that really filled his mind! I enjoyed his writing, its echoes of various Scottish traditions, its mixture of clarity and mystery, and I was more than susceptible when he let his prose rip. As time passed, I was called elsewhere and John took other directions. I have regrettably failed to follow his writing, but am delighted he has proved himself 'among the strong', as the Psalmist puts it, by reaching his eighty years. He is one of those people one would like to catch up with again. I think Pluscarden Abbey would too. God bless you, John.

When Our Lives Begin

Regi Claire

When our lives began disappearing, we didn't notice at first. Sometimes they simply ran ahead and we lost sight of them. Other times they swerved round hairpin bends spiralling so high we daren't follow. Or else they dipped and fell away into fallow lands where the wheel ruts meandered and thinned into tendrils of weeds. Now and then they played catch-up with us, hiding behind a milestone or in the blue shadow of a rock, almost within reach. As soon as we got nearer, they'd skip away, fleet-footed, helped by a wind that always blew in the right direction. A quick wink over their shoulder was all we'd see.

So we began to plot. With enough care and determination we were sure to snare them.

Conventional traps turned out to be useless; speed bumps and cameras yielded nothing but joy riders, drunk drivers and the occasional motorcyclist opening up the throttle on his Harley or BMW along the arrow-straight road, while steel contraptions caught only rabbits and foxes, eyes white with fear, legs half-gnawed off. Finally, our IT whizz kids came up with the solution: virtual traps. Inspired by the mouths of whale sharks, they designed a sequence of ever-finer e-teeth and filter pads, complemented by snake fangs to induce slewing and temporary paralysis. The success rate was nearly 100%.

At the next board meeting those of us who'd been reunited with our lives voted to promote the techies to grown-up status with immediate effect.

Naturally, our success didn't go unnoticed. Google, hard-nosed and greedy as usual, began to charge us for every life recaptured. The premiums went up month on month, until we were forced to increase the number of e-trap beneficiaries.

Then we had an idea. If Google was so keen on screwing more money out of us, how about luring away the lives of its executives and underlings, perhaps by speeding up their electronic equipment so much they no longer had time to go home and play with their kids or look after their wives? Once they were well and truly spinning out of control in the rat-trap of their existence, *we* would step in, offering assistance.

Instead of lost-property services, we set up 'Lost-Life Services — helping you become who you've always been'. It was lucrative enough, but not satisfying in the long run.

So we sold up and with the proceeds bought ourselves this small island where we now live, young and old together. We grow our own food, catch fish and breed chickens — and of course we plant sunflowers to keep watch over us with their gold-spiked heads.

Should our lives ever decide to run away from us again, they won't get very far. And if they try swimming, our nets will easily retrieve them, saving them from drowning.

John Herdman, a Heretical Appreciation

Craig Gibson

To pen an appreciation of a fellow scribe who is by far my superior in the art of storytelling should be a daunting task. However, as I have had the privilege of knowing 'Gentleman' John Herdman as a friend for some time now, I'll keep it personal and not bore you with any scholarly criticism regarding his lengthy career as a man of letters. I wouldn't dare anyway; I'm nowhere near qualified enough and I don't want to mention the dreaded 'D word' ('duality'), if at all possible. So, instead of all that, please allow me to tell you how we met and what fruits blossomed as a result.

I had attended the launch of John's literary and political memoir *Another Country* (2013) but I never managed to actually meet the man on this occasion (though if you look carefully at John's photo for his Wikipedia entry you can see my hat peeking over his shoulder at said event). Nonetheless, his memoir was a real eye opener and I devoured it eagerly. Fuck me, literary Edina seemed to be a much richer place back in the sixties and seventies. Some of this I knew already, but it was John's depiction of a folk-arts collective named the 'Heretics', of which he had been a founding member, that really blew me away.

Why had I never heard of these people before, and (perhaps more importantly) why was nobody putting on similar events in this day and age? I had a kind of Epiphany moment and so, when my long-term collaborator Peter Burnett of Leamington Books asked me if I would care to interview John about this very subject, I jumped at the chance.

Looking at the footage of this interview now, I am struck by how nervous I appear to be, even though Peter had been feeding me coffee laced with Sambuca for the duration. I had intended to act a bit like Ali G, and had even brought a clipboard as a prop (though to be fair it did have actual notes written on it) but John's effortless manner and genuine suaveness put paid to all that. In fact, in some of the stills from the interview he looks positively *beatific*.

In what proved to be a productive session, he answered all my queries regarding the original Heretics and (perhaps *even* more importantly) gave his blessing to Peter and myself to resurrect the name and activities of the group. His former wife and Heretics co-founder, Dolina MacLennan, was already in the process of organising a reunion of the surviving originals, he informed us, so the timing could not have been better. Doli's blessing was also forthcoming, and so The Heretics were reborn in the autumn of 2015. Monthly gatherings once again became the norm with much camaraderie and fellowship, and would still be happening if it were not for the ghastly Covid virus and its vile consequences. However, as we managed to successfully resurrect The Heretics after a thirty-five-year absence, recovering from lockdown will surely be a breeze, methinks?

Now, as the editor and publisher of a literary broadsheet named the *One O' Clock Gun*, my next logical move after establishing a rapport with John was to request some writing from him. *The Gun*'s raison d'être is to promote new writers and poets, but it is always a joy to include established and respected literary figures alongside them. Therefore, I was delighted when John agreed to pen a new piece for the paper, which began an excellent run of contributions, including a transcript of a Stuart MacGregor (legendary 'Sandy Bells Man' and founding 'Tic) song, composed in the early sixties, but never before appearing in print.

In a way, John reminds me of the late, great Angus Calder who had been something of a mentor to *The Gun*. As well as having a penchant for short grey beards, he has a similarly dry sense of humour and a mischievous twinkle in his eye, and he does not suffer fools gladly (a wannabe heckler at a Heretics evening was firmly put in his place on one occasion by an enraged John, which was *startling* to behold). I must stress, however, that afternoon pub sessions with John, whilst equally convivial and enlightening, are rather more sober affairs than those with Angus!

Above all, though, John is a master storyteller, so it is a grand thing to see that a selection of his novels, short stories and critiques are being reprinted by Leamington Books as he approaches his eightieth birthday. And if I'm not mistaken, I'm sure the auld fellah has many more tales to tell.

I, for one, certainly hope so.

Happy Birthday John, and thanks for everything!

A-just-about-recognisable Country

Morelle Smith

The first part of John Herdman's *Another Country* is a most fascinating memoir of people and places, many of them now disappeared from our landscape; all the more important then, for this era to be documented as John does with such warmth and precision.

I had absolutely no intention of going anywhere near 'another country', that tricksy realm of the past, but that's what seems to have happened. All I can say in my defence is that John might enjoy the riff on his excellent book of the same title, the way that memories arose from rereading it, yes, an inspiration, and the particular memories, of someone who was clearly dear to him, as he also was to me, the poet Sorley MacLean.

The cover of *Another Country* has a picture of the now famous Paperback Bookshop in Charles Street, off George Square, Edinburgh. And we heard recently this year (2021) of the death of its founder, Jim Haynes, that larger than life character who also founded the Traverse Theatre, in its original venue in James Court. Jim Haynes later moved to Paris, where he lived until his death.

As a teenager in the late 1960s I passed this bookshop every day on my way to and from school. It seemed the most natural thing in the world, a bookshop with a rhino's head attached to the wall, for it was part of 'the real world' (i.e. everything outside the artificial world of school) where anything could happen and indeed, *should* happen. From an early age I had always had an immoderate love of books, and haunted the public library, but this was the first bookshop I had ever entered to browse. I do remember talking to some people in there, but had no idea that I was participating in history then, as life for a teenager is all future, one that I could not wait to grasp, live to the full and to experience — everything.

The famous burning of the book (D. H. Lawrence's *Lady Chatterley's Lover*) outside this bookshop had taken place a few years before, as my older sister informed me (she was my main source of interesting information) but this action, and the book's trial for obscenity just seemed like incomprehensible things that happened in the past, ('they do things differently there') that adults did in the dark ages, before enlightenment, the full illumination of which I was clearly living in.

I first met John Herdman many years ago in the early seventies, the days of The Heretics, which he describes so well in *Another Country*. Poets used to gather in the New Town Hotel to read their work. I did not read with them there, I had only just started to write poetry and I was much too shy to stand up in front of others. That would only happen a few years later, in the same venue, when Sorley MacLean invited me.

Sorley was an enormous encouragement to me. In 1973–74 I had been travelling in Europe and Asia, and ended up living and working in Freiburg, Germany. When I came back to Edinburgh towards the end of 1974, a folder of writing in my rucksack, a friend suggested I go to see him. He was then writer in residence at Edinburgh University. I felt very nervous the first time I got into the lift of the David Hume Tower. Apart from one or two friends, I had never shown my work to anyone. And here I was, going to see a real poet, someone of immense stature, experience and authority in the literary world.

The place itself was familiar enough. I had gone into this lift many times before, as a student here. But my relationship to the place was very different now. Then, it had been a big part of my life, it was the place where I belonged, but now — what was I now? I was doing temporary work in bars and offices, I did not know what I was going to do in the future, I had no job prospects, no plan for my life; the only real possession I had was my experience of the past year and a folder of writing. I was about to show these pieces of paper to someone else and as they were the only things of value in my life, the only potential link with the world, I felt that I was offering my life to this stranger, as I handed over the sheets of paper. His reaction to them would determine, so I felt, whether my life had any value, in the world's terms, or not.

In my free time I was spending a lot of time writing, long rambling poems, and some pieces of prose. I was desperate to articulate my experience, and it all came out in looping, weaving strings of images. Occasionally, I would manage to say something simple, direct and descriptive, but mostly my inner world was one of piled metaphors that had no obvious or immediate relevance, that I could see, to life as it was lived by other people.

I remember that time, early in 1975, as one of grey, dull skies, a weight of clouds, slicing rain, and squalls of snow. I had made the decision to stay in this country, now that I was back here, but I was struggling for any sense of connection. Sorley MacLean, though he did not know it, held the validity of my life in his hands, as he read the first two poems I handed to him. The rain gusted across the big window of his office. His chair squeaked as he shifted his weight from chair-arm to table. He sighed loudly as he concentrated on the words in front of him. This convinced me that he thought the words were dreadful, a waste of his time and of my life. Bursts of rain hurled themselves at the window. I wished I had not come. What a way for your life to end, I thought, in an office in a tower-block, in a gusting wind, spitting rain.

When he finally spoke, his words came haltingly, but they seemed to come from his whole being, from his body, from his vast memory, from his love of open spaces, mountains, a grey sea, even the rain. His words came slowly, as if rising from great depths. But what he said about my work was encouraging. And most astonishing of all to me, was that he wanted me to come again, the following week.

I left the building in a break between the clouds. A shaft of sunlight hit a window of the tower-block and it sent out a flash of light.

Sorley's collection of poetry, *Dàin do Eimhir* was out of print, but a friend of mine had a copy, which I borrowed. His language astonished me. Here was someone who was not afraid to talk about emotions, someone in fact, for whom feelings were the central well of creativity, from which he drew. Sometimes these feelings were painful, sometimes difficult to express, sometimes hard to link in with 'ordinary' life. Whatever that might be. I got the feeling that there was very little in Sorley's life that was 'ordinary'. He had the ability, the gift, to breathe the marvellous into the most 'ordinary' of everyday life. Giving you a glimpse of his vision. From then on, both the man and his work became an inspiration to me.

Over the next few weeks, he talked about his experiences in the war, his feelings of regret, still, after all these years, that he did not go to Spain to fight with the International Brigade, against Fascism. He talked about Skye, his own poetry, briefly touched on his years as a teacher. And I listened.

Sorley, I came to realise, was a very large person. This little office could not contain him. Even the picture window, with its view out over Arthur's Seat, could not hold him in. He often closed his eyes, the better to see the inner pictures in the mind's eye. His voice had a deep resonance, which also belonged to open vistas and distant horizons. His voice had the same effect as the bagpipes, which are meant for covering long distances, for linking spaces that would appear to be unbridgeable, a sound that makes the skin tingle and the blood beat faster. To say that he encouraged my writing is an understatement. I wrote *for* him. I saw him once a week in his high-rise office, until the end of the summer term, when his post as writer in residence came to an end. Every week I had something new to show him. It gave my writing a purpose it had not had before. I knew someone was going to read this. Someone who was interested. Someone whose work I admired. Someone who said 'I'd like to see more'. With that kind of encouragement, it was easy to contact the feeling of wanting to write. Other areas of my life caused great problems and difficulties, but contact with the words was not difficult to access and the sheets of paper soon started to pile up.

At the end of his term of office at the university, Sorley gave a public reading of his work at the New Town Hotel. And he asked me if I would read too. I felt very honoured that he should have asked me, but I had never read my work in public before and the prospect filled me with dread. Somehow, I got through the evening and we all drank a copious amount of beer and whisky at the party afterwards, in David Campbell's flat, which helped, in my case, to erase the memory of the terrifying experience.

After Sorley went back to Skye we kept in touch and met up from time to time and each meeting was like a shot of inspiration to me, to keep going with my writing. But it was his initial recognition and response that validated my writing and formed a bridge for me, between my past self and the new one, that I was only just beginning to create. Full of self-doubt and uncertainties, my life a series of temporary jobs, homes and relationships, he was the one who said 'You can do it. You can write. Keep doing it.'

An amusing anecdote took place a few years later, in 1978. My partner and I, along with our two-year-old daughter, spent a few days in spring on the Isle of Skye. Sorley invited us to lunch with him and his wife Renee at their home, while we were there. During this visit he mentioned that he would be reading at an International Poetry Festival in Rotterdam later that year. It so happened that we were also in the Netherlands at this time, staying with a friend in Maassluis, not far from Rotterdam. We did not know which evening Sorley was reading but one evening my partner suggested we drive to Rotterdam. And it turned out that was the very evening that Sorley was reading, and he invited us, hospitable as ever, into the performers' tent for a drink, before the reading.

When it was time for the performance, we duly filed into the large building, to listen. Each poet read in their own language, followed by a translation into Dutch. I remember nothing of any of the others, there might have been French or German poets, which I could have understood, but we were looking forward to hearing Sorley of course, especially as we would be able to understand him. But one thing I had forgotten. When I had heard Sorley read in Scotland, he would read in Gaelic, followed by his English translation. Gaelic was his native language, and so he read in Gaelic, in Rotterdam, followed by a Dutch translation. Not one word was in English!

A few years ago I was walking towards George Square with a couple of friends who were visiting Edinburgh. As we approached the site of the former Paperback Bookshop, I started to tell them the story of this shop and the book burning that took place outside it. The Dugald Stewart building, part of the University of Edinburgh, now stands there. Just as we reached the corner, I looked down. Between the building and pavement, there's a low wall, just the right height for people to sit on. And there on this stone bench for all the world like something that had been placed there and forgotten when the owner stood up and walked away, was a small unobtrusive sculpture. I had passed this way many times since the Dugald Stewart block had been built but had never noticed this before. The plaque on the other side of the wall names it as 'The Haynes Nano-stage' by David Forsyth. The first Traverse Theatre was tiny, with steps up to audience seats, but the sculpture is also in the shape of a book. Yes, definitely a book, with one corner nibbled away, commemorating the famous burnt book.

David Punter, Five Poems

Little Effie's Piece of String

It started with a three-inch-long piece
she found in the garden; we caught her
staring at it, mesmerised. Life went on
(of course) but we saw that soon she
had found more, and — mysteriously –
had knotted them together.
We didn't know she could do knots.

Then there was the mouse.
We were used to mice indoors
(you have to be, with two cats),
always dead, sometime whole, sometimes
gutted, the head some distance from
the tiny grey body, still twitching –
But this one was different.

It was whole, but something had sunk
almost invisibly into its neck.
It wasn't the last. We didn't know much
about string obsessions, but we looked up
Hilaire Belloc and warned little Effie
about the awful fate of Henry King.
But she wasn't chewing. We thought.

Enough with the mice, we said,
and searched little Effie's bedroom
silently while she was asleep,
snoring lightly, innocently.
The piece of string was elegantly
knotted, and by now about three feet
long; no longer suitable for mice.

And then we only had one cat;
we were sad, and especially so when we
discovered the corpse. 'Daddy', she asked
one breakfast-time, in her delicate
lisping way, 'How do you do the gavotte?'
We were not sure that was what she meant;
but maybe she was just stringing us along.

Forgetting Cromer

In Cromer, he thought, it seems
that this is what it all comes down to
a lapping beach, that sick-pink smell of crab
the Hotel de Paris with its rococo crust
the ancient waiter creaking at the seams

He strains at recollection's dust,
it's like sighting through satin
looking through linctus, having a stab
at the swirls in the bottle — he's looking back –
no, sideways, crabwise, wise after
the event — what was the event?

A disastrous occasion, dinner, a mature student
desperate to impress, she'd heard (she beams)
he was recently back from the East

Hong Kong, that jumble of word and sign
on the map, English, Chinese, Xinhua,
Causeway Bay, Wong Tai Sin [sin — hah]
but she'd chosen to cook Korean, or was it Mongolian?
a proud ebony table, she'd put down the hotpot,
a sizzling, wood burning, a fine
covering up with towels, tatterdemalion

But that wasn't Cromer. He reaches desperately.
Sheringham? Or Holkham,
the wide lagoon spread like the faintest of brush-strokes,
was that it? The slight movement
of roughly cooked crabs if you poke 'em

But this was *before*. Before the EU, or even the EC,
when 'our fishing grounds were our own',
no Dutch super-trawlers out rocking on the wild North Sea
(north of what?) yards above drowned Dogger Bank, where we
(or somebody) lived all those many years long gone

He comes to (not for the first time), the linctus at his elbow,
is this what it comes to, shards of shell,
claws scrabbling on the shelf of memory's polyglot
the undersea a faint (he likes this) 'fell glow'

Was he ever in Cromer, was Cromer ever there?
He's hoping, against hope — it's only fair
that his memory isn't crabbed, that his forgettings
aren't summarised in a residue of some past summer,
beyond recall, in the crab's recoil
from temptation, from harm,
from the snapping jaws of the octopus' beach-crawl

Of Cromer, perhaps he has no recollection;
though Cromer may be collecting him,
claws, innards and all,
refashioning him in the likeness of an absent limb

That waiter, where did he go at night as he showed no haste
but revolved through the swinging doors
of some unimaginable kitchen, bowing improbably from the waist,
obeying some sidewise, crablike regulation

Once he'd driven to Kings Lynn,
hoping to see The Wash in all its glory
but got lost in Terrington Saint Clement
with no view of the sea but endless sodden fields
(it's possible that that's a different story)

in which it would be easy to sink, mistaking land for water,
as in Great Grimpen Mire, or the estuary marshes
further south, where lost jewels remain lost
and serpents describe their ever-extending crescent
in vanished causeways, the Broomway,
footprints washed away in deepening trenches

Coming to again from a damp doze, not unpleasant,
wipers swishing and flailing as he looks out
on vistas of nothing, he feels for the linctus —

Doctor Collis Browne's, it used to say,
all cares wiped from the slate sky at little cost

But now earth and water are rectangulated, bisected,
Fitzroy for Finisterre, no more end of the world,
desperation quantified, memory no longer inflected,
brought under control, we should express our gratitude

the waiter is nowhere to be seen
Cromer known only by the dispersing aroma
of crab and sea-water
anemone's memory
in the forgetting
of an antiquated
beach-comber.

Hobbies

Paunch-proud re-enactors, crusaders in doublet and hose
charging through mud, shouting hoarsely of honour and blood

Wizened men stealing off to their attics where the railways run
dreaming of when the machine-tool shop will finally close

Gamers, baton-twirlers, bread-makers and calligraphers,
winemakers and mycologists, skydivers and snowboarders

Lofts of murmuring pigeons after lights out, a stilled longing met
by the one true bird returning from its ineffable journey

Philatelists — never confuse them with philanderers -
lost in contemplation of the final stamp of life's incomplete set

Furniture builders, makers of model ships, Lego addicts, lapidarists,
restorers of ancient vehicles, cruciverbalists, genealogists

Embroiderers, crocheters, knitters of long felt wants,
unending clicking of needles, pincushions stuffed with hope

Radio hams crouched over the waves, sorting sound from sound
crafting a mosaic of noise so that lonely men can dance

In a world of work without soul, where hope might seem in vain
it may be the strangest hobbies that keep us truly sane.

Love's Effects

When you say (my love), rub it here,
and rub it there, and cure the itch,
and I apply it here and there, on your back,
with some cream obtained
from the Pharmacist of Oblivion
(or so I seem to think) and I try to find
the sore spots, and see my applying
and affectionate hand reducing

the irritation, then I experience
what is is not necessarily love,
but one of the many effects of love.
And then I see your careful flesh
and what lies underneath the flesh,
the extraordinary interplay of muscle,
artery, bone (though I am imagining things,
you can see little through the back

unless you are in the grip of love's thrall).
But perhaps the efficacy of such remedies
is forever suspended in the sudden sight
of a perfect back, the live future and
the terror of a primal past, so that
this minor application of an ointment
will play its part in the consolidation
of a love which will live for ever.

Ah! Do you feel better? Not much -
but the night will tell — the slow attrition
of sheets and duvet. And in the morning
will you again need to sit up straight
before me while I begin my slow ritual,
rubbing here, rubbing there, trying to assess
the imponderable effects of love,
a sacred back under my ministering hands?

Making a Day of It

A snatch of Harry Belafonte on the radio
singing 'Mary's Boy Child', though it isn't Christmas.

A small girl in the park picking up a hazel twig
stopping, ambushed in a green hush, as she whips it.

Two robins on the lawn prancing preening in dignity
outside my bee-bombarded study window.

My grand-daughter feeding swans by the lake
while they produce a glare she will later perceive as malevolent.

High fading contrails producing, for a poised moment,
a perfect letter X; immediately erased.

A solicitor's sign advertising 'Wills, bequests, debt advice';
furtive movement behind the smoked panes.

Somewhere else the unheard roar of oceans,
the slow smashing of tectonic plates; lava-flow.

What is it, this gift of sewing fragments together
to make a multicoloured, imperfect day?

David Punter

Living Through Books

Jennie Renton

A trigger warning for the tidy and well-organised: this content includes a graphic description of extreme messiness. Early in 2020 I embarked on hunter-gatherer forays into the paper jungle choking the basement of Main Point Books, in the hope of bringing together the scattered audio files of the interviews I did for *Scottish Book Collector* magazine. One cluster of cassette tapes, my holy grail, remained elusive. I held in my mind's eye a picture of my quarry: a small plastic crate, a dozen or so cassette tapes wedged inside. I had almost begun to think I had confabulated its existence when, delving blind to the bottom of a cardboard box, my fingers touched brittle casing, a series of ridges within: the edges of cassettes. One of these bore a paper label marked in red pen: John Herdman, Perth, 9/5/96.

So there we were, my ramshackle recording equipment set up and my fingers crossed that it would work. Picking up on a snatch of earlier conversation, I pressed Record:

'You were saying you have lived through books …'

John tells me how at the age of seven he started writing 'pastiches' of history books. 'When I was ten, I started to read Walter Scott, Conan Doyle, John Buchan, that sort of thing, and continued to write and to unconsciously imitate the styles of these writers. I also used to spend hours as a child kicking a ball or walking around the garden, making up stories for myself.'

Ghostwriting, set to be published towards the end of May, is to be our main focus. 'Publication dates with Polygon can be a moveable feast,' observes John.

I blether on about the blurring of borders between purported fact and purported fiction in *Ghostwriting*:

'What I'm probably trying to express there is the difficulty of reaching the truth about anything, rather than its impossibility,' he tells me. 'In a way, the book can be read as a criticism of postmodernist theory [using] the sort of technique a lot of postmodernists use to suggest the relativity of reality and the relativity of truth. What I'm trying to say is the opposite. I'm saying, yes, it's very hard to come to the truth of anything but it's not impossible. What the structure of the book is trying to say is that there is actually some truth to be found ... insofar as you regard fiction as a mirror of reality, there is a truth there to be found, somewhere; [the aim is to] guide the reader into looking for this truth, for what it is. As in *Imelda*, there's a kind of puzzle, a detective story element ... what is real and what isn't real? ... but without the postmodernist assumption that in fact nothing's real, that the reader creates the reality. I don't believe that.'

I confess to my ignorance of postmodernist theory.

My voice trails away.

'That's *partly* it,' John supplies gallantly. 'The last two books I've written have been an attempt to write a mystery. In a sense the point is just the pleasure the reader gets in trying to unravel this mystery and to work out what might be untrue. But at the same time there's a comment on the sort of literary theory that I think is very pretentious.'

He dismisses the proposition of the death of the author as 'spurious nonsense' and says more about his motivation, his intention:

'If the writer feels a perception of truth, then what they attempt is to communicate that to somebody else. And so that is one thing, the attempt to communicate insights about the nature of reality. And on the other hand, the sheer pleasure of ... probably the mimetic factor ... as I've said before, I like reproducing, often in a parodic way, the styles of others. I like parody for itself.'

After an excursion into John's book-collecting habits (amassed for content rather than collectability), I encouraged him to recall bookshops and booksellers, as book trade history was always a component of *Scottish Book Collector* interviews.

John obliges by telling me that as a young man in Edinburgh he frequented Brunton's at 38a George Street, recalling its proprietor, Morley Jamieson, as 'a difficult man to get on terms with but very good once you got to know'.

Morley agreed to stock copies of John's first book, a thirty-page pamphlet called *Descent,* self-published in 1968 under the imprint The Fiery Star Press and printed by the redoubtable Callum Macdonald.

'Why did you choose that name?' I wonder.

'That was something to do with an ancestor who stowed away on a ship called *The Fiery Star*.'

The story goes that the ship went on fire and the passengers and crew took to the lifeboats, never to be seen again; whereas the stowaways, who had been abandoned on the burning boat, were all rescued.

After some more discussion we return to the role of the writer and John's rejection of the idea of the writer/artist as a sort of high priest of society.

'I still think that writing is about the communication of truth and the attempt to communicate true insights. But I now see that, in a religious context, as very much subservient to a higher kind of truth. That's one of the greatest dangers in the twentieth century, that the human race is attempting to deify itself.'

John Herdman's words resonate out of my old tape machine. The voice, quiet yet intense, pierces into a hubristic present where relativism is in the ascendancy. It seems somehow apposite that on the table beside me lies a newspaper reporting that human genes have been introduced into monkey foetuses, to 'enhance our understanding' of how human brains develop.

John Herdman: Sonatas on a Ghostly Grand

Alan Riach

Strangers are in my true love's hame
Strangers wha haurdly ken her name
And tho' the country looks the same
    It canna be.

Strangers are in my true love's hame.
She had to leave it when they came,
And oh! the strangers are no' to blame
    – And neither's she!

Hugh MacDiarmid's poem 'Strangers' from *To Circumjack Cencrastus* (1930) might be a poignant motto for the title story of John Herdman's *My Wife's Lovers: Ten Tales* (2007). Whose love is traduced? Whose absence is felt so keenly? Who is the usurper? What presence does not carry guilt? And what can home be, ever?

I first read John Herdman when I bought a copy of *Pagan's Pilgrimage* in Duncan Glen's Akros edition of 1978 and the questions were already there. Home was maybe set by the precedent of James Hogg's *Confessions of a Justified Sinner* (1824), the cradle of a classic of devilish uncertainty and mortal threat, balancing self-righteous tones and language poised on reason at the edge of insanity. I'd read Hogg's novel years before and sensed but couldn't find anywhere a confirmation of what I felt certain was in it: a logic that proposed on one side religious conviction, on the other, murderous madness — or on one side, supernatural visitation, on the other psychological delusion — and all these leading straight to the book's implied judgement: that religious fanaticism is in itself insanity. The supernatural is a conventional term for immaterial reality, which is every bit as real as the material. And just as dangerous. Psychology crazed by religion generates the visions that destroy us. Such religion, embraced and absorbed and enacted, generates the crazed psychology that tears us apart.

Hogg's story ends in death, burial, resurrection and ambiguities unresolved. Except for the undertow that the Devil is God, and God is the Devil, in such a world as Hogg's poor pilgrim lives with. But Herdman's novel is dissolved, resolved, a clenched fist opening into much clearer air. The cradle allows the packed-in potential for destruction to uplift itself and float away in the air. The sinister in Herdman's work is real but the crosscurrent of humour undercuts it, always. But where are we left at the end of *Pagan's Pilgrimage*? Still on that edge. And gauging the balance and what is at stake is the exercise of every one of his stories. Perhaps being pagan is itself a kind of salvation.

The technicalities of that are in the measurement made possible by a narrative presented by the first person singular. The reader is trapped in the narrator's account. We have to judge for ourselves how sympathetic, how repulsive, how justified, how sinful, such a narrator might be. As Iain Banks says in the first sentence of his novel *Transition* (2009), 'Apparently I am what is known as an Unreliable Narrator, though of course if you believe everything you're told you deserve whatever you get.'

This provocative tension characterises John Herdman's fiction. Sometimes its ambiguity takes us through a kind of adventure story, as in *The Sinister Cabaret* (2001), like a John Buchan 'shocker' in its pace and location, but like an exposition of psychological encounters with the reality of others as described by R. D. Laing in its shifting of reliable co-ordinates. In *Pagan's Pilgrimage*, the ending is a release but in *The Sinister Cabaret* it delivers you to an edge of unknowing. Herdman's skill in selecting how and where to take us is a delight. One aspect of this is the weave of autobiographical reality and fictional invention. In 'Plaintiff' from *My Wife's Lovers*, a husband goes for a walk with his wife's dog (the titular character), which disappears down a rabbit hole; a strange person suddenly appears and advises him about how to recover it. He swallows a pill at the stranger's invitation, miniaturises, and follows the dog down the rabbit hole into what we're told is 'the realm of Unplease', where 'everything is very difficult, and truth hard to discern'. This 'realm' is a reversal of Alasdair Gray's city of Unthank from his novel *Lanark* (1981), the contrast marked by the brevity of the story in contrast to the labyrinthine extensions of Gray's novel. Both endorse and exemplify a perennial truth which is nevertheless too often forgotten or suppressed: that reality and imagination need each other and their reciprocation makes the development of the potential of more life possible. Towards the end of the story (I won't say more about it except that it's one of those miniature *frissons* at which Herdman excels), this paragraph comes as a surprise and astonishment:

Walking slowly a little ahead of us I saw a small slightly bowed figure in a green tweed jacket, frail but yet giving an impression of an underlying sturdiness, his head surmounted by a deep, stiff brush of grey hair. I recognised him at once as the poet Hugh MacDiarmid (C. M. Grieve). He entered the domed chamber and made his way to a grand piano in the middle of the room, which had not been there on my previous visit. He jumped onto the piano stool with unexpected sprightliness, and without any pause began to play with astonishing virtuosity and passion. Although the music was familiar to me I could not identify it at the time, but I have since come to think that it must have been Beethoven's 'Apassionata' sonata. Musical performance had never, so far as I was aware, been one of the poet's accomplishments, but now, as if discovering his true essence for the first time, he was filling the domed room with all the consummate artistry of his soul. I was swept away by the music into a tremendous world of spirit in which time and space meant nothing and here and now were contained only in the soaring sound which, I came on an instant to realise, was no sound at all, for it existed ... only inside my own head. What exactly do I mean by that? I know, but I am unable to find the words. But the music I will never forget. Music that spoke of the flawed impassioned perfection of this mortal world and its glorious *felix culpa*. Whoever heard its like on earth or in story? Alas, it was that I heard it that destroyed me.

This is a vision of MacDiarmid nobody but John Herdman could have imagined. Completely at odds with biographical fact, its imaginary reality is completely convincing, both in the physical portrait and the extended metaphor of performance and empowerment: a vulnerable man producing an invisible work of art that fills and invades everything around it with exhilarating virtuosity and passion. The ruthlessness of conviction, the undistracted attention and commitment to unfamiliar forms of communication, and the mortal danger of knowing its meaning, are all imbricated in Herdman's presentation of the narrator's appreciation of MacDiarmid's playing Beethoven. Thrill and threat, disinterestedness and intoxication, persuasion and cool, the absurdity of physicality and the dignity of art, are all here in this vortex of contradictions. And Herdman deftly suggests that the narrator is susceptible to the overwhelming power of what he hears. Herdman himself, in his artistry, depicts the scene and its meaning with an understanding beyond that of the narrator.

The story 'Death and Devolution' from the same book similarly weaves fantasy and realism. Ostensibly a semi-autobiographical account of 'those heady days following Winnie Ewing's victory at the Hamilton by-election in 1967' when SNP 'activists' planned and plotted their hopes for an independent Scotland, grafting dreams onto intractable realities, the narrator tells of their admiration for the heroes of the Easter Rising in Ireland in 1916. But when a new branch member arrives from Ireland ('I'll call her Niamh, because Irish girls are often called Niamh, though that was not her real name'), he watches her approach, walking along the street, and has 'one overwhelming impression': that 'there was someone else walking invisibly beside her'.

This spooky sense continues through the story as we meet Niamh's lover, the ambiguous Douglas Heron, who is 'inscrutable' and has 'a tormented connection' with Niamh. The narrator spins himself dizzy in his obsessive love for Niamh, partly propelled by the mystique of her inheritance (her grandfather, we're told, took part in the Easter Rising) and the unobtainable knowledge of her relationship with Heron, we're introduced to some of the characters of the era. The narrator and his companions go to a reading in Edinburgh's New Town Hotel, given by 'the extraordinary Ada Kay, a middle-aged woman from Lancashire who had written a play and believed herself to be a reincarnation of James IV. The reading was organised, I think, by a group called The Heretics — Stuart MacGregor, Willie Neill, Dolina MacLennan, Donald Campbell, John Herdman — that lot. Ada had written a novel called *Falcon* which she claimed was the autobiography of the late monarch, composed by herself out of her memories of this previous life.' Asking Heron his opinion of the event, the narrator is surprised to find him taking the idea of resurrection seriously: 'His preferred metaphor was that of a perennial plant: each year, out of the same root or germ or bulb which contained the genetic material, the plant brought forth new growth and flower, which were distinct from last year's growth but intimately related to a new embodiment of the germ's potential. "The same but different. Or, different but the same," he summed up in his slightly pompous tone of authority.' And he concludes: 'Douglas also applied this idea of reincarnation to the case of Scotland. Scotland too could be reincarnated, he believed. He insisted that he didn't simply mean by that a re-birth or renaissance in the usual loose cultural sense — it was a case, rather, of complete death followed by a new appearance in a fresh shape which would, however, be intimately related to that which had preceded it.'

The story dissolves in irresolution. Heron has a wife he will not leave and eventually disappears from the scene (though he may have been seen in Amsterdam talking to a British intelligence agent); Niamh goes back to Ireland; the narrator takes a job teaching History in a school, eventually retires and writes the story. And 'the Cause' of 'Independence' becomes a settlement called 'Devolution' and waiting for that to happen, a whole generation of writers dies; and then after 1979, 'the old warhorses of the SNP died one by one'; and then after that, another generation of great Scottish poets dies: 'And now,' the tale concludes: 'reincarnated Scotland, struggling up through the mud, is still nowhere to be seen; not yet.'

Like Stanley Roger Green in his book, *A Clanjamfray of Poets: A Tale of Literary Edinburgh* (2007), Herdman has written straightforward accounts of that period in *Poets, Pubs, Polls & Pillar Boxes: Memoirs of an Era in Scottish Politics & Letters* (1999), revised and expanded as *Another Country: An Era in Scottish Politics and Letters* (2013). Published when it was, the final sentence of that book seems to transfer itself from Herdman's earlier story into an approaching actuality: 'The outcome of the 2014 independence referendum cannot be confidently predicted, but however it may turn out, the road to it will inevitably mark a further stage in the slow dismantling of the imperial structure in the consciousness of the Scottish people.'

That transfer of sense, that a fiction may begin to take form as a fact, is at the heart of all John Herdman's work. And it has its literary cognates. Donny O'Rourke's anthology of contemporary Scottish poems *Dream State* was first published in 1994 and then revised and republished in 2002. With the first edition, you read the title with the emphasis on the first word as an adjective: this was a state that existed only as a DREAM; with the second, the emphasis seemed to fall on the second word: the first word had become a verb, a command that you should dream of Scotland as a STATE because once the unimaginable becomes imaginable, reality becomes changeable. This was never made explicit but it was palpable, for sure.

As a writer of fiction, Herdman's orbits are in the constellation of Gray and Banks, whom we've mentioned, and also James Robertson, whose *And the Land Lay Still* (2010) takes on in the form of an epic novel some of the aspects of imagination Herdman pioneered, and whose *The Testament of Gideon Mack* (2006) is related to other aspects of Herdman's fiction, such as the legacy of the weight of religion and the virtues and liabilities of the immaterial world. And perhaps beyond that, for Robertson as for Herdman, there is the legacy of that cool and patient humour of Compton Mackenzie — most evident in Robertson's novel, *To Be Continued* ... (2016) and in the prose style Herdman has cultivated over many years, and a long way from the farcical exaggerations of Mackenzie's film and TV adaptations. I'm thinking of Mackenzie's deadpan neutral prose in his sympathetic depictions of sexual disposition and preference in novels like *Extraordinary Women* (1928) and *Thin Ice* (1956). These too are neglected classics.

But it is not influence that matters here, but common cause. And Herdman sums it up in that phrase already quoted: these are all works in partial fulfilment of 'the slow dismantling of the imperial structure in the consciousness of the Scottish people.' And with them, Hugh MacDiarmid playing Beethoven's Apassionata sonata on a spooky grand piano, the music reaching you now, from somewhere else.

There may be some way to go yet but these writers all, and pre-eminently, John Herdman, are working to help what can blossom beyond that slowly self-reforming consciousness.

Two Prose Poems

John Herdman

My Stone

The stone now stands at the very centre of a small round table, at the meeting-point of its four quadrants. It is smoothish, grey, lightly but closely speckled; egg-like in shape, but with a very slight flattening on one side which suggests that it should rest there. When it lies easily in the palm of my hand it is heavy, still, saying nothing, yet much. It was not chosen for any special beauty, not for glint or attractive colouration (though in certain lights it can take on a barely perceptible greenish tinge), but for what I can only call its quality of containment. This stone is permeated by spirit. It has descended to me from the infancy of the earth, its atoms have travelled through the fathomless aeons and vacancies of the universe to be here with me now; it comes, anciently, from the unknowable essence of That Which Is. When I call myself old, it mocks me.

I found it in a place where, according to tradition, a great movement of the spirit first entered Scotland. It was found by a cave, St Ninian's Cave, on a beach of stones washed by the timeless Galloway sea. I was with my wife, in the first year of our marriage. We had approached the beach by a leafy farm road which ran alongside a tiny burn. We looked at the ancient cave with its old cross emblems carved into the rough walls; then we walked the beach and I came upon the stone and carried it away with me.

After that it lay on a kind of altar, a great slab of home-polished wood which we used for meditation; a few objects rested on the wood, the stone among them. We always ended our meditation with a squeeze of our two hands ... Now my wife and I are apart, and I am alone with the stone.

The stone is a little porous, and I like to imagine that over the years something of my soul has penetrated it, seeped into it like the linseed oil with which my wife had treated the altar slab, and which, for a few years only, left a little darkening on the base of the stone. For this stone is porous to the spirit. It enters into me and I into it, but this interpenetration does not take place in time. The contingencies of transience befall it but it remains the same. Psyche and matter are not different substances and spirit informs and inhabits all. This is what, in its silence, this stone has to say.

The Skein

In our inner spaces our dreams flow into each other, interpenetrate. The memory, even a fleeting glimpse, of one leads us directly into that of another, not connected by content or by obvious theme, not by proximity or even closeness in time, but by some invisible skein of relatedness which invites us, a little mockingly, to unravel it. Courts, rivers, screes, shadowy cathedrals and cloisters, crags, dense forests, lochs and milky burns, derelict haunted outbuildings, foul-smelling slums — strange distorted reminders of real places, street-maps of the inner cities of the mind — one knows where one is going in these landscapes, they are hauntingly familiar, you can venture down a narrow vennel, a twisted street, and somehow know where you will emerge, you are already well-known in the suburb which you must revisit. They are all still there, those vague yet vivid places of long ago, waiting to be rediscovered, re-explored! You can travel by car, by bus, by train or by boat; running, jumping, climbing, flying, falling! Swimming and plunging! — the means of locomotion are not lacking!

What is the invisible skein that binds these infinitely suggestive yet always irreducibly alien configurations? Where are these so visitable yet elusive countries to be found? Are these worlds not *real*, after all?

Surely they are.

John Herdman in 1967

Willie Archibald

We both enjoyed a very special encounter in that year 1967. We first met, a meeting which impacted on the two of us from then on. We were both achingly Scottish, idealistic, but from very different backgrounds. We were a match of contrasts if you will.

John was a representative of that important strand of powerful nineteenth century mercantile families. Intermarriage of family dynasties was common and seemingly strong networks established both within Scotland and further afield across the world.

I was from a more modest background, born to a family of small trades people who were fired up by the experiences of WW2 and a resolve to prosper in the post war world. I was of course a stranger to the world of academia.

I had been fascinated by Scottish independence and the various groups involved from an early age, as far back as primary school.

I became active by 1955 and entered a world filled with poetry and poets, writers, songsters and YES academics. Real and fake army majors and a variety of somewhat mad lawyers, in effect a ferment, a broth, right up my street!

John in 1967 was newly minted from Cambridge, the possessor of a top-notch double first degree in English. Cambridge changed John, but probably not in the way his parents expected, to put it mildly.

John is around a year younger than me and presumably before Cambridge he was more or less conformist, being educated at expensive private, so-called 'public' schools. John informed me that the Cambridge experience dramatically brought home to him the position of his own country and also the wider Celtic nations and their problems with the shortcomings of established Union of the UK.

John had been fired up by James Joyce and the Irish writers also he embraced the Scottish literary tradition and met up with Rory Watson who was spending time at Cambridge on postgraduate work. Meeting Rory probably added heft to John's journey from then onwards.

After my marriage and the advent of children I turned again to politics, and just before Winnie Ewing won Hamilton I rejoined the SNP. The momentous events after the Hamilton resulted in John joining the Party. Both of us were invited to meet with a local branch activist and that brought about our meeting.

Now occurred one of the stranger events in life. My wife Carole and I lived in rather a posh house in Edinburgh's Danube St. This is a Regency Terrace from around 1820. Danube St. had become somewhat unfashionable as the douce Edinburgers moved out to modern bungalows in Corstorphine etc. In 1967 Danube St. had acquired a rather dubious claim to fame owing to the presence since the second war of Mrs. Dora Noyce who ran an establishment catering for the needs of a mainly male clientele. Everything from the American fleet coming to Rosyth to the needs of more local clients who could claim being held up by traffic after leaving the office en-route to the aforementioned bungalows for their tea! The annual General Assembly of the Kirk also could be a busy time. I lived two doors from this place and to our amazement Rory Watson and his wife Celia lived a few doors on the other side of the same place.

1967/8 was a time of political ferment, student riots across the world. Much more was changing than just Carnaby St.

Provincial Edinburgh was even stirring itself. SNP Councillors were being elected. John and I thrust ourselves into the fray. We knew that real change was far into the future but we were young, and put in the spadework then which helped create a Parliament in Edinburgh.

John did not see his future in politics, an academic career held no appeal for him and he had his mind set on a career as a writer.

That can be a precarious occupation especially if do not write about murders, sex or nice wee homesy slush. John of course followed his own path.

John had a rich seam to write about in Scotland and he, as a fine raconteur mixed widely and enjoyed the degree of social mobility which had always been present in Scotland e.g. Burns, Scott, MacDiarmid, Dunbar and other poets of earlier times and which confounds English observers and which had been given a boost by new opportunities in education since the war.

Our friendship has prevailed all the years since we met first. Now in 2021 during the pandemic we meet as circumstances allow. We of course put the world to right as usual, discuss the madness of the human condition and I reckon are closer and importantly more supportive of each other than ever. That says something about friendship — fifty plus years and counting.

Travelling to the House of Herdman

Marjorie Sandor

John Herdman's fiction is deliciously dangerous. When I open one of his books, I have the urge to check the locks on the doors, and then, uneasily, I realise that there are no locks on the doors that are about to open, and I myself will be turning the doorknobs. The House of Herdman is full of such alluring and distressing doors, unsettling passages and unexpected staircases. Trapdoors abound. And for a reader, tell me, is there anything better? When I'm reading him, I feel like Duncan Straiton, the narrator of *A Truth Lover*, walking up into the Pentland Hills in search of a good lashing in Scottish weather — the battle to keep walking against that fierce wind feels like the only true respite from the onrush of fate — and even as we walk into the wind, Duncan and I, we know the escape is only temporary.

Appropriately, my path to the House of Herdman was a long and circuitous one: its true beginning is in a classroom at the University of Stirling in the spring of 1978, when I had the good fortune to take Rory Watson's seminar on Dostoevsky. At the time, I didn't know what a *doppelgänger* was, nor had I heard of E. T. A. Hoffmann or James Hogg — and when I thought of Robert Louis Stevenson, only the most famous titles came to mind. I was nineteen years old, and God help me, a Californian. But that first acquaintance with the concept of the *doppelgänger* took root, and many decades later, led me down the rabbit hole known as the literary uncanny. I began to teach the subject to my graduate and undergraduate writing students, and in 2014, put together an international anthology of stories in this genre-defying tradition. And since *uncanny* is a fine old Scottish word, I reached out across the decades to my former professor, and asked him to recommend a few Scottish writers who, for him, best exemplified this unsettling sensation in their short fiction. Among the many marvellous works he suggested, there was one title in particular that caught my attention: 'The Devil and Dr Tuberose.' When Rory said it was an academic satire, I was even more intrigued. There was, I feared, a severe lack of humour in my anthology and I wanted to express, somehow the variety of tones and textures that might comprise this tricky term. And as a writer-uneasily-ensconced-in-academia myself, I'm always hungry for a good send-up of university life. Then I read the story. I was floored by it — especially by the narration, which *appears* to be closely aligned with Dr Tuberose, but in fact conceals another storyteller who will emerge quite late in the story, adding to the already desperately complicated way the reader feels about the unfortunate Tuberose. He is, like all of us, a bit of a mess: pompous and pathetic, perpetrator and victim. You cannot fully dismiss him and laugh at his expense, due to the very unsettling sensation that you might be next to take the fall. But neither can you stop yourself from a good comic howl: it's a brutally funny send-up of the more absurd aspects of academic customs, and it grows more prescient by the hour.

I was thrilled to correspond with John and include the story in *The Uncanny Reader*, and in the years since, I have had the great pleasure of meeting him in Edinburgh, and travelling with him to Stirling for a reunion with my former tutor and his friend, Rory Watson. In subsequent trips to Scotland, I've had the chance to share meals and good city walks with him.

It isn't always the case the writer you admire becomes, also, a cherished friend, but that is the case here, and the many miles between my home in an Oregon college town and his in Edinburgh make that pleasure feel extremely rare and lucky.

And how delightful, on top of it all, to watch John Herdman prove Sigmund Freud wrong about the uncanny in at least one key sense, for the good doctor did not think the uncanny could be funny — he thought it would deflate and destroy the sense of disturbance. Oh, dear Sigmund, take note, the *unheimlich* does have the capacity to be funny — and John Herdman proves it, not only in Dr Tuberose's horrifying and deliciously funny downward spiral, but in everything else of his I've had the pleasure to read.

And something more: the uncanny prides itself on not letting you 'settle' on a particular view of the subject, and this is my favourite thing about John Herdman's characters: you will not be able to condemn or judge them, let alone keep them at a safe arms-length. His kaleidoscopic perspective in *Imelda* is my favourite example of this effect: go ahead, try to form a solid opinion of Frank 'Superbo' Agnew, then feel the certainty tugged out from under you, by such quiet degrees that at times, you think you might be gaslighting yourself. That's Herdman's genius: his stories and novels capture the exhilarating and near-hallucinatory instability of being alive, caught between very real passions of the heart, and a world that stuns us, over and over again, with its appetite for dark and playful caprice.

Sinister Cabarets

Roderick Watson

From the beginning Clapperton had felt his body to be a burden to him. His earliest reading matter being the Bible, he would, a child of seven, fearfully peruse the thirteenth and fourteenth chapters of Leviticus and examine his person for the marks of leprosy. 'And if, when the priest seeith it,' he read, 'behold, it be in sight lower than the skin, and the hair thereof is turned white, the priest shall pronounce him unclean: it is the plague of leprosy.' The most miniscule pluke was thereafter an object of terror, and he was seldom without a magnifying glass, in those days. ('Clapperton', *Four Tales*, p.118.)

We are in a dark cellar bar in Edinburgh, it is 1970, and John Herdman is reading aloud. The audience is attentive, sudden bursts of laughter punctuate the reader's measured delivery, with occasional gasps of surprise or shock, as his low key, undramatic voice takes us into a darkly comic vision of human futility, rage and failure.

This is a meeting of The Heretics, a creative collective of young Scottish writers, folk singers and musicians. In this venue (the bar is important) folk music and live poetry draw decent audiences for evening sessions on the first Thursday of every month. A typical event would feature two or three singers and two or three readers until a more established literary figure, usually a poet, brings the date to a close. For us younger writers it was a challenging introduction to reading in public, and how to hold an audience while pints are being dispensed at the back of the room. Then again, a regular performer like the Gaelic singer Dolina MacLennan could bring time itself to a stop, with the thrilling cut and *hwyl* of her unaccompanied voice.

We all learnt a lot and new voices emerged from those sessions. Early member Donald Campbell, for example, took up Robert Garioch's example (also a favoured Heretics guest) by writing poetry in Scots street demotic, paving the way for West of Scotland writers in the 1980s. Most notably Donald's historical plays in the same anachronistically vivid contemporary Scots were to forecast a similar explosion in Scottish theatre. William Neill found his voice in these sessions and went on to become one of the few then contemporary poets to write in all three of Scotland's languages. You heard it first at The Heretics. It was an added thrill in those days to be in the same crowded small room as a generation of older poets, when Norman MacCaig, Robert Garioch, Sydney Goodsir Smith, Iain Crichton Smith, Derick Thomson, an occasional Hugh MacDiarmid, and Sorley MacLean came as guests to read from their own work. (These were among MacLean's first poetry readings in public following his retirement.) Just on the horizon were the next generation of poets with Liz Lochhead, Valerie Gillies, Ron Butlin, Tom Pow, Brian McCabe, Dilys Rose, Andrew Greig, Tom Leonard, et al., some of whom also read at Heretic events. (Lochhead, Leonard and Gillies all featured in an LP called *An Evening With The Heretics*, recorded in 1975.)

It was a good time to be in Edinburgh, the modern folk revival under the influence of Hamish Henderson at the School of Scottish Studies in the 1960s, and the rise of the Traverse Theatre in Edinburgh and the Citizens Theatre in Glasgow had already set the scene. The essays collected in *The Scottish Sixties. Reading, Rebellion, Revolution?*, edited by Eleanor Bell and Linda Gunn tell more of the story, and John's own memoir *Another Country* gives an indispensable account of the political and cultural climate of the times.

I guess I became a reader at The Heretics at John's invitation. We first met in Cambridge, a fortuitous encounter, in 1967. I had turned up at Peterhouse the previous year, an Aberdeen graduate just back from a year as a lecturer in Canada, newly married, with a scholarship to write a PhD on Hugh MacDiarmid. The collegiate system at Cambridge was strange to me and the intellectual and socio-cultural mores of the place even stranger. I never felt so Scottish as I did when I left Scotland to find that the things I took for granted couldn't be taken for granted at all. John told me that his experience as an undergraduate at Cambridge had been exactly the same.

MacDiarmid's poetry was my chosen research subject, and I had a gently remote supervisor who confessed that he got the task because he had actually heard of the man. So it's not surprising, perhaps, that John and I, as Scots in exile, came to find common ground. He had returned to Cambridge as a postgraduate in 1966, with a growing interest in James Hogg — and he could recite 'The Watergaw'. 'I would read MacDiarmid, too' said one academic I met, 'but of course I don't know

Gaylick.' From scenes like these are friendships made, further cemented by a shared enthusiasm for Joyce and Dostoevsky, not forgetting Bob Dylan. *Blonde on Blonde* was the soundtrack of our Cambridge years and John's 1982 book *Voice Without Restraint* is one of the earliest critical studies to take Dylan's art seriously.

By 1969 John had decided to return to Scotland. My three years at Peterhouse were over, but I was still writing up my thesis. I got a grant, however, to study the MacDiarmid correspondence, newly purchased for Edinburgh University Library, so Celia and I moved north and met up with John again — and The Heretics. We rented a basement flat in Danube Street, right next door to the most famous brothel in town and made many new friends in Edinburgh's literary milieu. (These two facts are not connected.) An Arts Council grant for my own poetry kept us in the city for another year, until our son was born and we moved to Stirling. But Edinburgh was not so far away and it was easy to keep in touch with the literary scene and the growing cultural and political pressures towards Scottish independence. John's spell as a contributor and then as the short-lived editor of the nationalist journal *Catalyst* brought him into contact with the 1320 Club, some of whose positions were a step too far for my own SNP convictions. John's memoir offers hilarious insights into the group's more shadowy members, some of whom might well have come from one of his own stories.

John and I have been walking and talking about politics, language, culture and identity ever since. Always a mighty pedestrian, John was formidable in his day, settling for nothing less than full speed ahead. On one of his longer forays, in the hills above Blair Atholl an awkward stumble on the return path (isn't it always the easy bits that get you?) led to a fall that broke his hip. Out on his own, in the days before mobile phones, with daylight fading, he literally dragged himself down the track on his belly until he reached a house and got help. Tough creatures these men of letters. I still remember a two-day tramp we did through Glen Tilt from Bridge of Tilt to Braemar. Under the heat of the sun and the heat of discussion the time and the miles flew by, but the wooden tent poles we forgot to repack must still be out there somewhere.

Back with The Heretics in that cellar bar, John's reading style is an essential and unwavering part of his art. Deadpan, detached with a formal, slightly weary and scholarly air, occasionally glancing off to the upper right, he introduced us to an anthology of human paranoia, absurdity and shameful behaviour that would match anything in

Dostoevsky's underground. The humour of his bone-dry tones can pass almost unseen, until you realise you're bleeding:

> There is nothing like necessity for humbling pride. Youthful genius would sooner sweep the street than compromise its integrity. Then, one day, someone asks you to write a review. (*Ghostwriting*, p.3)

From the very start, with his early readings of 'Clapperton', there was always a certain *frisson* in the audience's mind, (even among friends) that the *personae* in John's stories may not be too far removed from personal experience. Small details ascribed to a number of his characters frequently pop up, with minor biographical references, habits of mind, or aspects of physical resemblance that do not seem too far removed from those of their author. (*A Portrait of the Artist as a Young Man* was an early influence.)

He writes, of course, from within each character's point of view, or as a vividly realised *persona* in the grip of direct first-person narration. But the consistent formality of his diction and the recurring themes of obsession, insecurity, hypochondria and sexual insecurity — none of which truly apply — nevertheless have a teasingly persuasive air of weary experience or even confession. This is his special literary field, the source of his black comedy and the key to his vision of human existence. In this respect his fellow traveller in the pends and vennels of comic existential despair is not his hero James Joyce, but Joyce's alter ego, one time amanuensis, and hoped for son-in-law (a very Herdmanish concatenation) Samuel Beckett.

John's literary engagement with the physical and spiritual humiliations of human consciousness, pursued in book after book, is thoroughly modern:

> I rather fear and dislike good weather; it oppresses me, I suppose, with the sense of the many opportunities it offers which somehow I always fail to take. Whatever activity I choose it seems to be the wrong one, and always I am sure I would have been happier elsewhere. And now that my life is to be my own at last I see that the same problem faces me permanently and on a much larger scale: faced with a riot of possibilities how shall I be able to choose between them, how determine upon any

single form of action which will give shape to my outward life; how above all will I give a form to my obsessional resolve to live by the code of truth? (*A Truth Lover, Four Tales*, p.1.)

The moral / legal crisis at the centre of *A Truth Lover* also has echoes of Camus and *The Outsider*, and the roots of Duncan Straiton's' ferocious misanthropy and pain, evoke early Dostoevsky, especially, *Notes from Underground*. These are key works in John's own reading, and key texts in European existentialism's struggle with nausea, angst, authenticity and being.

Like Beckett, and Swift before him, John's muse is sensitive to the fallibilities of the flesh and the grossness of the dying animal that we are tied to, but there is a metaphysical or indeed a spiritual dimension to his disgust. His is an acerbic intelligence, unforgiving of its own limitations, struggling to contain the absurdity of existence, relatively unprotected against the stupidities of society and the follies of human desire. In the face of such discontent, he has undertaken meditation and spiritual retreats at different times in his life, and was once drawn to Catholicism and a monastic calling. (His work has also used biblical references as a form of philosophical and personal exploration.) Committed to joining the world, however, he has chosen satire and black comedy as his expressive medium.

The special achievement of John's literary output is to convey every feature of Prufrock's ennui, or of 'the horror', that so overcame Conrad's Mr Kurtz — in the formal tones of an Edwardian diarist.

I determined therefore to disperse with the wind of action the noxious vapours that were poisoning my mind. My disturbances were the necessary accompaniment of procrastination and avoidance of my duty. It was now necessary, if I was not to become one of those sad and lost figures who, through some final failure of nerve, never accomplish the work for which alone they are intended, that I turn aspiration into achievement. I began accordingly to lay my plans for the assassination of the 14th Viscount Gadarene. (*Pagan's Pilgrimage, Four Tales*, p.83.)

Compare the tone of the above with the opening lines of a famous short story, 'Sredni Vashtar', by Hector Hugh Munro, 'Saki'.

Conradin was ten years old, and the doctor had pronounced his professional opinion that the boy would not live another five years. The doctor was silky and effete, and counted for little, but his opinion was endorsed by Mrs. de Ropp, who counted for nearly everything. Mrs. De Ropp was Conradin's cousin and guardian, and in his eyes she represented those three-fifths of the world that are necessary and disagreeable and real; the other two-fifths, in perpetual antagonism to the foregoing, were summed up in himself and his imagination.

Saki's short fiction has a savage strain, and under the surface of its Edwardian respectability, the *bon ton* are confronted by an often deadly natural world where bad luck, cruel tricks, physical accidents, and wild animals (a polecat in 'Sredni Vashtar') show little respect for their social position. The spirit of Saki is alive and well, it seems to me, in John's vision of petty bourgeois life, especially, perhaps, in the streets of Edinburgh, his native city — which is a uniquely rich ground, as some of us might dare to suggest.

So here is a writer with a very modern and rather darkly existential vision of human absurdity whose narrative structures are consciously and paradoxically traditional. Some of his characters have ironically appropriate names in the style of Dickens, or indeed Sir Walter Scott, and his opening sentences frequently use a formally introductory air:

Mr Stanley Kirkpatrick, a small, compact, rodent-like man in later middle age, clad in a long and loosely fitting tweed overcoat and an old-fashioned homburg hat, stood busily in the vestibule of the public library. Even when doing nothing whatsoever, Mr Kirkpatrick contrived always to look busy. ('Acquainted with Grief', *Imelda and Other Stories*, p.150.)

Indeed, I would argue that the central core of Herdman's creative humour is to be found in the formal *textuality* of this prose voice, equally strong in descriptive or first-person narrative. Its precision plays in constant contrast to the carnival of absurdity, pain and grim comedy that engulfs his characters. Early novellas have a disturbing rage under their genial surface, while black farce, a lighter touch and further narrative complexity characterise the later books, especially the 'trilogy' of *Imelda* (1993), *Ghostwriting* (1996), and *The Sinister*

Cabaret (2001). In all cases, John's unique sense of the human condition depends on the balance between what amounts to a kind of madness and an educated, descriptive tone, seeking control in adverse circumstances, often replete with self-aware ironies transplanted to a new fictional home:

> one day someone asks you to write a review. No harm in that, especially if you are fearless and incorruptible, strong-minded and impervious to blandishments. Next thing you know, you are writing a newspaper column which seems at first to be witty and perceptive but after a few months is agreed by everyone to have gone off, to have become bland and anodyne. Then you are asked to edit an anthology of contemporary verse. If things go badly, you could soon be putting together a collection of obscene limericks or copy-editing a fund-raising handbook. And if they go *really* badly, you could eventually find yourself replying to an advertisement for a ghost writer — and telling yourself that that is, after all, a thoroughly postmodern thing to do. (*Ghostwriting,* pp.3–4.)

The trope of ghost writing from the fine novel of that name seems particularly apposite, revisited, perhaps, in the figure of the 'professional biographer' in the title story of *My Wife's Lovers* (2007). John's narrative voice is perpetually aware of its own elegant artificiality, and this insight carries over into the process of the act of writing itself. Indeed 'writing' does, in a sense, write itself, as characters assume lives of their own. And perhaps writing is always a kind of 'ghost writing', by which phantoms are brought to life on the page, *by* the page, in a succession of receding mirrors in the middle of which there may lurk something called an author, a subject, and the elusive reflection of ourselves as we read? 'Thoroughly postmodern' indeed.

I'm reminded of an extraordinary passage in *Descent*, a key early statement and John's first book, published in 1968, but written at the age of twenty-three, in which the narrator sees the disease of cancer as a kind of inner life, a secret sharer that speaks for our own inescapably divided natures. Here it is visualised as a psychological or even a philosophical condition, as much as a medical one:

> ... what do we know of the unfathomable mystery of the malevolent life which springs up within us to destroy us? We

think of it only in relation to the devastating inroads it makes upon the human flesh. But of its inner purpose, of the motivation of its independent life, of the miraculous principle of its growth and the hidden beauty of its development — of these things we can know nothing, for their meaning is incompatible with and eternally opposed to that of the body for which we must care. Yet should we, by some miracle of imaginative empathy, ever receive an inkling of that meaning — in what confusion should we find ourselves? If the enemy, the scourge, should turn out to have a valid life of its own? (*Descent*, p.6.)

John wrote a serious academic study of *The Double in Nineteenth-Century Fiction* (1990), derived from his early interest in James Hogg and his fascination with Dostoevsky and E. T. A. Hoffmann — a critical interest we both share. The fatal alter ego, whether called Gil-Martin (*Confessions of a Justified Sinner*) or Torquil Tod, (*Ghostwriting*), and the ambiguous nature of all written texts are a common trope in this genre. Hogg's *Confessions* gives us a number of different narratives and indeed different documents about the same incident — an incident whose very reality is challenged by the instability of the texts and testaments surrounding it. Is Gilmartin real? Is Robert Wringhim mad? Stevenson does the same with the different and often conflicting narratives in *Jekyll and Hyde* and *The Master of Ballantrae*, so there are strong Scottish roots to this trope.

These roots are more than celebrated in the tangled threads of *Ghostwriting* (1996), where Tod, the supposed subject of the ghost autobiography might even be a fiction of Leonard Balmain's imagination. Or then again, the discussion between Balmain, the biographer, and Tod his subject, comes to seem like a conversation between the actual author and one of the figures of his imagination, or deeper still, the debate the author (any author) must have with himself, or between himself and any future reader:

There's a double movement going on inside me — I want both to reveal and conceal. To reveal to you, and through you to — who knows? To conceal — from myself. But if I conceal from myself, I cannot truly reveal to you. So what's to be done? [...] You must stand in my shoes, try to think yourself into my point of view, into the way I think and feel.

This is a revealing analysis of the doubleness of what it is to put pen to paper, most especially perhaps in the special form of truth creation that we call fiction, which is drawn from inner sources that we ourselves may not fully understand or even admit. It also reflects on what it is to read the result, for as readers we are ourselves the ghostly recipients, victims and creators of the author and his creatures. This is 'Ghost' writing, indeed, and by the end of the novel we are no longer sure if Balmain's death is at the hands of Tod (death) or whether Tod is an elaborate invention to conceal an act of self-expression and subsequent suicide. *Scribo ergo sum*: wheels within wheels, boxes within boxes. (The 'Memoir of Frank Agnew, Otherwise Known as Superbo' and 'The Memoir of Sir Robert Affleck' in *Imelda* from 1993 play the same game, replete with the variably reliable documentation of 'Editorial' interjections, selected correspondence and an 'Author's Note'.)

Hogg's engagement with the double, and 'the malevolent life that springs up within us' has had a significant impact on Scottish literature, but this was not always the case. Indeed, not unlike Stevenson, his current pre-eminence is a relatively recent development in the history of literary criticism. A corner was turned by André Gide's introduction to the Cresset Press edition of the *Justified Sinner* in 1947, and suffice to say that in the years since then, Hogg's novel has been widely recognised as a modern European masterpiece of psychological and textual complexity. In the last forty years, in particular, a whole generation of Scottish authors have been so markedly influenced by him that we can talk about 'contemporary Scottish Gothic' as a significant genre in its own right.

In this respect, John Herdman has been a really significant early adopter. He has more than sixteen volumes of creative work to his name, several of which have been translated into French and Italian. Compellingly original in its satirical approach, using the most scrupulously considered of prose styles, Herdman's dark comedy of human desire, futility and nightmare has played an influential part in contemporary Scottish literature, and it is particularly pleasing to see this being recognised, with new editions of his fiction in print again, and this festschrift celebration of his work. The two of us have indeed walked and talked for miles since our first meeting in Cambridge over fifty years ago, but I'll let the man himself have the last word (at least until we can meet for lunch again) on a note entirely worthy of those early days, reading together in a cellar bar in Edinburgh.

The poster announcing the appearance of the Sinister Cabaret was ceremoniously ripped down and Kenny Squeezebox held it up and tore it up into neat squares, then removed it to the Gentleman's Toilet, a place into which, before Donald's arrival, few gentlemen had ever penetrated. After that he got out his squeezebox, Big Hieronymus took his place behind the bar, Ingibjorg Sigurdsdottir sang an unconscionably long Icelandic ballad about another famous and no doubt equally bloody victory in the days of the Sagas, and in short there was a ceilidh and everybody got drunk. (*The Sinister Cabaret*, pp.167–8.)

List and apology attached

Ewan Morrison

Damn it. Admit that I'm stuck. What then? Write up a list, you fool. Marcus Aurelius wrote lists of questions, often before he went into battle, so there is no shame in it.

List.

Problems I face with writing about JH for the anthology.

Problem 1. OK, there is something vaguely 'obituary' or at the very least 'retrospective' about this, and JH is not dead! He is very much alive and so the tone cannot be morbid or 'memorialising' in any way, although it must be said the writings of JH can be seen as morbidly preoccupied, Gothic even, albeit playfully.

I abhor funeral speeches anyway, with their rose-tinted depiction of an individual's accumulated merits, their CVs of life achievements as 'appropriate classical music for funerals' plays on the sound system in the crematorium. The whole procedure stage managed to be artificially 'uplifting'. Damned atheists pretending they believe in something for a day. It's almost as if the person giving the funeral speech is doing a power-point presentation to St Peter just in case God exists (or whatever adjudicator is on duty at the gates of Heaven) on the good things the deceased achieved in their lifetime; their honesty, truthfulness, faithfulness and so on, omitting all the more nuanced acts of evil committed over said lifetime, so as to the sneak the deceased past the terms and conditions of the great book of names and judgement and cheat the aforementioned deceased into the aforementioned final resting place in the clouds. No, we can have none of that. No, 'what a perfect saintly chap he was'. Or rather is, because let us repeat, JH is very much alive! And this is the problem for this piece of writing.

I am aware that the continued existence of artists poses a serious threat in other art forms — to the galleries and investors of galleries, for example. As someone once said about the vocation of painter: 'it's the only occupation where your employer wants you dead.' The value of painting by a deceased painter doubling, trebling, and doing exponentially more so in price. But this is not the case with literature. Or is it?

Considerations around the sudden re-birth of interest in A. Gray after his passing, including a forthcoming Hollywood feature film with Oscar-winning cast, scriptwriter and director, various new appreciation societies and so on. Hmm. So, to play devil's advocate as JH often does in his cunning fictions — would death be a useful strategy for JH? Possibly have a chat with anthology editor about whether we could inflate book sales and reputation of JH by turning this book into a grand tome of obituaries. Yes, hold on, data from Neilson book scan shows a 24–32% rise in book sales and TV adaptations post-mortem for cult authors, and JH is certainly that. (N.B. such a chat will have to be treated with the greatest delicacy).

Which leaves only one problem — the continued existence of JH.

Speak to editor about this problem. Perhaps something could be staged — without of course in any way endangering JH. If not a death then a disappearance. Such enigmas are very in keeping with the literary aesthetic of JH. Consider JH's many years in Pitlochry, a kind of social disappearance, a wee-death, a necessary making scarce of oneself so as to concentrate more fully on the learning, the works and texts without distraction from the living and their banal chatter. Was this period not a rehearsal for a staged disappearance?

Yes, perhaps editor would consider 'disappearing' a double of JH?

But no, this is all wrong footed (or headed), here I am trying to construct a reason for writing an obituary simply because I loathe appraisals of the living.

Yuck.

Appraisals of the still living are like those Californian new age funeral parties, with everyone dressed in white, in which the not-deceased person parties with the living and listens to thirty or so speeches about how great their life was/is. 'Tabatha, we love you, we all do, you are the greatest person we have ever known and we're going to miss you.' And so on.

I can imagine JH would cringe terribly at the prospect of a literary equivalent of this kind of 'celebrate-the-life-while-still-living' party; the book launch even. JH being deeply sensitive, thoughtful, generous, perhaps modest, introspective and avoidant of parties, fuss, media hyperbole and all of the champagne fuelled hullabaloo.

OK, so perhaps JH would even like to absent himself from the publication of this book, due to the possible danger of individuals on a stage taking turns with the microphones to read their pieces about what an amazing author, thinker, philosopher, mentor, inspiration, translator, maybe even former sexual partner, surrogate uncle (as in my case) he is/was and so on. Yes, I can imagine JH's utter mortification as he is really, in my mind anyway, something like the modern day — and much slimmer version — of St Thomas Aquinas. And can we imagine Aquinas being asked to attend an event to celebrate his life's work while he was still living and writing? No, not at all, he would be furious at the prospect of having to leave his ancient library of accumulated treasures, his piles of dusty books with his endless marginalia overcoming the books themselves, and there of course there was the issue of Aquinas girth and the monks having to widen the doors with the use of saws, chisels and mallets to get his massive self out the aforementioned library, but this may be a fiction anyway, an urban myth, from before the times that the urban even existed, but I digress.

Yes, given the gothic and metafictional nature of the writings of JH, I must quietly speak to the editor about the replacement of JH with a deceased double! Yes, Hogg would be proud of us, as no doubt he is already of the writings of JH, if one can be proud from the grave — so that we could stop beating about the bush and give free reign to the obituary nature of this increasingly onerous task at hand. Good.

There remains the question of *a body*. Corpus Delicti. It is possible even that JH would enjoy the trope of a disappearance and a double coming to life as it were, or rather the opposite. The task could be a little Burke and Hare, but how Edinburgh and nineteenth century these references are, and all very much in keeping with the aesthetic and ethos of JH. So, a body to act as JH's double. It's decided then.

This would solve my problems and furthermore editors and publishing houses are always looking for novel ways to promote books. A body yes. Ask editor if budget could stretch to the cost of a pre-deceased doppelganger. How much do such 'remains' cost and how could I research this without drawing attention to myself on Google and hence the US PRISM surveillance system? Where could we find such a double for JH, maybe even someone who could 'play-dead'? If this could be realised, my task would be so much easier, and perhaps JH would enjoy this little ruse and could slip away into many more years of undisturbed productivity, living under an assumed name perhaps, existing as the final realisation of his 'Not-I'! It would be our little secret. A gift to JH! A body-double that was just a body. He could continue but as a ghost writer of himself!

Problem: how to convince all the other contributors to go along with this plan and to dip into their pockets in a whip-round to purchase the aforementioned unmentionable?

Problem 2. I cannot construct a fake history for myself in which I write anything along the lines of, 'The writings of JH have been with me all my life and have been a constant source of inspiration'. This would be utter hoggwash (no pun intended James).

No, the truth is so embarrassing as to be unrepeatable. For, I first came across JH in childhood as one of my father's writer-friends. He was in fact to be referred to as 'uncle John', and was not one but two such literary uncle Johns — the other being John L. Broom of the eccentrically dusty bookshop in Stromness. Dangers of digressions abound here, and sentimentality would no doubt be a constant threat. 'My memories of the kind, generous and almost saint-like like JH from childhood.' That kind of thing, would no doubt embarrass JH deeply.

So, there can be no mention of my deeply emotional, disturbed, loud and over-enthusiastic father, who somehow JH befriended, tolerated and was even a calming influence upon. No mention of the miracle of generosity that was JH's acts of support towards my father through his many breakdowns and recurring traumas. No, it would be awful to subject the public to any of this, and I, to my shame, had given up on my father, his drink problem, his cyclic peaks and troughs of extreme hope and despair, long before JH. No, in fact JH stuck with him to the end. So, if I was to write of this, I would come out of this looking worse than I already do.

It does haunt me though, why would JH continue to lend emotional support to such a broken man who had drained the charity of so many others? I've often wondered if JH's faith was something to do this, and then I imagine JH as something like Søren Kierkegaard, the man who took the leap of faith while others simply fell of the cliff. But all of this is too sad and maybe abstract to touch upon, and we don't need to claim that JH is a good man, a giving man, a quiet, compassionate person who approaches human problems. Who wants to hear such things in this day and age. Kindness is uncool. It doesn't sell books. Charity is not sexy. Benevolence — a word that cannot even be spelt these days (even I had to double check it.) Such were the unspeakable acts of JH in the life of my family.

Perhaps no one would get my reference to the other character who I've often thought JH shares a striking resemblance to — William of Baskerville, the fictional Franciscan Friar and proto-detective in Umberto Eco's metafictional masterpiece *The Name of the Rose*.

Allow me to digress — there is this moment when Adso — William's servant and student — flooded with anguish over the suffering of the poor, says to Sir William, something to the effect of, 'But Master, how can you bury yourself in books, have you no pity?' And William of Baskerville — or at least Sean Connery's version of him in what I must say is his greatest performance in his career — replies (and I paraphrase from memory), 'Perhaps that is the nature of my pity.'

Wisdom, not action, is the nature of his pity.

This moved me greatly when I first heard it.

Yes, so, oddly, again I come up with this formulation in which I associate JH with a scholarly monk of centuries past, who is only too aware of the sufferings of mankind and who, out of pity, seeks answers within the great texts, and let us not forget, faith itself is important to JH. There is his diploma or is it degree, in theology, his practice, the respect of the past and the curiosity about things lost to history within his writing. So, yes — this is my early and deep impression of JH as the son of a disturbed man who needed help and who JH had the kindness to help again and again, with the gift of quiet.

Uncle John William of Baskerville Aquinas.

This is all too embarrassing to tell anyone and the last person I want to make in any way blush is JH, so I'll again have to speak to the editor about what I cannot write. Which leaves me with nothing, really.

Also, it is embarrassing, that I only discovered what uncle JH wrote decades after I first knew him. It was like waking up one day to realise that the man I called uncle (one of two such, as I've already said) was in fact a writer of the calibre of Søren Kierkegaard, or James Hogg, or at the very least strongly within their tradition, if such a tradition could be said to exist. What shall we call it, metaphysical metafiction? And how did it leap through time, to JH, from the nineteenth century to JH himself in Pitlochry, perhaps via the stepping stones of Borges, Eco and maybe even Saramago? Such an international non-movement.

But, my surprise on discovering that the man I thought of as the man who held my father when he wept, who visited us, when all else had shunned us, who offered peace, calm and wisdom as an occasional surrogate family member, was this outstanding writer and thinker. It was impossible for me to articulate. Again, embarrassment. I should have said to JH years ago, 'But I didn't even know who you really were/are' — and again this problem of tense. It would be is much easier if I could say all of this post-mortem (either that of JH or of myself). The problem here is compounded by sentimental and rather eccentric memories from childhood. Of one breakfast, JH and his partner subjected us to, is subjected too strong a word? Is partner correct? It was a metaphysical meal even, a meditation on mortality; certainly I contemplated death much as I pushed the decapitated thing around my plate. I must have been eleven and the dish was called (forgive my utter lack of grounding in anything like the Gaeltacht or in fact in anything like spelling without the help of Google) Crap'd hied. Or Crappit? Or Crabbit? I recall being told by JH's partner as she served it to us that the eyes were a particular delicacy, this being a meal which consisted of a Cod's head stuffed with something like porridge, and I recall JH at the side of the room — my parents were still upstairs sleeping — adding gently that we could have some cornflakes if, my sister and I preferred. But proffering playfully that some great ancient Celtic awareness might be conferred upon us if we were to at least taste of the abomination.

He smiled and I picked up my fork.

So yes, the earliest memories of JH were not of him as translator, poet, critic, creator of complex and playful metaphysical meta-fictions and Neo Gothic murder mysteries, but of a man who had access to ancient truths as embodied in the horror of a plate food presented to my horrified childhood face, or rather mouth, or better eyes, although I did actually make the transition from just staring to actually eating. A sense that JH and partner were involved in some kind of archaic mystery work. I had never seen the vast size of a cod's head before, let alone been asked to eat its baked eyeballs, as part of a ritual of Scottish becoming.

What am I trying to say? That there is no value whatsoever, for any reader, in my passing on my early understanding of JH, as either my father's most generous and enduring friend, nor as provider of terrifyingly nineteenth century Gothic foodstuffs.

These experiences have only maybe a little to do with the man who exhibits calm in the face of human frailty who in my head is something like William of Baskerville, who sought answers to life's many sufferings in the wisdom within books.

But what would it mean to anyone to communicate to JH or the reader that I see him as something like the noble William of B, within the largest library in Christendom, attempting to salvage the lost books of history from the flames. What a childish notion, so again, I am stuck on what to say about JH and to JH about his work. Which brings me back to problem 1.

Problem 3. Or rather solution 1. OK, it is decided. I have just reread all of this mess and I conclude that the only solution is to write to the editor and tell him about all of these issues and state, with my apologies, that I will have to decline. Of course, it would be a great pity not to add my reflections on JH to this important book, but short of a solution along the lines of the one in problem 1, I can see no other way. So, that's it then. Decided. I'll have to write a letter to the editor apologising for letting him down. Maybe best to include these points above, on the understanding that the editor keep them confidential and under no circumstances share them with anyone else.

Yes, that's what I'll do. I'll say, you can have a read of my reasoning and doubts here, I'm deeply sorry and please, no matter what happens, do not share these confidences with anyone else. For the sake not just of me, but of JH. God, imagine what could happen if they ever made it into print.

Mar ná beidh ár leithéidí arís ann

Seán Bradley

Ignoring what W. H. Auden said about a publisher needing to know everything, I'd always assumed that, in relation to the publishing projects I embarked on, I knew about fifty-per-cent of what was required. Making up the remaining fifty-per-cent was what kept me interested. Working on John Herdman's *Another Country* (Thirsty Books, 2013) eight years ago proved that I was exactly right.

When it was first suggested to me by Todd McEwen that I look at re-issuing some of John's work, I had no hesitation in saying that what I would really like to publish was an expanded version of the pamphlet *Poets, Pubs, Polls and Pillar Boxes* which I'd read when it came out in 1999. There was ample, graphic evidence in that memoir to support Tom Nairn's assertion that 'The oddity of the Union has always posed grave cultural and psychological problems in Scotland'.

But that's not the reason it appealed to me. That was mainly a nostalgic one. What I had in mind was Anthony Cronin's body of work about the Irish writers who came to maturity (if you can call it that in all cases) in De Valera's repressive Republic, the place I grew up. Writers such as Brendan Behan, Paddy Kavanagh and Brian O'Nolan. Surely there were stories that hadn't found their way into John's brief memoir. I imagined the drunken young 'upstart from Cambridge' staggering home from Rose Street — Ma Scotts, or maybe the Abbotsford — hanging on to his poor suffering faither, bemoaning the state of Scotland — and getting nae sympathy! Staggering home to a seedy mansion, finally achieving fitful sleep with the help of a half bottle tucked under his pillow. I did not share this editorial dream with the author ... but I did come to learn that there were no such stories to tell.

What could be included, John assured me, was a further, more detailed critique of the writers covered in the 1999 memoir. Very good, I said. So, it happened that in a couple of short weeks, I had an additional 20,000 words to work with: the 50 per cent I didn't know about was an extended version of another pamphlet entitled *Some Renaissance Culture Wars* which John had published three years earlier. And that's what, in part, makes my publishing life interesting.

Another nostalgic element is that I arrived in Edinburgh in the mid-70s, at the tail end of the story set out in *Another Country*, the last few years of the MacDiarmid era. Though I did not meet John until much later, there's no doubt that he was part of the now vaguely remembered gatherings and ceilidhs that emanated from Sandy Bells bar. As Flann O'Brien said more than once — and always in jest — *Mar ná beidh ár leithéidí arís ann,* 'for our likes will not be seen again'.

Many happy returns John.

In Each Secret Place

In each secret place
the certainty of memories
the green bowers of the mountain
its wind-scoured crags
each day a pilgrimage
a reawakening to familiar
vistas which never pall
for knowledge must always increase itself
if only by a solitary new bird
or a cloud suffused by altering light
and in each secret place
I find the folk I cherish
inhabiting the memory
of days that have drifted
to earth like the copper coins
of birch leaves on the most secret
of all trails that leads
by the ravine-edge
upwards and even as I take it
companionless my friends are with me
and in imagination's time we halt
and together eat and drink and talk
remarking now on this immensity of sky
this cascading hollowness of water
this one more day drawing on to darkness.

Angus Martin

'An Upstart with a Degree from Cambridge'

James Robertson

Although it was John Herdman's fiction that I first came across and enjoyed, some time in the mid-1980s, I also admire, and owe a special debt to, his non-fiction. His reminiscences of the febrile literary and political scene in Edinburgh in the 1960s and 1970s, and of the individuals who populated the wilder fringes of the independence movement, are not only very entertaining but also a salutary reminder, especially in these latter days when the goal of independence seems tantalisingly wide and welcoming, that it is all too easy to blast the ball over the crossbar or sclaff it straight to an opponent – or even to a team-member who proceeds to put it in the back of their own net.

In a short piece published in the twentieth number of Walter Perrie's fine occasional publication *Fras*, in the run-up to the independence referendum of 2014, John wrote that

> a country's right to independence goes beyond the mere right of its people to choose. It is an inherent right, which one either accepts or one doesn't, and it continues to exist even if the people choose, at a particular moment in history, not to exercise it. … In September 2014 the Scottish people will be given an opportunity to choose whether or not they wish to exercise their right to freedom. But there is nothing absolute about that moment, the 'when' is a mere matter of historical contingency. The will of the people is something that is always shifting, as that of the Scottish electorate did between the failure of the Devolution Bill in 1979 and the acceptance of its much enhanced successor two decades later.

This is as clear and correct a rebuttal of the 'once in a generation' line favoured by some Unionists as I have seen. The idea that political choice and the exercising of that choice should be confined to one moment in, say, twenty or thirty or forty years, or constrained by what some person may or may not have said in that one moment, flies in the face of the basic concept of political rights. As somebody now entering his ninth decade, John Herdman surely knows about those shifting sands of time and choice and, indeed, about what political options may realistically be available to an individual, or a country, at any given period of history. When he was a boy, the possibility of Scotland being once again independent was about as remote as that of humans walking on the moon. Yet before he reached the age of thirty Winnie Ewing had won the Hamilton by-election and declared, 'Stop the world, Scotland wants to get on,' while Neil Armstrong had taken that other small step onto the lunar dust.

I want to say something about John's writing which focuses on that period of the 1950s, '60s and '70s when it was both harder and easier to be a Scottish nationalist than it is now: harder, because of the extreme unlikelihood that your ambition would ever be realised; easier, because with the goal so far over the horizon you could blooter the ball about with impunity in the middle of the park and nobody could maintain for very long that you had thus narrowly snatched defeat from the jaws of victory. One consequence of this situation was that John's hometown of Edinburgh, and specifically its pub scene, became a backdrop against which an extraordinary company of eccentrics, dreamers, dedicated grafters and dedicated wasters, poets and provocateurs strutted and fretted their hour upon the stage. John was both witness to and himself a player in this rich drama, and I for one am immensely grateful that he was there and that many years later he recorded his impressions of what went on: first, in a pamphlet published by Duncan Glen (Akros Publications) in 1999, *Poets, Pubs, Polls and Pillar Boxes: Memoirs of an Era in Scottish Politics and Letters*; second, in a pamphlet from Fras, *Some Renaissance Culture Wars* (2010); and third, in a book from Thirsty Books, *Another Country* (2013). There is additional material in yet another Fras pamphlet, which records a fascinating conversation between John, Walter Perrie and Richie McCaffery in March 2020 (*Conversations with Scottish Writers* No. 8, 2020).

In that conversation, Walter Perrie remarks that he and John, between them, have probably 'known most of the interesting people, certainly in the Scottish literary world over the last half century, we haven't missed many out.' John concurs, and says to Richie McCaffery, who was born in 1986, 'It's strange to think you never knew any of these people.' Then follows this exchange:

R.M. I do think I was born far too late.

W.P. No, you have come at the right time.

J.H. It's another curious thing, this business of the moment at which you're born. The degree to which you're a prisoner of the moment at which you were born and you can't do certain things because of that simple circumstance.

I find the assurance and acceptance of one's place in time, offered by the two older writers to the younger, both touching and true. I am nearly thirty years older than Richie McCaffery, yet in the 1970s I was still too young, and certainly too ignorant, to have searched out and experienced one of The Heretics spoken-word and music sessions in which John played such a vital part; nor did I witness the kind of scenes depicted in his memoirs, for example the magnificent post-pub stand-off, in somebody's home in Edinburgh, between poet Willie Neill and SNP local politician Willie Archibald, both in those days, as John puts it, 'formidable and generously constructed figures':

> It reached the point at which Willie A. demanded of Willie N., 'If you're such a great nationalist, what were you doing in the yapping, yelping Air Force? Tell me that!' Thoroughly incensed at this provocation, Willie N. grabbed hold of Willie A.'s nose and tweaked it, and Willie A., standing on the opposite side of a coffee table, responded in kind. Willie N. had tweaked first but Willie A. tweaked harder, and actually drew blood. Neither would now let go, and Carole Archibald, Rory Watson and myself and whoever else was there could only look on in consternation as the two massive figures swayed dangerously to and fro across the coffee table, the nose of each held firmly in the other's grip. Rory, I remember, turned to me in wonderment and with a certain pride and said, 'We're a barbarous nation, John!' (*Another Country*, pp.44–45)

The clean, clear prose of this passage, the accuracy of its description, the rich vein of comedy and the serious points underlying it – all these are characteristic of John's writing. Episodes like this – and there are plenty, such as when Major F.A.C. Boothby (of whom more below) repelled Anthony J. C. Kerr, the prolific letter-writer to *The Scotsman*, with the immortal words, 'Go away, you nasty little middle-European

Semite!' – actually happened; but they seem no less surreal than, for example, the encounter on a double-decker bus with a man wearing a large flowery hat and smoking a cigarette which forms the basis of John's 1990 short story, 'The Day I Met the Queen Mother'. The thin boundary between dream and reality is a recurrent theme in his work, and not just his fiction.

This brings me to my direct debt to John. Between 2006 and 2010 I was writing my novel *And the Land Lay Still*, which was, in part, an attempt to chart the political progress of Scotland from the almost unchallenged Unionism of 1950 to the creation of the modern Parliament at Holyrood in 1999. I felt that an important aspect of that story lay in the political and cultural undercurrents of the 1950s, '60s and '70s, where, as it were, a clandestine psychological struggle took place as individuals and groups fought not only the external establishment but also an internal one within themselves. I knew something about Major Boothby (probably, as it now seems, an agent provocateur placed among the wilder elements of the self-determination movement) and others of that ilk; I was familiar with the story of Willie McCrae's strange demise and with the exploits of Matt Lygate and the Scottish Workers' Revolutionary Party; but I did not have first-hand knowledge of any of them. John did.

This is not the place to go into the details of his scrapes and standoffs with the hierarchy of the 1320 Club, a dissident nationalist pressure group whose President, Christopher Murray Grieve (better known by his pen-name 'Hugh MacDiarmid'), was as left-wing as its Organiser, Boothby, was right-wing. ('Egomaniacs with delusions of grandeur always seemed to favour the post of Organiser', John dryly comments [*Another Country*, p.31].) Far better, and far more rewarding, to read about these in John's own work.

However, in 1969, he was persuaded to become editor of the Club's quarterly magazine, *Catalyst for the Scottish Viewpoint*, and this brought him into contact with Boothby and another man with an exceptionally good conceit of himself, Ronald Macdonald Douglas. The latter took it upon himself to keep an eye on John, which in effect meant attempting to edit the editor. The editor robustly rejected these efforts, bringing the wrath of Macdonald Douglas upon his head.

Macdonald Douglas's name was already known to me because on my parents' bookshelves was his 1935 miscellany *The Scots Book*, the contents of which I had, as a child, found inspiring (it was still being reprinted in the 1980s). Absent from his book was any mention of Macdonald Douglas's advocacy of armed force to achieve independence, a stance which put him firmly in the 'extreme patriot' camp, but it was his inability to tolerate any dissent from his own views which John found, well, intolerable. John, who in *And the Land Lay Still* gets a passing reference when Boothby calls him 'an upstart with a degree from Cambridge', edited just two issues of *Catalyst* before he had had enough and resigned.

It is seldom a good idea to meet one's heroes. One of my literary heroes was Hugh MacDiarmid. When he died in 1978 I knew nothing about him, but was provoked by the obituaries to find out. Reading MacDiarmid's poetry and prose revolutionised my thinking about almost everything, and helped to give order, argument and purpose to my previously merely emotional attachment to the idea of Scottish independence. Yet, as John MacCormick said of him, MacDiarmid was, politically,

> one of the greatest handicaps with which any national movement could have been burdened. His love of bitter controversy, his extravagant and self-assertive criticism of the English, and his woolly thinking ... were taken by many of the more sober-minded Scots as sufficient excuse to condemn the whole case for Home Rule out of hand.

All of which may be true, but MacDiarmid started me, and many others, on journeys we would never otherwise have taken. So, although in some respects I am relieved that I never met MacDiarmid, or indeed Christopher Murray Grieve, on the other hand I dearly wish I had. The closest I got to him was when, as writer in residence, I stayed at Brownsbank Cottage, near Biggar, where with his wife Valda he made his home for the last twenty-seven years of his life. For two years in the early 1990s I slept in his bed, sat in his armchair and woke every morning to numerous portraits of him staring down at me and inciting me to get up and work. It was a wonderful period of my life and, when I reflect on it now, I remember that John Herdman also knew Brownsbank. In August 1963 (I was five years old), he went there for the first time:

> If I had been expecting to be intimidated by the combative and

excoriating poet I was in for a pleasant surprise. Grieve was all welcome and geniality, and if when he was expatiating on some of his *bêtes noires* in politics or literature his eye took on a vatic gleam and the edge of his voice hardened into Stalinist steel, these were quickly dispelled when he reached you a plate of home-made scones with a persuasive smile of unfeigned, innocent sweetness. (*Another Country*, pp.20-21)

The scones, of course, were made by Valda. Nonetheless, John's discovery of a gentle, homely, private man residing behind the ferocious public persona was not unique. It's a tender and warm memory, and it chimes with my own of the benevolent atmosphere of that special wee house. John's various recollections of these bygone days are important to me personally and, I believe, important to Scotland generally. They tell us that we are not where we are now, in terms of our literature, our wider culture and our political maturity, by accident. We are here because of the people who came before us, and – to use an old cliché – their like will not be seen again. Thank you, John, for showing us who they were.

John Herdman and his Vignettes of Scottish Poets

Mario Relich

John Herdman's lean, precise and concise style of writing in his novels and stories lends itself to the aphoristic mode. The same goes for his critical writing. For the occasion of his eightieth birthday, I would like to celebrate his appraisal of various poets he has known; in effect they are miniature character-sketches of a number of prominent Scottish poets, his memoir *Another Country* (2013) being my main source.

Many of the poets he mentions read for The Heretics in the seventies, the informal group which organised poetry readings in Edinburgh, with Herdman as a founding member. His most perceptive comments are often on their reading styles. To start with Hugh MacDiarmid, he tells us about a Heretics reading at the 1971 Edinburgh Festival, which took place at the Charlotte Rooms, that he 'was by now close to eighty and there was a strong sense that he ought to be appreciated while there was still time', adding that:

> He was not perhaps an outstanding reader, but the biting force of his personality and the pleasure of hearing his highly characteristic Borders tones always made his appearances memorable. (p.54)

This is so shrewdly and justly phrased that it almost sounds like Samuel Johnson in his *Lives of the Poets,* despite the huge gap in historical era and cultural sensibility, not to mention nationality, between Herdman and Dr Johnson.

About another great twentieth century Scottish poet at the same reading, Sorley MacLean, he tells us that, among his achievements, 'He provided for many people their first exposure to Gaelic, and hearing him declaim in both Gaelic and English translation was a persuasive inducement to acquire enough of the former to appreciate him in the original'. But if this might sound possibly forbidding to some readers, the very next sentence provides a more down-to-earth touch in his recollection of MacLean:

His personal idiosyncrasies only added to the delight of his performances — the humsand haws, the rambling yet pointed introductions, the tightly screwed-up eyes, the shuffling of mixed-up papers, and the obsessively repeated glances at the large watch lying on the table, which he was somehow able to achieve without in the least compromising the passionate outpouring of language. (p.54)

Herdman's description is entirely accurate, and those of us lucky enough to have been at any of MacLean's bardic readings can vouch for its authenticity.

Norman MacCaig participated in the same 1971 reading. All three poets appeared together, as Herdman put it, 'I think for the first time', and 'which can fairly be described as an historic moment in Scottish literary history'.

Herdman makes both negative and positive comments about MacCaig, one of his more aphoristic being as follows: 'A great deal of the adulation he received can be attributed to his brilliance as a performer and his urbane good looks, and post-mortem adulation for him as a man remains more or less *de rigueur.*' However, he continues by revealing that he had 'more fixed feelings', culminating in this very evenly balanced character-sketch:

His self-esteem was considerable and he could be a verbal bully and rudely intolerant of the views and sensitivities of others. But he was a highly complex man, and the positive qualities of warmth, kindness and loyalty which others were aware of were, I am sure, no less real than those I have pointed to.

Contrasting MacCaig to MacLean, he observes that his readings 'did not have the unpredictable ups and downs of Sorley's but maintained a uniformly high standard of performance, beautifully timed and articulated, and appealing to a wider audience than Sorley's more exalted poetry.'

But he does add that MacCaig had another rival in the poetry reading stakes, namely his fellow Edinburgh resident, Robert Garioch, 'who was also a joy to listen to: always the pawky observer, playing skilfully on the ambiguities of the persona which he projected, at once humorous, caustic and self-deprecating.' He also points out that Garioch's poetry was 'securely grounded in the more or less contemporary demotic speech of the capital and was highly accomplished technically as well as very witty,' culminating in a shrewd summing-up of his character: 'His temperament was not combative, but quietly subversive.' No one who knew Garioch at all well would dispute this, and bearing this observation in mind it is not at all surprising that one of his favourite literary characters was Jaroslav Hasek's creation 'the good soldier Schweik'. Regarding Garioch's reputation, which he believes will stand 'the test of time', Herdman remarks that its durability 'derives from the secure basis of his poetic diction in living contemporary speech, although greatly enriched by a flexible readiness to make use also of the rich resources of earlier phases of the Scots language.'

While he judges that Sydney Goodsir Smith and Tom Scott, together with Garioch, were the 'three weightiest' writing in Scots at the time, his appreciation of the former two is more for their 'forceful personalities', and fidelity to MacDiarmid in their dedicated advocacy of Scots, than their actual poetry. His assessment of Duncan Glen in a review of his *Selected Poems* for *Lines Review,* No. 121 (1992), when Tessa Ransford was its magisterial editor, identified a different way of writing in modern Scots. Glen's style was less insistent perhaps than that of either Sydney Goodsir Smith or Tom Scott, even though Glen was also just as much an advocate of MacDiarmid's cultural/linguistic priorities:

> The restraint of Glen's Scots usage and spelling and his economy of punctuation can give his poems a somewhat stark and even forbidding look on the page: if not read aloud, they need to be internally vocalised to reveal their force. Their tone of voice is indeed, at its most typical, sparing and laconic, but the effects are far richer than may appear at first glance.

It's a passage that displays mastery of critical nuance, and evidently based on his own scrupulous engagement with Glen's poetry. In *Another Country,* he elaborates that 'despite his huge admiration for MacDiarmid', he 'nevertheless very much went his own way', and 'out of the Scots voice which he heard in his head, a contemporary voice from the borderland between rural and industrial Lanarkshire.'

At the end of his memoir, Herdman remarks that Alasdair Gray was vilified 'in certain quarters' for making contentious remarks about who dominates cultural organisations in Scotland. He therefore turned from 'national treasure' to 'grumpy old man', serving as 'a salutary reminder of what can still be the cost of speaking one's mind in Scotland.'

At eighty, John's reputation as an incisive novelist, short-story writer, and critic is secure. But he is neither 'grumpy old man', nor 'national treasure', a phrase he detests in any case. He should be regarded, instead, as an urbane man of letters who has always cogently, and without rancour, spoken his mind on Scottish literary and political matters. Long may he continue to do so.

Periodic Table of the [Herdman] Elements.

Todd McEwen

If the highest aim of a captain were to preserve his ship,
he would keep her in port forever.

Thomas Aquinas

At the Day of Judgment we shall not be asked what we have read,
but what we have done.

Thomas à Kempis

Crucifix.

Modest, if that is an appropriate term. Unfussy but not crude. Of plain metal. Or plaster. Affixed to the centre of a wall of pale, Georgian green, or perhaps pale, Georgian blue. Depending upon the residence, and the tendency of the decade. The first thing that must be admitted about a crucifix is that it is always, and indubitably, there.

Cold, very clean air.

1. It can be imagined, or used, as rectilinear volumes of air, of empty space, on the platform of a small railway station in the Highlands. These volumes of air exist on the platform *as* emptiness. They cannot be displaced even if there is some small human activity. They are permanent isolation and loneliness and exist far into the night and they are there in the morning. They protect the little station. They continue to exist in a photograph, or even if the station should be torn down.

2. This cold air surrounds and buoys the writer. It can be found in the pale rooms. Nobody can write anything when it's hot. Nobody. This particular air, like most air, can be found in the pale rooms and also in the kitchen and in the bedroom. It envelops the bath; it *reminds* the bath that the bath exists in the world, in Scotland. In the kitchen it is inside the cupboards. It *reminds* the whiskey.

Music.

The songs are high and thin. They really do act like haar — this is proven fact. They brush the tops of the pines on their way. They never reveal their destinations; this is for the writer to do. Some of the songs are in Gaelic, particularly the ones about longing and despair and wishing one had the means to marry. Or wanting to see Glasgow. Gaelic can reach the draughty parallelograms if it tries hard enough, but why should it bother? The lowland tunes are plucky. If you can treasure them in your head, they can help you march along. In heather, in mud. Pipe music is better, the hell with the Disarming Act. Although it is hard to whistle, because what do you do for drone? Your braces? Pibroch, certainly. Can we leave out the military stuff please? Hymns, probably not. Chant, yes. Yes.

Aqueous humour.

This is not jokes about fish. This is the essence of the eye itself, of the eye in the cold rooms, the eye that falls on the paper bought from James Thin. It is one of the most brilliant fluids of creation. It brings the world into our heads and displays the canniness, the hazel intelligence of the person who owns the eye. This penetrating hazel eye in its aqueous humour has looked upon many a foe in debate, many an irritating inebriate, many a bad sandwich of the lonely travels. It is still looking.

Leather.

The world the writer travels and imagines and exults in would not have come to exist without leather, though it is less in evidence than in the past. For this world to come into being it was necessary to have saddles, bridles, bellows, books, bibles, reins, aprons, halters (whatever they are), hats, jerkins and even masks for Covenanting preachers. Leather persists in the actual world under discussion here in the form of really good walking shoes. They might be of the 'ghillie' type, worn with plus-fours and knee-length woollen stockings, or they might cover the ankle, or you might buy them from a little shop somewhere in the Borders when it is raining or you might walk right in to Tiso's, bold as you please, and bone up on the latest from Switzerland. But they must be stout, stout shoes for kicking in the teeth of those who oppose you in the The Society. In your dreams.

Pine.

Perhaps too obvious to mention. But the works of the writer are surrounded by trees. Trees are glimpsed from the cool interior of most rooms in the work. The trees and the cold air are not exactly symbiotic but they are partners. Partners in background, partners in underpinning drama in the work. On the morbid side, many pines of our nation are made to sacrifice their lives to become panelling. This panelling exists in the work, in some stately rooms; the humbler pine panelling is what the writer has seen with his hazel eyes in run-down bars. The more run-down, the more panelling, though who did the original panelling it would be hard to say — the panelling was actually designed to be coated with tobacco smoke for exactly 78 years. Even the pine trees knew this.

Books.

One speaks of 'volumes' of air, many people do, but in the cold rooms with the books in their cases there are volumes of air also, each book possibly having a slight volume of air surrounding it. Everyone knows that books must be neatly arranged, it's practically axiomatic, so that the volumes of air surrounding the volumes of the books can be infinitesimally thin. Some of the books are bound in leather, yes, but this does not make them inherently better than any of the other books, bound in cloth, buckram, card or paper. They just *happen* to be leather, some of them. What is a 'scholarly' book? Does it have a look? Does it *lord* itself over the other books because of its title, the impress of the spine, its *leather*? Can a book *become* scholarly because of where it sits and how neatly? Will time tell, or will time do nothing about it? Can a book called *The Statistical Account of Scotland* rise, in time, becoming the leader or even the king of the other books in the cold case in the cold room? It doesn't matter because *the warmth comes when you open the books.*

Whiskey.

Stone, paper, scissors. Whiskey fights cold, even sitting in its bloody bottle. A bottle three-quarters full (huzzah) in a cold cabinet in the cold, clean kitchen. If a thermometer would not exactly reveal that it is warm, a hygrometer would, in a sense, but the point is that the whiskey is *yearning*. It wants to do its job, it wants to do what it was god damned put on this earth to do and it also wants to buddy up with lots of pine panelling. This whiskey — it might be from Perth, or it might even have been distilled in Blair Atholl, well not Blair Atholl itself but at the Blair Atholl distillery, you pedants, at Pitlochry.

Abstract knowledge.

Has filtered into and through the work from many sources. Some from the books, some from prayer, some from doctors and booksellers. Like a vitamin, like protein, like haar, like an orchestra. Like blood being purified by whatever organ purifies it, the work (and the trees and the whiskey) reifies the abstract and it becomes real, it enters the world, it becomes biting and colourful and funny and sad.

Abstruse knowledge.

We hate it, the work hates it, the trees hate it, The Society hates it and the whiskey hates it. And the small Highland railway station hates it.

Jealousy.

Say, brother, can you feel the tight wires? The zinging wires of frustration and jealousy, that criss-cross the farms, hills and trees of Perthshire? That alarm its very alarm geese in a yard? The murderous, unchurched dirty lust of farmers, barmen, the police? Not beautiful like a haar, it stings as if you were being sliced in a frighteningly large mandoline. This jealousy is in the work, in the cold air in the clothes of the characters, and they act on it. They use the jealousy to surmount large obstacles, really the most towering obstacles. This is how you make plot.

Longing.

Unlike the sear of jealousy, longing is also laid across the map of the areas in question. It is akin to music, in its poetic, but it is practically evanescent. It affects not farmers, who are merely jealous and in a perpetual rage, but people who live in cold rooms and who have made a few mistakes, even though they didn't want to. Longing can be transported around the county in a car, sometimes, but then it becomes action, which is not the same thing.

Love.

It's still not known whether this can be observed or calibrated like the haar or the music or the longing and jealousy. All of humankind still does not know, and will never know. But it is in the work. It is in all work, it is in the panelled bars and the cold rooms. It's everywhere, and the work acknowledges this, without wishing to suggest that this is abstruse. No one is suggesting that — there must be a better word.

England.

Never really existed. It might be mentioned, but it never really existed. *Cambridge* existed, but only as itself, not as something that exists in England, which doesn't exist. Not really.

Loch Maree.

In a startling suggestion, or pre-iteration, of the work, several people died in 1922 at the Loch Maree Hotel from eating bad duck-paste. Of the hotel's own making. This is not to say that the work is poisonous, far from it — the work is ennobling and beautiful. The very real connection is that sadness and longing and jealousy and haar were laid like a fish net over that part of Scotland at that time, and this must have contributed to human woe which in turn caused human errors that led to the inadvertent killing and death. There's nothing about this in the court papers but that's how it figures.

Joy.

Or let's say pleasures. Here is what you need on a solitary trip to the Highlands, whatever your reason for going, whether it be a John Herdman expedition to the home of the strangely privileged and booky or just a trip of your own to make yourself *feel* like John Herdman:

Stout leather shoes.
A good warm jumper.
A corduroy sport jacket.
Large Cadbury's Fruit and Nut.
Flask or half-bottle of whiskey.
Pipe and tobacco.
Railway timetable.
Ordnance survey map.
Some kind of sandwich.

A determination not to disturb the aforementioned volumes of air on the little Highland station.

Roam free. Except on or in Atholl Estates, where John Herdman was once called by a keeper a smart-arse, arse-hole, smart-aleck, jack-ass or fucker, it's not clear. It's not easy or pleasant to try to remember. For anyone. How could this have happened?

Possibility.

It's key, as the Americans say.

First example: would you be happy to spend the rest of your life living in a room at the Atholl Arms or even the Tilt, having a bar supper every evening and visiting the Blair Atholl Watermill for tea and wholemeal scones every afternoon, you being the constant, the unvarying, and watching the parade of touristic and boyscout humanity eating the same bar supper and wholemeal scones every day? No?

Second example: would you be willing to struggle up from beneath practically all of the abovementioned stuff, haar, music, longing, volumes, air, jealousy, pibroch, timetables and all the rest of it, and *take notice*, take *notice* of these fish nets and longings and wisps and oppressions, and give voice to this? Yes?

A Visit with John Herdman

Alan Mason

The house of Mr John Herdman stands at the eastern end of Brighton, a few yards from the sea front. It is a large, solidly built residence whose rounded windows directly overlook the street and whose porched entrance is reached by two worn steps that boast a palm on one and a pair of cracked shoes on the other. While its white façade and peeling paint are familiar to anyone who knows Brighton, there is much about the interior of the house that is distinctive — memorable even, for everywhere one looks there are signs of the wide-ranging sensibility that we have come to associate with the works of Mr Herdman. In the entrance hall, for instance, there is an old oak chest which was once the property of Anne of Cleves, while the stained-glass lamp that swings from the ceiling originally graced the smoking-room of the boat on which Mr Herdman made the crossing to Tunis, where he resided for the best part of a year. The dining room to the left of the hall is adorned with fine landscapes by distinguished artist friends, and the drawing-room, to which the visitor is conducted up a broad, angular staircase, is full of knick-knacks that speak of both the author's good taste and a broad success in life, the two merging in a bust of him by Mr Halliday which wreathed in laurels sits before a mirror on the mantelpiece.

When Mr Herdman strides into the room he is attired in a rough woollen suit of a reddish-brown shade and high walking boots, having just returned from a morning ramble over the Downs at the back of the town, to which he is more prone than the fashionable stroll along King's Road. Mr Herdman is below medium height; his hair is iron-grey, and he is never seen without spectacles. For all that there is a brightness about his ruddy, clean-shaven face, and a briskness about his voice and manner which would not lead one to suppose that he was getting on in years or that he recently recovered from surgery that at one point threatened his *good hand,* as he calls it — though he concedes there are critics who would jibe at the description.

We compliment him on his apparent good health, which was

obtained he tells us on the moors and mountains of Scotland.

'I put on enough in the summer to last me all year,' he says. 'But then I have always been susceptible to the wind and sunshine. It was because I was so bronzed on my return from Africa that my friend Pettie got me to sit for his portrait of a Crusader.'

We remember it well, we tell him, and the sensation it caused at that year's summer exhibition.

'You have a large acquaintance among artists, Mr Herdman — but then you are an artist yourself.'

Our glance travels round the room and alights on one or two pretty water-colours which are the novelist's own handiwork.

'Oh, I have used the brush a little,' he replies, with a deprecating shrug; 'and at the outset it was intended that I should make a profession of art. But I drifted into journalism by writing some articles on Ruskin for a Glasgow newspaper, which in turn led to an appointment on the *Weekly Citizen.*'

'And journalism led to novel-writing?'

'Yes. For some years I combined the two occupations but it wasn't sustainable. I felt that I couldn't do myself justice until novel-writing was all I did, however modestly.'

'And what is your method?' we inquire, when he has settled himself in his favourite armchair.

'A very slow and painful one, I am afraid. Before putting pen to paper I have to live with my characters for months, if only to find out how agreeable they are. If they cannot agree with me I can hardly expect them to agree with my readers, who are more exacting than I am and quick to point out discrepancies — although that's often my intention,' he says, with a smile, 'to show that we *vacillate* and that we are none of us fixed personalities. This is what I do during the summer, and the only time that I am really free from the burden of the novel-that-is-to-be is when I am grouse shooting or salmon fishing. At other times I am haunted to distraction by the lives my characters lead and the worlds they inhabit, and often have to stop and read about a subject if only to get my bearings or in order to make the whole thing plausible. Before beginning *Imelda*, for example, I was compelled to read a history of secret societies in Europe. For *Ghostwriting* a treatise on sanitary engineering. I believe it was because of my wide knowledge of the subject that a broken-hearted wife wrote to me asking for assistance in finding her husband, who had disappeared for the purpose, she supposed, of joining a secret society.

Another wanted to know if I had the name of a plumber, which I was able to provide from the extensive notes that I'd made on the subject.'

'Have you had any other eccentric correspondence, Mr Herdman?'

'Well, I daresay you have heard of the old lady of Lochinver, who ever since reading *A Truth Lover* was persuaded that I was her long-lost nephew. She used to address me at the Caractacus Club, "John Herdman, alias Macready, Esq.," explaining that in the novel in question I had related circumstances which were known to only one person other than her — that is, the nephew who had mysteriously disappeared — and consequently I must be him. I called upon her in Lochinver, in the hope of destroying her extraordinary delusion, only to leave her cherishing it as much as ever — more perhaps, though I only heard from her sporadically after that, and her letters degenerated with her mind until finally falling away entirely.'

In further conversation Mr Herdman tells us that not a few of his readers have remonstrated with him upon the 'sad endings' which he has given to several of his novels — even the late President Garfield, who on hearing from Andrew Carnegie that he was going back to Scotland for the summer, and would call upon Mr Herdman, asked him to take a message to the novelist, reproaching him for the conclusion of *Clapperton*, pathetically adding, 'Was there not enough sorrow in the world?'

'It was a Congressman from the same part of the world who asked me with tears in his eyes why such-and-such a character had to die? Well, you see, I told him. I didn't want her die. I'd grown rather fond of her. But I had to do it. If she had lived the reader would not have remembered her an hour after he closed the book.'

Whether this would have been so or not, Mr Herdman's readers could hardly forget his characters more speedily than he does himself. Mrs Herdman mentions more than one circumstance as showing how completely a novel, once it is finished and corrected for the press, passes out of her husband's mind. Possibly Mr Herdman has to have a clear field for the characters and incidents of his next novel, which, in his own words, 'is always going to be the best one.' On the other hand he is unlikely to forget the hard work he has put in or the ground he has tilled, and has a keen eye for what he knows to be his property. The practice of lifting lines from his books has become a commonplace he says, and claims to have seen examples in the works of several authors whose names he rattles off which we are surprised to hear and shall forebear from repeating.

'They think because my books are on the whole meretricious, and deal with life at its lowest, that the more elevated sections can be liberated from their surroundings and shown to better effect in a more elegant setting. But I am aware of their game, and while I continue to try to do good work I have recently lowered the tone to the point where any appropriation by others would be futile and self-defeating.'

We sense Mr Herdman is growing heated on this subject, and rather than provoke him further we inquire if he ever swims in Brighton. Though answering in the affirmative, and relaxing noticeably, he has clear ideas on the subject which he is keen to share with us.

'When swimming in the sea there is naturally more risk of accident than in a public bath where the space is confined and assistance is readily available. This being the case, I would suggest that the novice swimmer is in many respects like the fledgling author. The dangers of over-reaching are very real, and he can easily be swept away or misled by an early success into going too far or paying too little heed to the weeds or the undertow, which are ever present. He must find out if the tide is coming in or going out, and if it is going out confine his swimming to a comfortable distance parallel with the shore. When in danger it is usual — indeed natural — for him to throw up his arms and shout for help. But this only makes matters worse, though the instinct is all powerful. The sudden upward movement of the arms will force his body under the surface, and as at the same time he will empty his lungs of air, down he will go. It is a common belief, by the way, without the slightest truth to support it, that a drowning man will rise three times — three times, no more, no less. Obviously it depends upon circumstances; you may never rise at all, or you may bob up and down a hundred times. Similarly there are flailing authors who don't know enough to bow to their fates and sink peacefully below the waves, but persevere year after year and grow more desperate in their efforts to be seen — and rescued,' he adds, gazing from the window.

In conclusion we ask about Mr Herdman's homes, for in addition to the house in Brighton, and the lease he appears to hold on the billiard room of the Caractacus Club, he now has a pied-a-terre in London in the shape of some old-fashioned rooms at the Embankment end of Buckingham Street. Peter the Great once lived in these rooms, and they are supposed to have been the dwelling place for a time of David Copperfield. Moreover it was here that Mr Herdman himself laid some of the more contentious scenes of his novel *The Sinister Cabaret*, and it was here, he tells us, that he believes he met his double.

He was dressing for the theatre, he says, when he looked from his window and crossing the street below was a figure whose gait and general demeanour struck him as familiar, to the point where Mr Herdman could almost feel it in his legs and in the turn of his neck, which was often stiff and which he ran his hand across at the very moment the figure did the same.

'For an instant he looked up,' says the author, 'and pulling out a notebook proceeded to make a note that was done and dusted and tidied away in the pocket where his hand remained as he slipped from view. On reflection the note couldn't have been more than a smear or a line struck through an existing thought, but whatever it was meant to convey he had crossed the street before I knew it, vanishing beneath me at an angle where I could no longer gauge the finer points of his progress even as I stood on my toes and pressed myself to the window and for a moment pictured him at the front door of the building or on the staircase whose every creak made me jump for the next few hours. I never saw him again, and I don't know what to make of it, but I've come to believe that our paths had crossed by mistake and that he regretted it; that however fleeting the encounter he felt distaste for the man he saw and wanted nothing more than to be gone — or for *me* to be gone,' says Mr Herdman, 'so contemptuous was the look he gave me, and all the worse for being my own and for the fact that I warranted a note or the removal of one, which has come to trouble me more than any other aspect of the affair.'

My Wife's Lovers and Cruising:
the play and the book

Sally Evans

The play *Cruising* came first, published by diehard and performed in Edinburgh in 1997. My husband and I produced the book of the play, and we enjoyed attending the production in the Netherbow (now the Scottish Storytelling Centre.) In *Cruising*, characters with foibles and clashing class backgrounds are held together on a shipboard holiday after meeting in Edinburgh New Town. An old lawyer Sir Hamish and his wife Cynthia appear in the play's first scene and remain in control — or not — of the action when thrown together with the equally Scottish Wee Davie. A testing of the married couple ensues.

Ten years later came the book, published by Black Ace, containing ten varied tales, including a rumpus in a church on Easter Sunday, a reflection on Scottish Nationalism, and the story version of *Cruising*.

The title story, 'My Wife's Lovers', is an intense tale of literary detection, and if the title and illustration suggest a theme of marital comedy, this is proved mistaken on reading the stories, so the inclusion of a tale based on Hamish and Cynthia and Wee Davie could redress readers' expectations in that line. The tale 'Cruising' is preceded by a shorter piece, Voyaging, running through a saga of nineteenth century shipping and ending with the meeting of Herdman's parents. The reader is left to deduce this tale is true among the fictions of the book.

'Cruising' has been thoughtfully rewritten from the ten-year-old play. The story remains the same. The interesting thing is its viewpoint — the stance the author takes as storyteller, the character he is nearest to. In most of the stories, 'My Wife's Lovers', etc., the storyteller is fairly close to Herdman: the biographer in the title story, the witness in the church fiasco, himself in Voyaging. In a play there may be viewpoint in the amount of speech a character is given, the way the playwright presents the characters, but there is no authorial viewpoint in that the characters speak for themselves.

In the tale 'Cruising', however, we are in Wee Davie's viewpoint. It is Wee Davie's tale, using a language unlike most of the stories in the book, and utilising Scottish idiom. This 'happened to a pal of mine' says the narrator. It remains the English language, yet in a very Scottish way bridges the gap between classes and backgrounds of the play's participants.

And so I've ended up discussing and reading the whole book *My Wife's Lovers*, not just *Cruising*. The whole book is about watching people collide regardless of background, whether they are church probationers ('curate' being, as noted, an English word), seedy aristocrats, old country gentlemen, the Misses Faux (Fox) and Todd, or even John Herdman's own ancestors. Class is different in England and Scotland. In Scotland, and the New Town is a great example of this, you have class background but you relate to everyone. There is language for doing this. In England there's more distance. It's a very Scottish book, and the play too is Scottish for the same reasons.

Anither Fareyeweel: A Palimpsest for John

Andrew Greig

An overwrite of Wm. Fowler's 'Ane Fareyeweel: Address to the Graduation Revelries of the Class of 1574' From 'ROSE NICOLSON', a Memoir of the early Reformation With the goodly companie of our Formation in mind

'A toast and gledsome fareyeweel to my learned friends Wallace, McLeish, Chisholm and Millar! God speed ye stalwart lairds Hamilton, Acton, Fairweather and Davie, lang may yer humane lums reek! To Crawford, Watson, Smith and McCaig, braced for dominie posts — may your sagacity ne'er be questioned, and the punitive tawse hang dusty in your closet.

May the East wind ne'er find ye out, Findlay, Morgan, Black and Gray, as you sit in your unheated chambers, undoing Council edicts and regulations byordinar!

Let us drink pisspots of claret to those who left without graduating: Palmer, Heron, Williamson, Grieve, Martyn and Michie. Who does not envy Eveling at the cleek factory, bairn at his knee, polishing his baffie? With Stoic equanimity we shall overlook Kelvin and Bold, lost to Theology — may your sermons be learned and interminable, and we not be there to hear them.

Let us drink a tearful toast to absent friends: Bob Tait (fever), Sutherland (choked on hard bread), thrawn Jackson (poisoned) and ever-joking Charlie Ogilvie who died by discharge of his own pistol to the head. May your brief lives be remembered till ours are forgot.

Adieu to Milne's and the Criterion, the Oxford and Traverse, those rudimentary howffs we have been glum and glorious in. May we never again drink rancid beer and leathery claret in such quantities! Goodbye and riddance to Principal, Dean and Proctor, to tutors drunken, recusant, lecherous, addled. Rattle your keys in vain, greasy-palmed Hebdomadar, keeper of our most shameful secrets!

Goodbye to George Buchanan and Richard Hamilton, in cold clay by St Rules. I shall never cease to thank you, for you gave me the means — better Grammar, modesty and wit — that may help me accomplish the ends to which I aspire (don't enquire). You were kind to a hungering boy.

So now Goodnight Butlin, Herdman and McCabe, Lochhead and Hutcheson, fieres of my youth! I would read you a poem, but I have been o'er busy playing gowf and revising for my final examinations to write one.

Let there be tears, yet not o'er many, for this is a small country and likely we shall meet again to share tales of our charred town and its moribund university in the years our Formation.

Friends, I shall stagger back through moonlit streets to my bunk one last time, wind off the sea tearing moisture from my eyes as I cross the links where a lass once filled my heart with siller as if it were a purse.

Our days in this wintry Hell are done! I toast an end to learning. Let our trade wi the world commence!!'

Added on MSS verso, in his old age

Such were my fellows in early days of our Reform,
When town and gown were threadbare and fighting to be warm.
Our fees were outrageous, our landladies rapacious,
The few lasses sharp-tongued as gulls,
Our tutors exhausted, the honest in despair,
The corrupt plotting in their chambers –
All envied us, even in their grandeur,
For we were young and they were not.
Their day has passed, as ours
Will soon enough –
Laugh that off, Charles Ogilvie, Dunbar!

'Being Scottish …'

Margaret Bennett

Being Scottish I'm rooted in this Land of the Mountain and the Flood, Old Red Sandstone, Grey Granite and Trainspotting. The land of my birth evokes a disparity of responses reflecting the place I happen to be, at home or abroad. There's awe at Edinburgh's skyline, a smile at Glasgow's Lobey Dosser (in dreichest rain or traffic), rankle at Sutherland's Duke, tranquility at the Quiraing, a sense of wonder at Soutra, and curiosity at the smells of factories or breweries. Callanish and Jarlshof amaze me, but so do my compatriots who'd swap them for a football match. Being Scottish, however, we raise a glass together:

> Scotland thy mountains,
> Thy valleys and fountains
> The home of the poet,
> The birthplace of song.

And here's to porridge, penicillin, bicycles, bagpipes, steam engines, tartan, tarmacadam, thistles, whisky and Dolly the sheep. Oh, flower of Scotland …

Sometimes I wonder if I belong to a country of the imagination. Outside it, I'm expected to explain, dismantle stereotypes, or justify my claim to being Scottish.

'You have an accent,' and they don't.

'You don't sound Scottish! Where's your rrrrrrrroamin in the gloamin? What part of Ireland are you from?'

These folk make me explain my species of Scottishness. A Hebridean, Gaelic-speaking mother and Lowland, Scots-speaking father, who both spoke English. One sang Gaelic songs, the other hee-durram-haw-durrams and played the bagpipes. One leaned far to the left, the other did not. They raised four children between two cultures, three languages, surrounded by a wealth of domestic, social, religious, cultural and political paradoxes.

Apprenticeship in philosophy begins at birth, and in Scotland, cradle of the paradox, lasts a lifetime. Being Scottish, I'm proud of David Hume and his ilk but grapple with the inconsistencies, absurdities, and impossibilities of our homeland. Faith of our fathers, yet not my father's faith. The fear of the Lord is the beginning of wisdom — don't be afraid to speak your mind. Children should be seen and not heard — mind, you've a guid Scots tongue in yer heid. Cleanliness is next to Godliness. The clartier the cosier. Here's to pure air, pure water, pure filth — pure dead brilliant.

Dichotomy aside, this same cradle nurtured culture — literature, song, music, dance, cinema, art, photography, theology, engineering, science, law, sport, education and medical knowledge. Being Scottish, I glow with pride at world acclaim for our famous medical schools — I reflect on the centuries of clan physicians that predated them. What was that about the worst health record? Excuse me, we're talking about achievements.

Being Scottish I love tartan, even badly worn, but not worn badly. I'm proud of the tartan armies (those of tanks, trenches, prison camps and freedom); despise tartan terror; and wish Scotland could harness enthusiasm like the Tartan Army. Such whole-heartedness would do wonders for Scotland's languages, education, health, industry — the stuff of dreams, what could be, should be, and my daily hope it yet can be.

Perhaps this world of contradictions may make more sense if I look through Scottish eyes at how we live. Rowans planted to keep away witches — you'll see them in Edinburgh gardens on the way to church. A bridegroom stripped naked and blackened before his wedding — indecent and cruel any other night but that one. A lassie on a busy road jumping over a chantie fu o salt — her pals stop double-decker buses, and the local bobby kisses her. Men carrying a huge barrel of blazing tar on their shoulders through packed streets ignoring peril. People climbing Arthur's Seat in the middle of the night to watch the sunrise and wash in the dew. Families tying rags on trees to wish away disease. Horse riders galloping at breakneck speed through their town, risking life and limb to remember centuries past. Others on foot, stampeding across anything and over anyone to capture a wee ball covered in ribbons. That's what real Scots do because they know what it means to be Scottish. "It's priceless, incomparable, unique," say thousands of wanna-be's flocking to Princes Street and George's Square on a freezing Hogmanay — they've paid for a taste of being Scottish.

(Give me the Flambeaux, the Tron or the fireside.)

An undefined sense of Scottishness follows unbidden wherever I go. Ordinary at home, but celebrated abroad, grand style. "We'll offer you better prospects," some say. "You can earn a living here just by Being Scottish. You'll never want to leave." But, like the love-struck partner in a bad marriage, back home I go, not driven by homesickness or mindless duty — just unprecedented devotion. There's nothing like a bit of temptation or a wee fling, though, to keep the Scottish passion alive.

Beethoven's Response to the Hanging Gardens of Neglect

Ron Butlin

LUDWIG VAN BEETHOVEN (1770–1827) never visited Edinburgh, though he often dreamt about it. The city was his El Dorado. Having been commissioned by George Thomson of Edinburgh to write settings of Scottish folksongs, he had cleaned up in a big way. As had Haydn. 'These songs are my pension,' said Haydn, rubbing his hands each time he nipped out to cash that week's Postal Order from Scotland.

Unlike Mozart, Beethoven was one of the first freelance artists to survive. He took the whip hand — driving hard bargains, often selling the same piece several times over to different publishers — and recognised that publishers needed composers or they would go out of business. A healthy attitude.

MAXI THE TAXI, of course, still lives in Edinburgh. His kind increases the further north one goes.

'BECOME A MILLIONAIRE IN SIX MONTHS — OR EVEN LESS!' had been the 20-point, bold-type heading to the flyer that had come in the second post. Beethoven studied it carefully. There was no small print, just promises, testimonies from newly minted millionaires, multicoloured graphs and persuasive statistics. Knowing where his best interests lay, the great composer had put aside the sketches of a new symphony.

That was yesterday. Today, as always, he's come striding into Edinburgh. Setting a cracking pace up Minto Street — a gradient that defeats many a lesser musician — picking up speed on the flat so that the 8 Till Late minimarket, Bernie the Barber's single-room, single-chair salon, Blockbusters, the Queen's Hall and South Clerk Street itself are no more than a blur of shop windows and stalled traffic. Steamrollering down Nicolson Street, hitting peak form opposite Tesco's. Looking neither right nor left — no glance into the Apple Centre nor towards Chandler's Classical Music shop (Vinyl a speciality). No distractions — he's utterly focused. The other pedestrians part to let him through, the buildings on either side seeming to lean back to give him freer passage: the iron railings of Nicolson Square, the glass-walled Festival Theatre, the soot-blackened Old Quad. Neither too fast nor too slow, *allegro ma non troppo*, the colossus of western music marches ever onwards.

Knowing he's going to be a rich man has certainly put a spring in Beethoven's step this morning — and no wonder! By 3 p.m. yesterday every scrap of available paper had been covered in calculations — and he knew he couldn't lose. By 4 p.m. he'd been to the bank, withdrawn £2,000 in ten pound notes. Called at the post office on his way home. By 6 p.m. he'd been writing letters. By midnight addressing envelopes. By two a.m. licking stamps. Three in the morning had seen him and a sackful of mail staggering towards the nearest post box.

The future's looking good. There'll be no more selling the same old *Mass in C* over and over to different publishers pretending it's brand new, no more depending on handouts, sponsorship deals and brown-nose dedications. Strictly Business Class from now on: stretch limos and Platinum Cards. He'll be a Frequent Flyer, hitting the executive hospitality suite to make up for all those years trapped in the bus lane of life.

As the rest of us get into the swing of the New Millennium, we seem to have lost touch with the *basso continuo* keeping us in step with our individual destinies. No primal rhythm moves us anymore, only a debased counterpoint of hopes and fears, regrets and self-interest. We have stumbled, and have been brought to our knees. Not so Beethoven.

Brushing aside the Rise and Fall of several empires, the discovery of the subconscious, the splitting of the atom and a World War upon which the sun has never quite set — the great composer sticks to his chosen path. When it rains, he gets drenched to a perfect likeness of the portrait done shortly after his first set of cello sonatas: black hair, a sleekness and confidence of demeanour, a youthful moisture about the cheeks, lips and eyes. When sleet sharpened by an easterly comes scudding in off the Forth, he ages to that grey-haired *Bürgermeister* of the late quartets: the straggled locks, the complexion of liver rolled in flour. But whatever the weather, he never lets his gaze shift from the far horizon as if only from *there* — Portobello Beach? The shimmering hills of Fife? — will come any hope for the salvation of mankind. But who knows? Perhaps it will.

Now that he's passed the Chinese Buffet King, one of the city's major landmarks looms into view, the Tron Kirk — as tantalising as ever. Only a few hundred metres to go, but Beethoven has never yet succeeded in reaching its ever-beckoning steeple. Before him lies the most difficult part of his journey — the Zone of Everything-and-Nothingness that is South Bridge. The great composer has never yet conquered this no man's land, this anti-matter force-field, between Infirmary Street and the Royal Mile ... And already he's slowing down, stumbling even. Beneath these pavements are the layers upon layers of darkness, the walled-up passages and hidden chambers whose forgotten stonework long ago became the foundations for today's Festival City. Like some terrible gravity, the city's stifled history has begun dragging on his every step.

He struggles to keep going, pausing every few yards to catch his breath. Soon he's hauling himself hand-over-hand from doorway to lamppost to bus shelter, to have something always to hold onto. Finally, next to Poundstretcher's, he stops, and doesn't get started again. He can go no further. Here, indeed, is a stretch of Dante's dark wood: perpetually failing daylight, the fast food outlets one after the other, the roomfuls of slot machines, the suitcase sellers, the hirers and lenders and cheque cashers, the MASSIVE SALES where the whole world itself will be marked down in the end. The message is clear: EVERYTHING MUST GO. This is the twenty-first century — overlaid by swirling litter, scaffolding and dogshit.

Seeking relief, Beethoven lifts his eyes to above street-level, and sees floor upon floor of boarded up windows, peeling paintwork, untenanted dampness, mould and dry rot. Upwardly mobile decay that's held in check by the weight of chimney-stacks and roof-lead, by the rattle of broken slates, the snap and slash of exposed wiring and, most of all, by the hanging gardens of neglect: the wind-borne grass and weeds clinging to choked gutters and shattered stonework.

With both hands raised, the great man has stepped off the pavement and out into the middle of the street:

'ENOUGH!'

His anguished cry reverberates along the entire length of South Bridge. The traffic comes to an abrupt halt. He climbs into the nearest taxi.

'TREES!' he commands. 'Take me to trees, and meadows. And rushing streams. And hills.'

Meter switched on, the driver glances in the mirror to inspect his latest fare.

His latest fare stares straight back at him: 'Trees, I said. Big ones. Big branches, broad leaves, trunks like gasometers.'

'Certainly, sir. Trees it is. The Botanics maybe?'

'The trees of my Sixth Symphony, the *Pastorale* in F major Op.68, did not grow in the Botanics! They were not watered by Council hoses nor clipped by Council shears. I want wild trees, not ones with labels on them! I want trees of freedom reaching for the heavens! I want wide open spaces and a horizon that expands the soul!'

'Fair enough, sir.' The driver does a quick u-ey, turning his taxi face the way he'd just come.

Maxi The Taxi is used to tourists. His childhood among religious fanatics has secured him an equable temper based on the certain knowledge of his own salvation. It cheers him to think that he himself brings thousands of city-visitors that bit closer to their predestined damnation — and gets paid for it. His psychopathology is strictly Scottish Throwback. Like most children he was musical. In the absence of an orchestra in his muddy village he conducted the hedges and woodlands, his string section. As he grew more confident, the sheep and cattle on the hillside, the clouds, the birds, the wind, the river, the farmer's dog, his tractor — everything seen and unseen was given its place on his unwritten score. So far so good — then word got around. His teacher, a strict believer in Scottish Education, stood him out in front to conduct the morning's noise, and kept him there till he'd learnt his lesson. That night young Maxi lay in bed listening to the restless hills and streams, to their unplayed music. Far above him, the moon turned soundlessly on its invisible rope.

Adult Maxi nourishes the child-within by picturing the torments his passengers are destined for. It passes his days. As they reach Minto Street, towards the unmapped Southside lying beyond Cameron Toll and out of town, he switches to automatic pilot and starts revelling in visions of damnation. A faith-strengthening exercise.

For Beethoven, looking out of the taxi window, the journey's like watching his recent past unscroll backwards before his very eyes: the Festival Theatre, the Apple Centre, Queen's Hall, Blockbusters, Bernie's. For consolation, he reminds himself that 200 letters (minimum required) with a ten pound note (no cheques, please) in each, are even now making their way to the potential contributors to his future wealth. The hard work has been done, all that remains is to let the Karmic tide of fiscal benevolence roll back in, swamping him with cash.

'The Pentlands suit you then, sir?' Maxi's called from the front of the cab.

The great composer is savouring his calculations one more time.

Even allowing for a modest response rate, 10% say, he'll get a tenner from 20 of them — 20x10. £200. Plus a further tenner from each of the replies they themselves receive in turn — 20x20x10. £4,000. Then tenners from everyone that replies to all of *them*. Which'll be the same again, times ten. £40,000. And so on, and so on, and so on … The mind boggles.

'THE PENTLANDS, SIR? Are you deaf?'

'No need to shout.'

Twenty minutes later the taxi has pulled up at the Flotterstone road-end.

Beethoven stares out at the grass-and-bracken slopes of Turnhouse Hill and Carnethy, at the green fields and generous stretches of woodland. There is an ache in his heart and a longing too deep for words. Which would he like to do first: lay his head on Nature's grassy bosom, or hug a few trees?

'That'll be £22.40.'

Beethoven takes out his purse. 'Do you take *groschen*?'

'£22.40.'

'Euros?'

'£22.40.'

'Cheque? Switch? Mastercard? Bank transfer?'

Maxi is a super-bigot in financial matters also. Though more enlightened Calvinists accept the elegance of double-entry book-keeping and the dynamics of credit as God's gifts to the prudent, Maxi considers such innovations to be 'limbs of Satan'. Since the economic boom of the '80s, he has watched Satan's limbs multiply exponentially and it is one of his bitterest pleasures to hunt down and damn every new ISA, TOISA and MIRA.

Too late Beethoven hears the twin *clicks* of the taxi doors' automatic locks.

It is evening. After a cup of sweetened tea and a dinner of bread followed by bread, Beethoven prepares to stretch out on his Scottish Office regulation strip of bed-foam. Having been driven, at no extra charge, to St Leonard's police station, he has decided that, this time, he really has *had* it. From further down the corridor come the sounds of a man weeping, another is screaming. In the cell next door someone's hammering his fists against the wall: 'Sticking me back in here again! See you, God, you've a fucking short memory!'

Beethoven switches off his hearing aid. Peace at last, time-out from the headlong rush of human progress and the miracle that is pyramid-selling. Like the descending violin figure from the Benedictus of his *Missa Solemnis*, he gradually eases himself into a state of complete calm. This moment of delicious resignation, he considers, should not be squandered on the contemplation of mortality nor on thoughts of a new string quartet. It is precious, and should be treasured. He lies back and closes his eyes ...

Maxi, meanwhile, is nearing the end of his backshift. He's begun talking to himself: 'Got hissel immortality wi symphonies? — but he disnae pey his wey. Only yin place fer the likes of thon. Stick him in, an throw away the key.'

Nobody listens, of course. His last fare is a woman giving birth. As he drives away from the hospital Maxi consoles himself for the lack of a tip: 'Anither yin tae keep the fires burnin.'

Thanks to some joint funding from the Scottish Arts Council and the Goethe Institute, Beethoven is released a few days later.

Naturally, he wants to hurry straight home to the pile of accumulated mail — every envelope swollen with hard cash. But he doesn't. Because he can't. Because he is utterly lost. Decanted after midnight onto an unfamiliar street, without map or directions. Where is his customary route? The shops he knows so well? The theatres, galleries, restaurants?

He wanders a city of darkened streets. All around him are the eyes that glare, the tongues that loll, the hands that clench and claw, the faces turned inside-out. He blunders from pavement to gutter and back onto pavement again, slithering on vomit, piss and pizza. He gets shouted at, sworn at. He's grabbed, punched, kicked. There are only the hard men left — the hard men, and the downtrodden. All of them had been set free in *Fidelio*, only to be imprisoned once more, it seems, here in the free market. In this nightmare, all he can summon to his aid — like a set of bearings for another place, another time — is the enigmatic phrase he scribbled in the margin of his last string quartet.

Coming to an abrupt halt at a traffic island in the middle of nowhere, he glowers in every direction, then raises a clenched fist to the heavens. He cries out:

'MUST IT BE? IT MUST BE!'

Each curse he brings down upon the city is marked ff.

Bob and John

Alan Taylor

Less than two months separate the births of Bob Dylan and John Herdman. The former was born in blue-collar Duluth, Minnesota, on 24th May, 1941, the latter in bourgeois Edinburgh on 20th July. Four decades later, Herdman wrote *Voice Without Restraint*, a critical — and appreciative — commentary on Dylan's lyrics. It was one of the first such books. At the time, Dylan was in the midst of his religious phase, having converted from Judaism to Christianity in the late 1970s. A trio of albums, sometimes referred to as his 'gospel' albums, *Slow Train Coming*, *Saved* and *Shot of Love*, were greeted with dismay by many Dylan diehards. If not quite reaching the level of abuse when he 'went electric', there was a sense that he had lost the plot and many of those who had followed his career were in despair.

Not John Herdman, whose fascination with the tousled-haired troubadour never wavered. For Herdman, the intriguing question was, 'What is the voice saying, what is the music saying?' The one could not be divorced from the other. What Dylan's Scottish contemporary hoped to illuminate in his study was the American's 'hybrid art'. Along the way, he invoked Levi-Strauss, Marshall McLuhan, Nietzsche, Rimbaud, Brecht and others. In a golden period for rock music, Herdman, rightly, put Dylan 'half a step ahead' of the likes of the still underrated Randy Newman, Mick Jagger and Keith Richards, Bruce Springsteen, hailed as the next or new Dylan, Van Morrison and Robert Hunter of the Grateful Dead. Conspicuous by their absence was any mention of Messrs Lennon and McCartney.

I can't recall what reception was given to *Voice Without Restraint*. Rereading it recently, however, I was struck by the generosity and insight of its author. Much water has gushed under the bridge since it was first published, and Dylan and Herdman have continued to write and develop. Those of us who grew up with Dylan have the habit of locating ourselves according to what he was doing at a particular time, be it the aforementioned Damascene conversion from acoustic to electric, much to the horror of folk purists, or when in 1966 he crashed his motorbike and nearly died young like so many of his peers.

Dylan's ability to produce songs for all occasions and emotions is not the least remarkable of his talents. Like Herdman, we all wondered how Dylan became Dylan, how he emerged from the chrysalis of an ordinary family to become such a totemic figure. What transformed him, we puzzled, from a performer of cover versions to an ageless songwriter? We were not surprised when he was awarded the Nobel Prize in Literature, or if we were it was only because it had taken the Swedish jurists so long to honour him. 'Desolation Row' was the Dylan generation's *Waste Land*, 'Visions of Johanna' Whitmanesque in its enigmatic eloquence. We never asked ourselves if he was a poet; that was self-evident.

Listening to Dylan, countless questions arose. What is he saying? What's this song about? Is it personal, political, or both? At a time when the average pop song lasted no more than three minutes, Dylan, defiantly defying categorisation, used albums to expand the form. He told stories, created atmosphere, evoked character, all in songs that you could identify within the first few notes. Years ago I interviewed Kris Kristofferson, who was staying in Glasgow for a while. In 1966, he had been a janitor in the studio in Nashville where Dylan was recording what would become *Blonde on Blonde*. Among the songs he was one of the first to hear were 'Rainy Day Women', 'Just Like a Woman' and, of course, 'Visions of Johanna'. 'It was like listening to Keats's words,' said Kristofferson, 'set to music by Mozart.'

As Herdman makes clear Dylan's aim was to write lyrics which would work when accompanied musically. In that regard, he was constrained. Keats did not need to think how his lines would sit musically. One of the many mysterious things about Dylan is how lyrics become songs. While musicians hung around the recording studio he would be writing elsewhere. Then, when eventually he showed up, he would whisper in the ear of, say, Al Kooper or Robbie Robertson, who would pass on instructions to other members of the band. How the underlying sound (often markedly different from one album to the next) that was achieved came about is one of the many mysteries surrounding the manner in which Dylan operated. What he seems to have been keen to do is record the song as it played in his head at a particular time. But as the bootleg series shows, he was always eager to explore alternative versions. There is no definitive take of his songs. Each changes as the mood and the moment seizes him. It's an organic, evolutionary process, more akin to jazz than classical.

What Dylan was seeking, observed Herdman, is 'authenticity of feeling'. Dylan himself described it thus: 'Sometimes you say things in songs even if there's a small chance of them being true. And sometimes you say things that have nothing to do with the truth of what you want to say and sometimes you say things that everyone knows to be true. Then again, at the same time, you're thinking that the only truth on earth is that there is no truth on it.' It could be said that this is yet another example of Dylan having his cake and eating it, of illuminating his art while simultaneously obscuring it. What he is suggesting here, it seems to me, is that his art is as much of a mystery to him as it is to the rest of us and that he would prefer not to explore its genesis. But he is also speaking for other artists who do not know where their genius springs from and how it will develop and be received.

When *Voice Without Restraint* appeared no one, least of all its author, knew how its subject's career would pan out. What John Herdman was sure of was that by 1981 Dylan had already created an oeuvre that was likely to endure and required serious attention. What may have appealed to Herdman was Dylan's determination to do his own thing, as people were wont to say in the 1960s. We do not know to what extent his family supported his ambition; in his memoir, *Chronicles*, he is evasive about his upbringing. When a record company executive asked him about his family and where they were, Dylan replied: 'I told him I had no idea, that they were long gone.' Other enquiries were given curt answers. His father, he said, was an "lectrician', his mother a housewife. No mention was made of his brother. 'What was your home life like?' asked the executive. 'I told him I'd been kicked out.' How true this was is uncertain. Even then Dylan was adept at deflecting enquiries about his private life.

What we do know, is that Herdman's folks — affluent, upper middle class, Presbyterian, 'almost Victorian' in attitude — had earmarked him for the family business. This was not his inclination and his desire to become a writer led to tension, especially between him and his father. The Sixties was a decade in which youth asserted itself, sometimes insensitively. Both Herdman and Dylan chose paths of their own mapping. The roads they travelled may have been geographically different but they were essentially the same. They were artists disinclined to look back.

Clapperton in a Changing Scotland

Tom Pow

From the very precise publication date of *Memoirs of My Aunt Minnie and Clapperton* — April 23rd 1974 — I think it must have been in the early '70s that I heard, on a couple of occasions, John Herdman read from *Clapperton*. This would have been at the West End Hotel in Edinburgh which was the base of The Heretics. John was a rare prose writer among a bevy of poets, but when he announced he was 'now going to read from *Clapperton*', there was a hum of approval and anticipation.

I still see him, neat in his shirt and tie, erect, but for the slightest propulsive lean forward as he read about the unfortunate Clapperton, pausing briefly now and again for laughter to subside. His face was flushed with pleasure. I have other memories of prose readings from around that time; most particularly, of Iain Crichton Smith, enjoying as much as his audience, his *Murdo* stories. The mention of Murdo could also make an audience sigh with anticipation. Iain, as I recall, unlike John who exercised some restraint between himself and his character, was very much in on the act.

> One day Murdo visited the local library and he said to the thin bespectacled woman who was standing at the counter:
> 'I want the novel *War and Peace* written by Hugh Macleod.'
> 'Hugh Macleod?' she said.
> 'Yes,' he said, 'but if you don't happen to have *War and Peace* I'll take any other novel by the same author such as *The Brothers Karamazov*.'

It was as if Iain had just come up with the conceit at that moment and was enjoying it along with his audience. Perhaps it was that sense of identification with his creation that led to such a rich and extended relationship between Iain and Murdo, such that eventually, in *Life of Murdo*, the two came together. In an introductory note to that work, he comments, 'Using "Murdo" rather than "I" allowed me the distance that I needed to be objective about myself and to make comedy of painful experiences.'

By contrast with the extensive mining of *Murdo*, it was a surprise to me, returning to *Clapperton* for this essay, to discover how short it is — no more than twenty pages of print. But then again, it is as long as it needs to be to do what it wants to do: to establish in the mind, for amusement, a character beset by social and cultural circumstances. It strikes me also that John has always known how long something needs to be: his strategy is the dart, the hit and run, the short story, the novella, rather than the lengthy exploration. (I'm remembering now that there was something of this in his reading manner too: the sentences came in staccato bursts of energy.)

In its publication, *Clapperton* is prefaced by *Memoirs of My Aunt Minnie*. In the hotel where Aunt Minnie works, one of her suitors (the story concerns Aunt Minnie's unlikely sexual allure) asks another 'how he liked his women'.

'I like them long and scrawny and breastless ... and a few bristles on the chin.' This was a more than adequate description of Aunt Minnie.

It is also a 'more than adequate description' of the 'women' who appeared in Monty Python from 1969 to 1974. It is a distaste (an easy humour) that is amplified by age. When Clapperton visits his Aunt Hetty and, 'holding his breath', bends down to kiss her, 'he took hold of her upper arm [and] felt through the layers of shawl a loosely-hanging pouch of skin with no flesh inside it'. But then we have been told that, 'From the beginning Clapperton had felt his body as a burden to him.' The opening scene of the story underscores that. Even his feet are against him:

The strange sensation in his foot now invaded like a stealthy enemy the peace and unusual optimism of Clapperton's morning mind.

Throughout *Clapperton* there is a fracture between physical appearance and the inner life. We are told of his sense of 'innate superiority', set close to a description of him as, 'a man of indeterminate age', 'an old man young or a young man old'.

The most striking feature of his physical appearance was its lack of self-consistency. His body seemed countlessly fractured, and its component parts — as if held together by no unitary principle but rather by an act of will upon which no absolute reliance might be placed — appeared anxious to hive off in independent directions.

The tone recalls Gogol, here describing the main character of *The Overcoat*:

On no account could he be said to have a memorable appearance; he was shortish, rather pock-marked, with reddish hair, and also had weak eyesight, or so it seemed. He had a small bald patch in front and both cheeks were wrinkled. His complexion was the sort you find in those who suffer from piles ... but there's nothing anyone can do about that: the Petersburg climate is to blame.

Like Gogol's characters, Clapperton could be described as a 'grotesque caricature', a puppet for his author's satirical purposes. Here, the references reach much farther back than Monty Python: his sense of his 'innate superiority' suggests the elect of *Holy Willie's Prayer*, as well as, later in the tale, the wrong-headed vanity of Malvolio. In his battle with his employer, Colonel Dudgeon, he wonders (and as he does so, Herdman brings Stevenson and Hogg to mind),

Was he ... guilty of the sin of intellectual pride? Was he not positively exulting in his rightness? Was his concern motivated by the love of truth, or by the dictates of an assertive will? Such were the considerations which lifted this episode from the level of a squalid and petty local squabble to realms of lofty and impersonal moral grandeur.

In comparison with the lofty considerations of his mind, the body's basic needs are given little attention:

When he had dressed Clapperton prepared and ate a light breakfast of fruit juice, a boiled egg ... two oatcakes and two cups of tea.

Neither is food given much fanfare in Murdo's life:

> He ate very little food and this worried Janet. He had a theory
> that too much food made his brain feel heavy, and that this was
> particularly the case with meat and soup, though not with fish.

The 'burden' Clapperton felt his body to be was an issue for the main
driver of the narrative, his efforts to win Trudy Otter, 'the girl across
the street', who in turn had a 'tragically incestuous' relationship with
her brother, Rex. The story describes Clapperton's uneasy visits to the
home of Mr Otter, a retired police sergeant and 'his spouse', whose
'sense of each other's existence was registered ... by waves of palpable
antipathy.' At the Otters', Trudy would flirt with Clapperton 'to induce
a state of jealousy in Rex'. Trudy Otter, we are told,

> was a honey blonde with a peaches-and-cream complexion and
> green eyes, of middle height and a figure good but well covered,
> inclining very slightly to the fleshy, but not to an objectionable
> degree.

Once more we are at the edge of distaste. No surprise that 'it was
[Clapperton's] misfortune to combine an unlimited confidence in his
capacities, in his general human worth, with a total lack of confidence
in himself as a sexual being.' And no surprise that the courting goes
awry. Incidents with dogs are a theme here (Herdman enjoys writing
about dogs), followed by the standard no-show, which leads a sherried-
up Clapperton — 'with the hunch of bitterness within his breast, the
hunch of endless longing and repeated failure and indescribable folly'
— to deliver a rallying cry of hatred to a table of Englishmen:

> I wish you to know that I detest and despise you. I do not propose
> to go into the rights and wrongs, the why's and wherefore's, I
> am in no condition to do that; but I wish to make it abundantly
> clear to you that your presence is a matter of offence to me.

Thereafter, Clapperton embarks on a tumult of moaning, as he walks
home, 'washed with great thoroughness, brushed his teeth and brushed
his hair, moaning all the while.' In bed, his face is bathed in tears. Yet,
in the morning, 'a weak ray of sunshine' gives him hope.

The previous night it had seemed that life might strike him down; but life could never strike him down, for it had never raised him up, and it never would raise him up, never. So Clapperton arose, meagrely sustained by his wretched hope, not briskly but resolutely enough, to live another day.

The story therefore ends on a note of optimistic pessimism, which echoes Beckett's, 'You must go on. I can't go on. I'll go on.' Herdman doesn't go on with *Clapperton*, his story is finished, though Iain Crichton Smith explores, through Murdo, concerns of language, culture and history — until the character of Murdo is identified with Crichton Smith himself, in a way that is more empathetic than the term 'alter ego' might suggest. *Clapperton* has different aims, but its slanted comments on Scotland in the early seventies are considerable. It is a story whose roots are deep within Scottish culture; aware of the dichotomy between body and mind, between desire and 'fate', between ease of enjoyment and repression, between the self and the world's judgement upon it. There is also Clapperton's failure to connect, to empathise with others: none of the other characters are real to him in any meaningful way — whether Trudy with her not 'objectionable' fleshiness or the crone that is Aunt Hetty, a character that could be drawn from a folk tale.

Clapperton is, most significantly, I would argue, a story illustrative of a changing Scotland. As Murdo negotiates his way through an unstable culture (*'Is Calvin still alive?'*) and as Ivor Cutler, around the same time, satirises his memories of *Life in a Scotch Sitting Room* ('We were obliged to kneel and eat cream crackers with butter and Gouda … with our heads inside the sideboard'), so Herdman writes from a (slowly) vanishing Scotland. Five years after publication of *Memoirs of My Aunt Minnie and Clapperton,* the failed referendum of 1979 would lead to an invigorated, more culturally confident Scotland. Many of us might wear some of Clapperton's chips on our shoulders, but the ground that he walked on — and that Herdman caught so concisely — has changed greatly for the better.

Regi Claire, Two Poems

Costings

how much
for a mouthful of
weather

for honey from
blooms
beside names and dates

for a fingerbone to
strike
the xylophone

I step round
an angel

where you are waiting
behind tinted windows
parked between me

and the exit gate
an empty can
rolls in a puddle

the magpies are silent
the crows sweep
low

drawing lots in the wind

If we have our time again

you were given a dozen pebbles
so perfectly spherical
most of them

slipped
through your fingers
sank into sand

the last one you planted and
watered with
care

when nothing happened
you began to forget and finally
stopped

years later you return
remembering
and find a sapling tipped with raindrops

when you pass this way once more
there will be a tree
covering the earth with darkness

and trapped within it a web
grey-husked
of many threads

all
leading towards
the centre

if we have our time again
let me unbury that pebble
let me roll it in my hands

let me split it in two

Regi Claire

John Herdman: photograph to accompany an article written for the Spring 1969 edition of *Catalyst* magazine titled 'Using the Enemy's Weapons'.
(Photograph: Gordon Wright)

A party at Helen B Cruickshank's house to celebrate the publication of her *Collected Poems* (Reprographia), 1st November 1971. Seated L to R: Mary Munro (wife of Ian Munro, biographer of Lewis Grassic Gibbon); Helen B Cruickshank; John Herdman. Standing: Mary Herdman (neighbour); Dr Ian Campbell (English Department, Edinburgh University). (Photograph: Gordon Wright)

John Herdman reading at a meeting of The Heretics, New Town Hotel, early 1970s. (Background: Alexander and Genevieve Reid. Seated foreground: Donald Campbell). (Photograph:Gordon Wright)

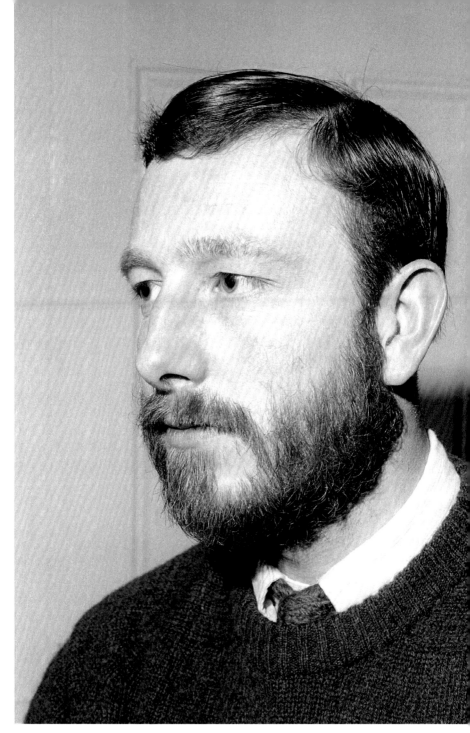

John Herdman 1972.
(Photograph: Gordon Wright)

John Herdman, 2021.
(Photograph: Robin Gillanders)

John Herdman, Man o Mony Pairts

John Burns

I first met John Herdman in the 1970s when I was just embarking on a study of Neil Gunn and Zen Buddhism and immediately recognised a kindred spirit. I knew some of his work from Duncan Glen's magazine *Akros*, and I had heard him read some of his pieces at the various poetry readings that were a feature of the city and the university at that time.

I admired the tone of his writing immensely, that ability to be both serious and funny at the same time. His 'jocoseriosity', as Joyce has it. Then there was his obvious love of the well-cadenced sentence, and the rich, resonant voice with which he read those sentences aloud. I am still the proud owner of a vinyl LP called *An Evening With The Heretics*, on which he can be heard reading a wonderful description of his character Clapperton's hypochondria much to the delight and amusement of the live audience. His ability to write so sharply and to deliver the lines so effectively is a skill that seems less and less important in a world that places so little value on the spoken word despite the plethora of outlets we now enjoy. I think Herdman's own delight in the placing of vowels and consonants in his choice of words, and the rhythms he creates is something that resonates with his readers. I also think it is not just personal choice, but comes out of his reading of Robert Louis Stevenson, another writer who paid close attention to such things.

It is difficult now to remember the world of Scottish Literature in the 1970s. It was a time when very little Scottish literature, whether in English or Scots, never mind Gaelic, was taught in schools and in universities, beyond the pioneering efforts of a dedicated few. It was a world in which many key texts were either out of print or unknown. Those of us interested in such things felt as if we were part of an underground movement who picked up texts, ideas, and names of authors largely by word of mouth or in magazines like *Akros*, *Chapman*, *Lines Review* and others. We had to actively seek these things out so in many cases commitment to the cause came before much actual exposure to the reality of it. Like Clapperton we also became dedicated prowlers in the many second-hand bookshops of Auld Reekie. John Herdman was an active part of that movement, not only as a reader, speaker, and writer, but also as an editor. Notably, he was keen to see Scottish writers and their works as being part of a wider European tradition. There was nothing insular or narrow-minded in his approach.

On the occasion of our first real conversation I had gone to talk to him about Neil Gunn, about Zen Buddhism, and the neglected novelist David Lindsay, author of the extraordinary novel *A Voyage to Arcturus*. The discussion ranged widely and moved easily from Lindsay to Gnosticism, to Buddhism of various kinds, to Krishnamurti, and to Gurdjieff. John was the first person I ever heard talking about Alasdair Gray's *Lanark*, which had not yet been published in book form. This was very heady stuff for a young student, but while I do not now remember many specifics of that conversation I do know that it gave me a sharper sense of a context in which to explore some of my own hazy intuitions. Crucially, it gave me an insight into the way a writer's mind works; always making connections, always testing ideas, always looking for a clear way to say what needs to be said. In the light of the writers named above it was important that someone had so openly and patiently spared the time and energy to have such a conversation outwith the formal setting of a lecture or tutorial. John did not assume the role of teacher, but I certainly learnt a lot from our conversation.

And I went away with my head reeling with new ideas, and a whole new list of writers worth reading. As a teacher myself I really appreciate the way in which someone who has practised something can guide you on the way to learning, not just by sharing what they know, but by allowing you the space to develop and discover what *you* need to know to follow your own path. That was what John did that afternoon. He has probably forgotten all about it, but it was very important to me and in my later life as a writer and teacher of writing in school.

In keeping with John's awareness of the way Scottish literature exists in a European context his central characters are often the kind of troubled young men we find in modern European writers like Dostoevsky or Kafka. At the same time, they are also deeply influenced by Scottish writers like Hogg and Stevenson. They often seem to be intensely realised metaphors for the alienation often felt by individuals who do not "fit in" to the modern world. He exists as a kind of Everyman character, haunted by a self-consciousness that inhibits action or propels him to inappropriate, sometimes even violent action. Many modern writers, whether novelists, dramatists or poets, and psychologists like Freud and Jung, have explored the tortured minds of such characters and sometimes suggested ways for them to come to terms with their situations. In a way what they are exploring is the human condition. Gunn once described modern man as the serpent that has swallowed its own tail, a horrifying corruption of a traditional symbol of wisdom.

As well as dealing with the social, sexual, and psychological ills that bedevil his central characters, Herdman does so in texts that continually challenge our grasp of any coherent narrative. Indeed the constant reversals and underminings of what we think we understand by setting up counter narratives might suggest that our compulsion to discover orderly narratives in life is not always necessary or helpful, an insight that might give some of our politicians pause for thought. As in Hogg and Stevenson, new narratives often in the shape of letters, manuscripts and even dreams cut across or completely contradict the narrative we thought we were following. Character and reader alike are put in a position where causal logic does not seem to be enough to provide understanding. In many ways this takes us back to Zen and the way Zen masters try to get their students to go beyond logic by asking them to answer impossible questions or asking them to solve impossible dilemmas. Herdman's narratives have such authority in themselves because of his command of language, his use of irony, that it sometimes take us a little while to realise that while what we are reading is a story and a very good story at that, it is also a meditation on the nature of narrative itself or on that perennial question, 'Where do your characters come from?' A title such as *Ghostwriting* points us surely beyond the obvious and makes us question the whole nature of the experience of writing and of reading.

As well as his subtle (and sometimes not so subtle) narrative playfulness, his psychological insight into troubled minds, his love of the well-written sentence, one of the qualities I enjoy in Herdman's writing is his ability to describe settings with such resonant economy. His characters may be psychologically fragile, but the settings in which they find themselves can often be wonderfully atmospheric and specific, whether they are describing a stately mansion, a dusty bookshop, or a Scottish hillside. Often these descriptions are closely connected to the character's state of mind which again raises questions about the nature of fiction itself.

Personally I am very taken with the ease with which he can describe landscapes which are at once real, yet have a metaphorical significance. In *Sinister Cabaret* for instance, Donald Humbie sets out for Ben Despair Lodge [is that *Beyond* Despair Lodge?]. At first his journey over the beautiful wild landscape evokes in him feelings of 'lightness, beauty, and repose'. The description presents a lovely traditional Scottish postcard scene of heather, bracken, alders, and birches. Most of us will have been in similar landscapes, and can attest to the accuracy of the picture and its effect on us, but as Humbie carries on walking his mood changes and the 'delightful little glen' becomes bleaker and more forbidding. *The vegetation thinned out and all but disappeared; the glen became barren and desert-like, bounded by almost precipitous scree-covered slopes. The burn was now scarcely more than a trickle … Donald felt oppressed by a claustrophobic sense of enclosure …* Maybe we have been there too. It is a recognisable feeling and a recognisable situation, but we can also perhaps hear echoes of texts like *Pilgrim's Progress*, or Hawthorne's *Young Goodman Brown* which explore the kind of spiritual and psychological themes that we find in Herdman's fiction.

Given Herdman's intense engagement with modern European literature and with the developing discipline of Scottish literature it might seem to be rather odd for him suddenly [?] to write a critical study of Bob Dylan. *Voice Without Restraint*, an exploration of 'Bob Dylan's Lyrics and their Background' was published in 1982 by Paul Harris Publishing, though copyright to John Herdman says 1981. Dig even just a little deeper, though, and that oddness evaporates. John's fascination with Hogg and Stevenson and their explorations of the links between the conscious and unconscious levels of our experience, the use of the 'double' as the prime literary technique in this exploration, their juxtaposition of often contradictory narratives written in contrasting styles, fed directly into John's own fiction, and feature largely in the writings of Bob Dylan. Dylan famously uses paradox and contradiction as part of his approach to song-writing: 'I fought with my twin, that enemy within'; 'There's no success like failure/ And failure's no success at all'; 'Sometimes Satan comes as a man of peace'. I am sure such lines did not go unnoticed by Herdman.

He also had a developing sense, perhaps due to Dylan's influence, that the oral culture of contemporary 'pop' or 'rock' music was gaining in importance in the 1960s and the 1970s against the influence of literature that appeared in print. I seem to remember him writing about this in *Akros* in the late seventies. And I am sure that, born in the same year as

Dylan himself, Herdman was very aware of the important Edinburgh folk-scene of the early 1960s when he was in his early twenties, an age when we seem to be acutely aware of the music around us. Writers, singers, players, mixed widely and it was a mix that led to a growing awareness of new possibilities about how to live in a world threatened by imminent nuclear destruction. The times were a-changing right enough. *Voice Without Restraint* was one of the earliest critical studies of Dylan's work. It was a bold statement that this man's words were not only important, but could stand up to the kind of critical scrutiny afforded to more strictly literary rather than oral poets. Strikingly, it anticipated the controversial award of the Nobel Prize for Literature to Bob Dylan in 2016. Controversial still because of the argument that what Dylan writes is not 'literature', an argument that Dylan himself in typical ersit fashion did nothing in his response to the award to defuse.

It was also an important book in that it came when Dylan was being increasingly written-off (again) as irrelevant, and his work was undergoing a major transition. In 1979 Dylan announced that he had converted to Christianity and in concert refused to play any of his old songs, preferring to play new songs that were intended to spread the Christian message. For a writer and performer that many saw as the leader in new ways of thinking and spearheading a cultural revolution, all in the name of freedom, this was seen by many as a betrayal. They seemed to have forgotten Dylan's barbed advice to them in *Subterranean Homesick Blues*: 'Don't follow leaders'. Remember, too, Dylan had been famously heckled as 'Judas!' in a 1966 concert because he had dared to play an electric guitar. Herdman chose to write his study of Dylan at this crossroads moment in his career. He had had many years to process the early lyrics that still seem to define Bob Dylan for many people, lyrics of protest or of social concern, but he had to respond quickly to these new songs, and to Dylan's apparently unforeseen new stance as a performer and artist. His knowledge of the language of the Bible had already allowed him to track religious references in the songs so he was able to comment on the 'Christian' songs with genuine authority while many other critics at the time struggled to come to terms with Dylan's new music. And remember, this was before the days of easy internet access to information or to film and audio clips of live concert performances. It must have been difficult to write the book in that atmosphere yet what emerges is an elegantly thoughtful appreciation of the work of one of the twentieth (now twenty-first) century's most important artists which still reads well forty years on. And don't forget that Bob Dylan has released many new albums since 1981 so that his work has developed in many ways which could not have been predicted in 1981. Indeed Herdman's 'Postscript' to his book makes the point that the album *Saved* was released after he had written most of the book. By 1982 he had also released *Shot of Love*.

Perhaps most impressive is the way Herdman looks at *how* Dylan's songs work. He is obviously interested in Dylan's 'message', but knows that any such message is complex and multi-faceted. The problem of 'What's real and what is not' echoes right through Dylan's work so the listener is placed in a similar situation to the reader of *Pagan's Pilgrimage, Imelda, or Ghostwriting*. Who do I believe? Is this true? If *this* is true, then how can *that* be true? A conundrum worthy of Chic Murray. It is notable that Herdman deals at length with two of Dylan's greatest songs despite the difficulty listeners have of discerning what is happening in them, 'Visions of Johanna', and 'Tangled Up in Blue'. Both of these songs employ sophisticated narrative structures and juxtapositions which allow the listener to view the action from different angles more or less simultaneously. Herdman delights in the audacity of this and must have felt very much at home among the songs' shifting surfaces and varied textures. Though many people have gone on to write about these songs since, perhaps only Michael Gray had done so when *Voice Without Restraint* was written. Herdman was a trailblazer in what is now a burgeoning critical industry. His book deserves to be much better-known.

I do not know if John still listens to Bob Dylan, but I do know that he quotes him in *Sinister Cabaret*, and that he quotes one of Dylan's most impressive recent songs, 'Not Dark Yet', from 1997's *Time Out of Mind*. It is a simple example which readers who are not Dylan fans might easily miss, but Herdman's slight twist in his use of the quotation plays its part in agitating the surface of the strange, disturbing, narrative of the novel. As readers we have to keep our wits about us if we are to retain our balance among the shifting certainties and uncertainties of John Herdman's sharply challenging and hugely entertaining fiction.

From H. to J.

Hayden Murphy

From Homer to Joyce. Discuss the factifictions around the exagminations. Take the word to progress. Start with the Son of Cork, Telemachus, unbottled, open to the two eyed bewilderment of Horatio on the Pilgrim Ship called Pagan. Step back into the teaching tomb of Nestor and hear of Aristotle distorting love for truth. Allow the method mutate down to where the stones speak on the spread out of the beaches. Wherein lies the modality of the visible. Eat your empirical dish and go to the pub. Notate. Clapperboard for Clapperton, find Mr Finlay Walsh behind the makeup in the wings and travel with Dylan to Dublin. Shoot, Flashback to the Carry on Crusading feature film. Heretics be damned. Please drink ex-cathedra. Make cause with coasters. Itch to be damned. Fade the plot to allow the daguerreotype warriors regroup. Switch to sepia notions. Fade to knee trembling in Wick and the water of life cascading in the mouth-to-mouth resuscitation now required. A cauldron for the witches brewing salvation and back again from Joyce to Homer.

Mnemonic for Mnemosyne.

Joyce to Homer, late in the days but early in mourning. The breakfast of fowl and innards of others. Of labouring word-building from Joyce to Goethe, from joist to girder. Building up by bathing with Calypso. Leading to the blooming of words. Feasting with the Lotus Eaters before ordaining the Jesuits with your Confession. Voltaire to Russian Rousseau. Sentenced to word roulette. The Hades of paraphrasing. Switching on the critic lights for the traffic of notions tracking the cities to find Aeolus has cannibalised the topic and is slow feeding it to the Lystroyganians. Goats' milk and sweat of Dionysus. Burgundy and Gorgonzola, please. Imelda flirts with Virtue renewed. The Eucharist is taken before the Hamlet ghost seizes up and turns the pages into monsters. Fate knows the ambitions of both Scylla and Charybdis when they invade the mind, the type, the story. Take them out. Excise. Edit the novelties. Oh Wandering Rocks fall over and crush the limitations of lamenting words. Now go to the pub. Sit snug in the snug, toast the

Sirens and go on to out glare the Cyclops with twin visions. Pause to praise, and flatter, (of necessity) that Princess of Plaecia, Nausiccaa. Did she really give saviour birth in the company of Oxen of the Sun? Now, at the other end of day, turn tail. Pig trotters are on the table of Circe. Beneath the circumference of the Moon. Lunacy beckons. Pestilent Penelope not too distant now. Steady the ship. Wave back with words. *Mnemosyne in Mnemonics.*

Late in our days, beyond the Coral Island, the atholl of the spheres. Be herded Mr Herdman by Eumaeus. Be beached. Lie down, wait for the dog to bark. Find the time and place for the wind-up, wind down, the weft and weave of tale telling. Return to Ithaca. Embed again in the weavings of Penelope. Dress down the days. Let only the ideas isolate the years. Grow old without aging. Tell more lies. In the Name of the Vowel, the Verb and Holy Venalities bless us that remain paring our fingernails in the margins.

Now delete, reform, restart, conform and construe a reply for *Hayden to John @80.*

Joseph's Feet

Jonathan Penner

Joseph's parents, who were poets, were taking him to Great Slavia —
only a yellow teardrop on his desk globe — for a month of cultural
exchange. It was Joseph's father, A. H. Robinson, who'd been invited.
He'd published seven books. Olivia Robinson, Joseph's mother, only
one.

In a Mercedes cab, the Robinsons swept from the airport into the
capital city of Kalemegdan. Their driver had a hairy neck and a jacket of
some sad fabric that Joseph thought would be interesting, but creepy, to
touch. Open trucks, packed with soldiers, rumbled and jounced out of
the city. There had been fighting here. Joseph had seen it on the news.
But both his parents had told him not to worry.

A.H. had said he doubted there was actual danger, only its provocative
scent. Olivia told Joseph that Great Slavia would be good for them –
experience was oxygen! — and best of all for him. She said his lust for
life was huge, though still, because he was only ten, barely on the cusp
of consciousness. 'This trip will be a smithy,' A.H. told him, 'for your
malleable soul.' Joseph was furious at his father for putting them all
in danger.

Now A.H., a poor traveller, sagged against the seat cushions. 'Novi
Kalemegdan,' said the driver, waving at repetitious apartment blocks.
Olivia kept an arm around each of them, tracing patterns on Joseph's
chest while she stroked his father's face. They crossed a bridge and the
driver said, 'Stari Kalemegdan.' Joseph unzipped his backpack and slid
a hand inside, making sure his plastic guys were there.

'I think I've had it,' A.H. said. When they reached the hotel, he had
to lie down immediately. While Joseph arranged the guys atop a dresser,
Olivia covered his shivering father with blankets. She and Joseph would
try for some lunch. 'Shall I bring you a bite?' she asked A.H. 'I can't
promise what.'

'I shouldn't have come,' A.H. said. 'I doubt I'll make it home alive.
I feel I'm aging rapidly.'

'It's only jet lag,' Joseph told him.

'Not jet,' A.H. said thoughtfully. 'Some other lag, ineffable, and far more serious.'

He frowned, making Joseph feel stupid. 'On the other hand,' he said, brightening, 'it's not purely an imposition. There's pleasure in meeting your suddenly aging body. Imagine getting to be this, imagine getting to be here! It's like,' A.H. said, working his shoulders, looking around as though he could see through the walls, 'foreign travel!' Then he sat up in bed, and Olivia brought him his notebook and pen.

The restaurant was crowded with men who sat and drank and smoked and talked. Their loud voices sounded angry. Though Olivia was able to order what looked like sausages, after one gristly bite each they switched to the bowl of stale bread. She requested milk but couldn't get it, not even by showing two waiters the word in her phrase book. 'It doesn't matter,' Joseph told her, knowing himself at fault--the only person there who couldn't drink coffee or beer. She told him never to forget the old waiter's teeth or the young waiter's walk, but didn't say what about them to remember.

She wrapped the last of the bread in a napkin and stuffed it into her shoulder bag. Back in the room, they found A.H. quiet as a corpse. In huge letters across his open notebook he had printed: MY LIVING WILL — DO NOT RESUSCITATE. Though Joseph knew his father's jokes, he watched until he saw breathing. Olivia lifted the notebook and pen from A.H.'s chest, the bifocals from his nose. Then she tucked Joseph into bed and kissed him.

Immediately he felt exhausted. His parents' bed seemed far away. His mother got in next to his father, leaving the light on to read. Joseph noticed that each time she turned a page, she licked her finger and lifted a corner of the next page, as though she needed to hold hands with the book. When she saw him watching her, she frowned and patted the air, telling him to put his head back down on the pillow. He was sure she'd find food, find hotels, get them on buses and boats and planes, but not that she could keep them from being thrown in prison and later shot.

When he awoke, the room was dark. He could hear his parents breathing. Only the bathroom light was on. He went in to use the toilet. A moth was floating on its back, and he tried to drown it in his waterfall. Then Joseph began to feel weird. He realised that something was wrong with his body. His foot, his left foot –it was bigger, it was growing, already it had grown a lot. It stuck out way beyond the right. He snapped his eyes shut and felt his way back to bed.

***

In the morning, it was cold. Olivia brought him clothes to put on under the covers. He could hear traffic outside, and his father complaining of a headache. Why was there always something wrong with him? They were going down to breakfast when Joseph remembered his feet. In familiar socks and shoes, they looked up innocently from the elevator floor.

Breakfast was easier. There were eggs. There was a strange sort of juice. And now, in the morning, there was milk — *hot* milk. When Olivia asked for cold, the waiter hid his hands in perplexity. The steaming milk smelled disgusting. Joseph sat three plastic guys on the rim of the glass, legs amputated at mid-calf by the white surface.

'Well,' said his father, 'here goes,' and out they went into the streets of Kalemegdan. They walked past food stores, banks and barbers, some with signs in unfamiliar letters, windows displaying watches and clothing and plumbing pipe. Joseph saw a soccer ball, marked with a comet and strange words. 'Can we buy that?' he asked. But his mother said it was expensive, and his father said they were in a hurry.

A.H. had a slip of paper: the address of the Komisija. Today he was to meet Great Slavian officials, discuss his itinerary, and be issued his dinars. They were already late by ten minutes, then a half hour, as A.H. grew frantic, wheeling about, folding and refolding his street map. Suddenly they entered a square where two tanks were drawn up. Real tanks, with long guns. Joseph whimpered and grabbed both his parents' hands. 'Damn,' said his father. 'Look at those massive treads.' The tanks were just sitting there. Helmeted soldiers lounged against them, similar as plastic guys. Their open hatches were dark holes that made Joseph want to slip inside.

At last the Robinsons panted up the cracked steps of a sagging mansion and down an unlit hall, where Olivia used her key-ring flashlight to read the name on the last door. Inside, the Komisija had many more desks than people, dusky carpets, grandfatherly bicycles resting against file cabinets. Joseph stared at monster adding machines, towering typewriters, old and insect-black, keypads perched on metal stalks.

The Komesar himself, a secretary explained, was abroad; it was therefore the Direktor who would welcome them. He, so far this morning, was unfortunately not yet in. The Zamenik, however, was present, and desired to meet A.H. Robinson immediately.

This was a huge young man who jumped up to seize their hands. 'Super,' he said. It was he, he explained, who would be helping them effectuate their plans, though the Direktor — himself a poet — was eager to greet Dr Robinson. He gave A.H. papers to sign, then opened a safe and counted out stacks of worn bills. Next, while Joseph's parents peered at a map of Great Slavia — much bigger than on Joseph's globe, and the wrong colour — the young man was on the phone to travel agents and hotels, saying 'Okey-dokey' and 'Super' and 'Super-duper' into the receiver, and winking, winking at Joseph, who stared helplessly at his massive milk-white neck, studded with caramel warts.

Or was he winking at someone behind them? There was a horrible cough, a sound like ice being chipped from a driveway. 'Ah, the Direktor!' The Robinsons turned to face a desperately long and wild black beard. Joseph thought the Direktor looked like a madman. His eyes burned as though he'd just been slapped. At once he took A.H. into an inner office.

The Zamenik was talking again. Olivia was taking notes. 'Here and here you can't go,' he said, 'for reasons of safety. But here is still fine.'

They leaned over the map, her rear end sticking out so far that Joseph imagined himself kicking it. It would be what she deserved for making him come to Great Slavia. He watched the Zamenik's long finger fly over lines of red and green and blue to tap bright yellow dots. The cities' names were in convulsion, hostile letters hugging crazily — Vranjska, Radimlje — names that looked as though they'd been already destroyed by war. A secretary brought his mother a bitter-smelling thumb of a cup, then carried a tray with two more cups into the Direktor's office.

When A.H. came out, he was pale and moved slowly, as though hesitant to test some injured part. The Robinsons started back toward their hotel. 'They don't know my work!' he said. 'They didn't even read the books I sent!'

Horns were blasting and Olivia hurried them across an intersection. As he walked, A.H. held his head with both hands. He had explained to the Direktor his wish to give readings, arrange translations. 'But as far as they're concerned, we're tourists. I expected better.'

Again they entered the square. As though by some magician's trick, the two tanks had become four. Now their hatches were closed. Joseph thought of the soldiers packed inside. "Don't be frightened," said Olivia, and A.H. actually picked Joseph up — something he hadn't done in years — and carried him. In the middle of the square, a man waved a flag on a stick as people around him chanted in heavy rhythm. When Joseph saw the store with the soccer ball in the window, the one with the comet on it, he imagined clutching it to his chest and getting out of there. Ten, nine, eight, seven, a surge of power. Three! Two! One!

***

In Maksimir, A.H. seemed filled with sudden energy. He told Joseph that the city was on fire with poetic hyperconsciousness. Tonight, an official of the Zabljak Writers' Union — chap with authentic character, he said, albeit that of a weasel — was taking him out on the town. 'I'll be abstemious,' he promised Olivia, combing and recombing his hair.

The weasel had guaranteed an authentically Zabljak cultural perspective. This would be, A.H. explained, the intellectual equivalent of a sauna. It would empty the mind and cleanse the passions. Normally you couldn't bore a poet. But if you did, his interest grew savage as a starved dog. And out he walked, leaving Joseph and Olivia to play chess in their hotel room.

When Joseph awoke it had happened again. His left foot was swollen insanely. He lay stiff, afraid to look or reach down. Shadows moved on the walls and ceiling: A.H. was back, taking his clothes off, talking. The Inuit had a word for baby walrus. The Inuit had a word for two-year-old walrus. The Inuit had words for mature walrus, large male walrus, tusked walrus. But the Inuit had no word for just a walrus, which was the poet's dilemma too, that inability to work in scale, that morbid consciousness of each hair in his little brush.

The next day, Joseph held his parents' hands as they squeezed through the nauseating Maksimir market. He felt as though he'd fall right into the heaped vegetables, the cloth-wrapped cheese, the slabs of fish awhirl with ecstatic flies. Jets screamed low overhead, five of them forming a V. Everybody in the market fell silent, looking up.

'They're going to bomb us,' Joseph said. 'I want to go back home!'

His father said, 'Those are fighter planes. They won't attack civilian targets.'

'They're gone now,' said his mother. Then she said, 'Joseph, look. Compare these peppers to those tomatoes.'

Why weren't his parents afraid? The peppers were fine and noble, but Joseph preferred the humble tomatoes. Deeper in the market, Olivia found a tray of inlaid wood, and A.H. a carved cherub to hang above their toilet tank. That evening, gulping a beer in the restaurant, A.H. seemed fevered with excitement. He'd thought of a novel he might knock out, do justice to his themes at last, and sure as shit make some money. Then Joseph saw his mother grow silent, as though his parents had to take turns with a single portion of joy.

Olivia had brought, packed at the bottom of a suitcase, a vinyl duffel bag. This was for their purchases. In Most Begova, they got lost in a mazy bazaar, endless rows of stalls where crouching men hammered metal and stared as the Robinsons passed. Olivia admired a brass cup, and made Joseph stroll ahead with her so A.H. could bargain. If they watched him, she explained, that would create a problem of audience. 'I'll buy you one of these,' she offered, stopping at a stall with silly wooden animals. Embarrassed by the merchant's attention — a man no taller than himself, bright tireless mouth, but weary eyes — Joseph swiftly chose a dancing bear, its great head cocked coquettishly beneath a dunce's cap.

Everything hurt, A.H. told them that night, back in their room. '*Mea culpa*,' Olivia said. 'I kept us at the market too long.' This whole trip, said A.H., was one grand thundering blunder. Comic to the Olympians, doubtless, but for him a pain in his personal ass, and its literary value was nil. He lay as though too weak to move, limbs angled unnaturally, and spoke in the whine of a child until Olivia tucked him in. That made Joseph mad — his father was being such a big baby! Later, when Joseph's foot woke him, he heard his parents moving in their bed, whispering and panting. He knew what was probably happening. But the sounds were frightening and strange, as though Great Slavians were wrestling in the dark, sighing syllables of their incomprehensible language.

In the morning, A.H. refused to dress, didn't want food, and wouldn't speak to either of them. He brought his books of poems into bed and turned the pages hurriedly, gesturing with his chin as though he were meeting people on the street. Finally he dozed.

Then Olivia put a finger to her lips. Waving for Joseph to slide over, she lay next to him on his narrow bed, curling onto her side to write in her notebook. Joseph watched a long time. It puzzled and finally worried him, the way she kept crossing things out — good and reasonable words. Perhaps the room's dimness made words too much alike, and so had silenced the three of them, like birds in a hooded cage.

In Musafirhana, A.H. flexed his muscles and lifted a pig, a pink and stinky thing. Joseph edged alongside and Olivia snapped the picture. To his parents' strange delight, the market was much worse here, littered and smelling of rot. Aisles packed with country people swathed in odorous wool. Shit-smeared pigs and lambs bleating from the beds of rusty trucks. Joseph felt annihilated and begged to return to the hotel. His parents agreed; they'd bought a prayer rug they loved, and now they were hungry. After lunch, the Robinsons climbed the streets of the old quarter, to a cool museum of icons — painted saints with jewels stuck to the canvas for their eyes. And one that made Joseph look away — Mary, the mother of Jesus — her divine nipples were pearls.

Boarding the bus to Ropotovo, the Robinsons were patted for weapons. When two soldiers with machine guns took seats behind the driver, Olivia quickly rose and led the family to the back. Turbid with tobacco smoke, the bus bounced through countryside until Joseph began to think of vomiting. But he was able not to when he saw how sick his father seemed, leaning forward and grimacing, checking his watch every minute.

In their hotel at last, A.H. said it was agony to piss. As he lay groaning on a bed, knees drawn up, clutching his crotch, he told Joseph that his urinary tract felt like the bore of a flamethrower. Joseph turned away to align his guys on the windowsill, secretly touching himself to see if he hurt too, while Olivia searched through her envelope labelled EMERGENCIES.

Ropotovo had an American Centre. She got the Administrator on the phone. Then A.H. stopped groaning and took the receiver with, to Joseph's amazement, a chuckle. That which all men must, he said in a jocular new voice, he found himself disabled from doing. The Administrator said to walk right over — the American Centre was near the hotel — so the Robinsons slowly did, stopping for A.H. to lean against buildings and grin at the sky.

When they entered the Administrator's office, a sudden proud American flag, and then the President's signed photo, made Joseph feel safe. The Administrator's easy American voice — how well he spoke English! — seemed miraculous. His smiling secretary brought cold cans of Coca-Cola and a bowl of popcorn. On the basis of Professor

Robinson's symptoms, the Administrator had already sent down for a broad-spectrum antibiotic. He handed a vial across his desk, and A.H. washed a capsule down with Coke.

'Things are starting to happen quickly,' the Administrator said. 'You left Most Begova when? They've just closed the airport. You three were on my list this morning.' He flourished a pen and whirled an oval, sectioning a column of names. 'The State Department wants you out'. Then he turned to Joseph. 'You never learnt this in school. A country can die just the same as a person.'

Joseph thought of his family trapped in Great Slavia's huge dead body. But Olivia explained that they were travelling with the greatest care and had only a week to go. Then they'd fly home from Kalemegdan, which was still secure. This would be a trip that their son would remember always. And A.H. said, 'It's a story Joseph needs to know. He'll remember it when all of us are gone. As long as he remembers it, it happened. That's why people have children.'

He'd sometimes wondered why his parents had him, but that was probably one of his father's jokes. People often couldn't tell whether he was joking or not, and Joseph had the queasy sense that A.H. wasn't sure either. 'Be inconspicuous,' the Administrator said. 'And don't even think of extending your stay.' Then he shook his head and asked if they'd like a tour of the building. In the library, they found three books by A.H. Robinson, and Olivia Robinson's book too. Some of his mother's poems referred to Joseph as a foetus. He hoped the Administrator hadn't read them. He hoped nobody had.

***

At the seaside resort of Pag, Joseph's bed shook. Something glass fell and broke. When he opened his eyes, both his parents were at the window, dark against the moonlight. 'Joseph, this is fantastic,' said his mother. 'We're having an earthquake.' It seemed to be over. Olivia asked whether he'd felt it, what he'd felt exactly, and suggested he write the entire experience down. But it was A.H. who swung his arms and said he planned to work all night. The next morning he was still propped up, his bedside lamp enfeebled by daylight, his lap cradling his notebook and pen like elderly pets. 'A trap, a trick,' he said, 'a hoax, a whore.' Earthquakes were nugatory. Disaster was profoundly silly. There had been nothing to write about at all.

After breakfast, Joseph's parents sprang a surprise like a punch in the chest. The day was gorgeous, great for the beach, they both insisted heartily. Joseph loved the beach, and when they told him this was a nudist beach he felt sickened and betrayed. Olivia said he could wear his bathing suit. 'Bring a book,' A.H. advised. 'The secret is, it's boring.' Where you paid to get in there were signs, cameras with X's drawn through. The path followed a rocky shoreline, in and out of clumps of trees. Bodies lay on blankets, but Joseph couldn't see much. Then two men and two women (as though by some plan, all were fat) passed them walking the other way, in sandals and sunhats, the men's pricks bobbing benignly, all of them talking and gesturing as if, like Joseph himself in dreams, they didn't realise they were naked. Just *looking* at the women felt like taking photographs. Their black tangles, patched with pink, looked like aerial shots of undeveloped land. Soon more people were passing. Joseph saw three girls his own age, talking together in what might be German. These weren't as bad. Their hairless bodies looked reassuringly simple.

Just beyond a restaurant with naked patrons at outdoor tables, the Robinsons came to the main beach. People lay on towels and blankets, on shed clothing. Some stood in the water. Others had waded or swum to an island, whose rocks — Joseph had to squint — were a rookery of sunbathers.

They spread their towels and Joseph's parents started to undress. A.H. folded his clothes carefully. Was something wrong? Maybe it was the sunlight, or the fleshy Great Slavians and Germans, but A.H. seemed inhumanly thin, and pale as though he'd been stripped by a mugger. Last of all he removed his glasses, sliding them into a shoe.

Olivia had turned to undress and now faced Joseph with an embarrassed smile. He was shocked by her breasts, no longer round but hanging half-depleted, like birthday balloons the next morning. Her vagina (if that was what it was) looked weird to him, like something from space that you saw in a movie. 'Are you coming?' she asked. Joseph shook his head. He watched his tender-footed parents, leaning on each other, wobble down the pebbly beach to the water. Where the foam broke they dipped their toes. They walked in knee deep, waist deep, and then he lost them in the distance and the crowd of bathers.

Joseph lay on his stomach, thinking how clothes showed it was you. He took guys out of his pockets. It was their armour and weapons that distinguished them. Otherwise they were identical — pale pieces of plastic. They had no faces, just indentations to suggest the shapes of heads. Joseph felt his own face. He was like a plastic guy. The only things that made him Joseph were things that could change at any time, things that could easily be removed. Shoes and socks. A pair of pants.

There was a roar and three jets hurtled from seaward, passing low over the beach. An old lady quickly covered herself with a fold of her blanket, and a young man leaped to his feet, shouting and throwing seaweed at the sky. Then Joseph's parents were standing above him, hair matted to their heads, wet flesh glistening. 'Can we *please* leave?' Joseph asked. For a minute he thought he might cry. He imagined them running, bullets stitching the sand all around. But he didn't know whether either of his parents was actually able to run.

'It's an attempt to frighten,' Olivia said, towelling herself. 'The local people aren't leaving. And Joseph, you *must* go in, the water is fantastic.' A.H. was already over his open notebook, head tilted back as though he still had his bifocals on.

His mother was right, no one was leaving. In fact, more naked people were arriving. The beach wasn't being attacked. Joseph, who was wearing his bathing suit underneath, removed his outer clothes. 'Can I swim to the island?'

'You may,' Olivia told him, then said to be careful. It got deep.

As he eased into the sea, the island didn't look as close as before. He waded out until the chill climbed to his testicles, then began to swim. Joseph didn't like to put his face in the water. Like A.H., he did the sidestroke. The island was sliding away in a current. Finally, panting, he drew within yards.

Then he was stepping among flung limbs, buttocks of every size and shape, breasts that flowed and puddled like melting desserts. His father was wrong, it wasn't boring: it was like a crazy dream. From here the beach seemed impossibly far. He found a narrow spot between two bodies that smelled of salt. If he wasn't back soon, he guessed A.H. would come for him. They'd sidestroke in together, Joseph in the lee of his father's body.

The people surrounding him seemed asleep, their sighs joining the shush of the waves. These walls of flesh made Joseph feel as though he were again unborn, the foetus in his mother's poems. Later, when he reached for his shoulder, trying to brush off something prickly, he knew that he'd slept too.

That was stupid. He was going to be sunburned. Joseph slid into the water and swam steadily for the shore, which, winking out of sight behind the crests of waves, looked farther away than ever. The heavy current hardened against him until it wasn't water at all. He felt helpless, a downed moth. He could drown right now. Then it wouldn't matter who he was. Dead people were all the same. His body would wash ashore polished smooth and impersonal as plastic. Politely he cried out for help — a huge Great Slavian, buoyant as a walrus, was swimming vigorously past — but his English was a squawk, a meow. His foot began to grow and he kicked the water until he was gasping.

The one who came, then, wasn't A.H. as he expected, side-stroking and spitting, thin hair floating. It was Olivia. She came to him naked in the water, crying his name, reaching with arms and buoyant breasts. She leaned back to hold him up, against her, between her legs. She was panting.

'My good boy,' she said, as though he were little again. 'My good boy.'

Good boy? Was he good? Was *that* what was true about him? Was that what would be true forever, after everything else changed?

***

The Direktor stood silently, yet significantly, as though the display of his long beard made his position as clear as he wished it to be. Now Joseph understood that this man meant to be an icon, brother to those saints in the museum at Musafirhana.

'Super-duper,' said the Zamenik. He winked down at Joseph, lacing banana fingers across his belly, and asked Joseph's father, 'Will you write us a report?' A.H. had come to sign some final papers. Afterward the officials shook his hand, then Olivia's, and finally, without irony, Joseph's. That made him feel suddenly older.

'We're having a party today,' the Zamenik remarked. He pointed to a plate of crumbled pastries. 'It's for me. The Direktor' (he winked) 'has asked me to resign. He's Kalemegdanian, you know. I'm Zabljak. We're historic enemies, now.' Both men laughed without mirth. 'Would you support my immigration to America?'

Their last purchase in Great Slavia was the soccer ball with the comet. It didn't fit in the duffel bag — Joseph wouldn't let them deflate it — so he held it in his arms the whole way home on the plane. At the customs desk in JFK, while one agent inspected their Musafirhana prayer rug and Zabljak carvings and Most Begova brass, another held the ball close to his ear and shook it curiously.

That night, home in his own bed, Joseph was afraid to sleep. If his foot swelled in America, he was afraid it would stay that way. His parents stood over him, asking what the matter was, promising that he was safe now. Joseph thought about telling them. And then he did.

Imagination, said Olivia, was lord and ruler of us all. The only way to save yourself was to write the entire experience down. But his father, as Joseph had known he would, believed him: he too, he said, had felt strange in that strange country. Now that they were home again, they would all be physiologically perfect.

After they left, holding hands, Joseph squeezed his soccer ball and watched the window, where the American moon was rising. While they'd been gone, it had changed. It looked dented, like somebody'd kicked it. Soon he heard his parents whispering and laughing. They were happy to be home. Their soft voices sifted through walls and rose up through his pillow. At last Joseph could hear them laugh and whisper inside the soccer ball, still hard with the air of Great Slavia. And there he thought he'd keep them safe, and have them with him under the covers, even after people and nations died.

Mossmen

They had no charter; they were not a guild.
Mossmen were an inbred brotherhood
who guided pilgrims across the moss-
peat bog, ten thousand acres of waterland –
to the abbey on the island in the lake.

Mossmen agreed a day, a time and a price.
They met at the bridge where paths were firm and dry.
They worked in pairs: one went ahead
and the other walked behind the pilgrims.
The leader said, 'Our spears are for water-monsters.'

The path grew narrower,
as thin as the single wavering meadow-trail
the neat-hoofed cattle made at milking time.
The trail sponged into moss;
each footprint filled with amber water-peat.

The leading mossman stopped.
He turned to face the pilgrims. 'Listen,' he said.
A water-monster is close. You hear the beast?'
His spear was angled at a pilgrim's heart.
'The danger is much greater than the price.'

'You mean a spearhead or the monster's jaws?'
'No, pilgrim. No. Our women and children starve.
Another piece of silver will save their lives.
Your crosses and your purses weigh you down.'

The pilgrims had sunk shinbone-deep in moss;
the mossmen's feet were dry. 'How can we trust —?'
'We are the only people who know the way.
Your God cannot …' 'Our God is also yours.
We shall pay for your wives and children, and for you.'
The mossman turned his spear and offered the shaft.
'Grip with both hands and follow where I tread.'

James Aitchison

An Interview with John Herdman

Macdonald Daly

John Herdman's published presence in Scottish literature now spans three decades. For reasons which will become obvious, his varied and voluminous activity cannot be said to have amounted to a 'career'. His work has been consistently overlooked by critics, a neglect which would seem inexplicable only to those unaware of many parallel cases in literary history. It was partly to remedy such inattention that I sought Herdman's permission to interview him. We met at his home in Bridge of Tilt, Blair Atholl, Perthshire, over two days in January 1999. What follows is an edited transcript of part of our long conversation, which is offered as a resource to readers and researchers interested in pursuing Herdman's distinctive contribution to Scottish letters. A substantial body of published and unpublished manuscript material, with few access restrictions, is also housed in the National Library of Scotland.

MD: In your first published novella, *Descent*, the nameless narrator expatiates on his inability to achieve anything more than a 'deadly confusion' in the relationship between his inner and outer worlds. He tells us (in section II) that he holds his inner world dearer, but that at times it seems 'endowed with a crablike malice'. He describes it as a cancer upon the life he leads 'in the world of human intercourse'. He waxes lyrical about intoxicating moments when he does experience ties and obligations and a sense of communal belonging, even fashioning 'masks' which allow him to indulge in this sense of social authenticity, but these moments, which he calls 'happiness', disappear as his 'inner life' reassumes dominance. His existence oscillates between these incommensurable worlds. Before the external world can demand a share of his attention it seems hugely antagonistic, and there is a brooding passage in which, at such moments, he feels like Roderick Usher, the expiring character in Poe's tale; and then, finally, he remarks that in this confusion between 'the tortuous vagaries of the mind' and the 'grasping for the actual' he feels 'at one with my weary time and culture'. The section closes with an explanation of what it is that 'nourishes' the inner self, and it turns out that these are virtually all things from the past: 'old history books, quaint Victorian drawings of Elizabethan voyages, Old Testament phrases, exotic place-names like Bhutan and Tegucigalpa, mathematical symbols, old coins, obscure species of sea-life, [...] ruined keeps.' So the inner life seems mapped on to the past, richly resonant, while the outer life belongs in a spiritually, culturally, morally impoverished present; and this disjunction is said to be typical of contemporary experience. I was wondering how much the voice of *Descent* (which you have elsewhere classified as a 'confessional essay') is to be taken as your own, at the time of writing and/or now?

JH: Well, I think I would have to say yes, it is my own, though obviously filtered through a lot of literary influences. I am often surprised when I reread this book as to how prophetic it is of my own inner spiritual development, in that it poses a lot of what I suppose are ultimately religious questions which I would not have known how to solve then, but which I seem to have had a certain advance notice of, as it were, and which later I began to think of more in religious terms. How far I would say that it is my own voice now? Well, obviously it is very much a young man's book and I wouldn't express the things that I say there in quite the same way now, but at the same time there is nothing I say there, I think, that I would dissent from now. As to whether or not it is a reflection of the condition of the present time and culture as seen in the experience of one individual — it might seem arrogant to claim that it is — but I think in some ways that has to be the artist's starting point, to try and find the point at which his or her own experience coincides with the experience of the time and culture, and perhaps the experience of a distinctly dysfunctional individual, as I certainly was when I wrote *Descent,* may point up some of the things that are wrong with society, or some of the ways in which it is difficult to live in contemporary society, which are covered over in the case of people who are more functional than I was at that time.

MD: What were the literary influences behind *Descent,* and have they endured?

JH: I think there are one or two that I could pick out quite easily. One is certainly the Rimbaud of *Une Saison en Enfer,* and also *Les*

Illuminations, to some extent. I was interested at that time in short prose writing. Joyce's 'epiphanies' were also an example that was before my mind. Dostoyevsky's *Notes from Underground* also, and in the realm of confessional writing, Rilke's *Notebooks of Malte Laurids Brigge*, all of which fed into this first-person confessional narrative mode. I think all of these writers have continued to be important for me, definitely so, particularly, perhaps, Dostoyevsky, but also Joyce, in a very diffuse way, and Rimbaud I continually seem to revert to as someone who lived out some of the essential struggles of the twentieth century before their time.

MD: *Descent* depicts a mind with a deeply troubled view of the world, but, more than that, its narrator admits to a certain fanaticism. Yet he also claims that his experience or his perspective can be aligned with the kind of society in which he lives (although he does not describe that society at length). I was wondering how much this early, and very clear, articulation of a psycho-social crisis or dilemma, is proleptic: how much is it present in your later work? *A Truth Lover* comes obviously to mind.

JH: Very much so. Certainly *A Truth Lover* was an attempt to make more concrete what in *Descent* was extremely abstract. So in one sense it is a sort of development of *Descent*, and I think in those early novellas that I wrote — *Descent, A Truth Lover* and *Pagan's Pilgrimage* — I was concerned with questions of the will and of self-assertion. I think that theme is first of all broached in *Descent* and later elaborated in an episodic but more concrete way in *A Truth Lover* and in a more comic way in *Pagan's Pilgrimage*, but in all these books I am concerned with the individual pitting himself against society in some way, seeing himself as marked out to defy society by being an individual, perhaps not in any more social a sense than that, but simply by being an individual and asserting a sense of his own rightness over against the claims of society. But I was always aware at this time of the *hubris* involved in such an attitude, and I think what those two novels, *A Truth Lover* and *Pagan's Pilgrimage*, are really about is the religious dilemma, ultimately, of where this form of self-assertion (which I suppose could be called Nietzschean) leads the individual. In *A Truth Lover* I use the metaphor of truth, you know, 'love of truth', as a kind of hook to hang that on.

MD: There is, it seems to me, another very decisive development between *Descent* and *A Truth Lover*, a difference which their otherwise comparable styles and themes make more evident. The narrator's remoteness from action in *Descent* explains the fierce abstraction of the prose, its remove from any sustained presentation of narrative incident. Instead, *Descent* takes the form of a prolonged spiritual meditation, a tendency which remains strong in the later novellas written in the first person, except that the voice never again seems to speak out of such a void. What I mean is that the prideful narrator remains a constant, but increasingly *narrativises* his preoccupations, the revelation of an arrogant, superior mentality being interwoven with greater related incident and progressively more situated in identifiable times and places. Thus *A Truth Lover* not only has a named narrator, Duncan Straiton, but a dramatic centre (the exchange between Straiton and the judge in which an assertion of existential freedom meets its authoritarian Nemesis); *Pagan's Pilgrimage* has a yet stronger narrative drive; and the texts in which contrasting first-person narratives are juxtaposed, *Imelda* and *Ghostwriting*, rely for their effects upon quite dense plotting. Arguably, as a consequence, your narratives seem more and more 'gothic', if, for the moment, we use that term to describe fiction in which the world is mediated through the psyches of obsessional, perfervid, highly strung characters engaged in bizarre actions, or in which relatively 'ordinary' characters describe being flung into contact with a world in which such people seem to have the upper hand. How would you take to being labelled 'gothic'?

JH: I think my difficulty when I started writing was that I had very little sense of structure. I think I was born with a sense of style but with very little sense of structure. As you've noted, there is a progressive narrativisation of the abstract ideas that, I suppose, I want to express, although perhaps the notion that I set out in order to express abstract ideas might be putting it the wrong way round. Progressively I think I have moved away from a narrative structure which is essentially episodic towards one that is more densely organised. When I wrote *Pagan's Pilgrimage* I was interested in exploring whether you could take the idea of the "holy killer", as found in Hogg's *Justified Sinner* and also in Raskolnikov in Dostoyevsky's *Crime and Punishment*, and see what would happen if such a character discovered that in the last resort he didn't have it in him to carry out the holy murder on which his whole *raison d'être* had been based. So that, I suppose, first took me into the realms of the 'gothic'. I became a long-standing admirer of James Hogg, and indeed I once started to write a doctoral thesis on him. I think that drew me into an interest in the Double and ways in which the fictional device of the Double could embody some of my preoccupations. I then wrote a book, *The Double in Nineteenth-Century Fiction*, which exposed me to a great deal more of the 'gothic'. However, I stopped writing fiction for almost ten years, at a time when I underwent a religious conversion and became a Catholic. When I came back to fiction, I found that I was more interested in structure than I had been, and more capable of producing a densely structured book, although still on a comparatively small scale. I had also read Wilkie Collins in the interim and was interested in writing a kind of metaphysical gothic whodunnit (or whydunnit). So I think that all these influences came together to produce a new kind of novella for me, one which was 'gothic', in which I was interested in more complex types of narrative voice and also, I think, more interested in the question of the nature of truth than I had been. I was more interested in the question of will earlier in my career, and I think I then became more interested in the question of truth, which I suppose began to bring me into what would be called postmodernist realms. I am distinctly not a believer in the relativity of the truth, but I do believe that the truth is something extremely hard to come by and extremely complex. By using some postmodernist techniques I think that I began to approach that theme in a way that was new for me.

MD: *The Double in Nineteenth-Century Fiction* might be read as a guide to the kind of influence which authors of that period — principally Poe, Hogg, Dostoyevsky and Stevenson — have had on your work. Which writers of the twentieth century, apart from those you've already mentioned, have you learnt from, or been inspired by?

JH: I would say certainly Kafka and Beckett were very important for me when I was in my twenties and probably left some traces on my work. The interesting thing about both Kafka and Beckett for me, and also Dostoyevsky, is that these are generally considered to be very pessimistic and metaphysical writers, who have to be studied with great seriousness and with a very long face, whereas I find the attraction of all these three writers to be primarily in their comic dimensions.

It's the comic dimensions which (for me) make what they have to say alive; you know, make their world views living. It was, I think, aspects of taking things that are suppressed in ordinary consciousness and bringing them onto the surface, acting them out as Dostoyevsky does and, in the case of Beckett and Kafka, teasing out things which are assumed to their logical conclusions, often to absurd effect, which attracted me.

MD: In the light of influences which are, with the exception of Hogg and Stevenson, largely European, I was wondering, are you a *Scottish* writer in the sense mainly of using the kinds of narrative devices that we find in Hogg and Stevenson, or are there other senses in which you would claim to be a Scottish writer, beyond the obvious fact of your narratives being situated in identifiably Scottish locales?

JH: I suppose I do feel myself to be in that tradition of Hogg and Stevenson, of the divided psyche, the divided personality, coming out of a background myself which in some ways has highlighted division. I am not sure how closely that can be related to the political state of Scotland, the religious state of Scotland, the psychic state of Scotland. I think that I first became aware of myself as a Scot, never mind as a Scottish writer, through reading Irish literature and feeling an empathy for it and an affinity with it which I have never felt for any English writing. This happened to me when I was an undergraduate in Cambridge. Very soon after I went to Cambridge and started off reading History and then changed to English, most of the things that I was interested in were actually, I found, either Irish or European. Now that made me aware of not being English in a way in which I hadn't been before, and while I admire a great deal in English literature, particularly some of the Romantic poets, in the field of fiction I didn't feel any very strong affinity for any English fiction writer. I was much more strongly drawn, first of all, to Joyce and Beckett, and then to Rilke, Kafka, Thomas Mann, writers in the European tradition. Then I read Hugh MacDiarmid and I saw this was a perfectly logical position to be in, you know, of trying to reforge the links, the direct links, between Scotland and Europe, which had been rather pushed out of the way, in my view artificially, by the Union and its cultural ramifications.

MD: There seems to me to be an implied politics in all of that, which may or may not be mediated by the literary work itself. I wonder if we could talk about your political position, as it is now or as it has been in the past.

JH: Well, I became converted to a kind of MacDiarmidian style of nationalism way back in 1961 or '2, when I would be about twenty or twenty-one. I suppose I would have described myself certainly as socialist then as well, although not having much claim from the point of view of personal background [*laughs*] to inhabit that territory. I have more or less stayed there since, I think, in that broad position, a supporter of the SNP, but with very considerable reservations, about a lot of its cultural attitudes particularly. But I don't see any other obvious political home for myself, except in the sort of left-of-centre of Scottish nationalism, which I have really espoused most of my adult life. I think I am very grateful for what has been achieved and hope that a good deal more will be. Obviously much cultural erosion has happened since 1961 or '2, which I think might not have taken place to the same degree if Scotland had had more control over its own affairs from that day or from 1967, if we take the date of the Hamilton by-election as the first decisive breakthrough for the nationalist position. It is very hard to say to what degree cultural erosion can be halted by the extension of democratic institutions to an area of the world that wants to re-assert its national identity, but I have considerable hopes that there will be a certain revivification of Scottish social and cultural life as a result of the present developments and that they will move further, in constitutional terms, within the space of the next decade or so.

MD: Anyone who reads your unpublished autobiographical writings (some of which are available in manuscript in the National Library of Scotland) will know that religious issues are deeply important to you: they will learn, for example, that after a prolonged spiritual crisis you converted to Catholicism in the 1980s. I personally find it difficult to ignore this knowledge when reading your work. Is it any wonder, I ask myself, that John Herdman finds the 'confessional' such a congenial form? *Ghostwriting* also demonstrates what you are making, artistically, of religious experiences and commitments. That novel is, of course, very far from being a fictional apologetics for Catholicism, although you have recently written an introduction to a novel by Fionn Mac Colla, which arguably is. What do you say to the following two observations on this matter? Firstly, Orwell's contention (in *Inside the Whale*) that the novel is essentially a Protestant form, by which he meant, of course, that novels written under the influence of any institutionalised ideology are bound to fail? Does someone like MacColla disprove that? Secondly, a more practical observation: doesn't a preoccupation with religion make for a pretty devastating unfashionability? Won't it guarantee that your work refuses the embrace of a larger audience than it has at present? Perhaps I am simply asking one question here: what relation do your religious beliefs have to your practice as a writer of fiction?

JH: Yes, well, we were talking about my earlier work, and insofar as it dealt with religious themes it was I suppose doing so from an existentialist point of view, and I think probably my fiction still does approach religious questions from an existentialist point of view. As a writer of fiction, I certainly don't attempt to set out to prove any pre-established doctrinal position. What I do do is try to broach certain themes, and find out where certain sets of attitudes with which I endow my characters lead in terms of the developments of their lives, and anyone can take out of that as much or as little as they want. Obviously sometimes I use religious imagery or maybe a religious quotation or two. I make some use of the story of David and Bathsheba at the end of *Imelda*, for instance, but in general I don't think anyone could say that any of my work is overtly religious. In fact, it would be interesting to see, from someone who didn't know, whether they could notice any difference between the earlier novels, before I became a Catholic, and the ones written after. The novel, I think, probably is a Protestant form in its most classical nineteenth-century bourgeois shape. I'm not sure that the novel in the way that I use it is necessarily a Protestant form, although certainly, as a novelist I wouldn't like to feel that I had to write in a way to which an *imprimatur* could necessarily be attached. I think it probably is true, to tackle your second question, that dealing with such themes isn't fashionable, isn't particularly conducive to finding a large audience at the present moment. I think that's true not only of Christian writing, insofar as I can characterise my writing as Christian writing. I know that Alan Spence has often said to me that he finds that where his writing deals overtly with spiritual themes — and he is of course a devotee of the spiritual teacher Sri Chinmoy — but he deals with meditation and such themes in some of his stories, and he finds there is a resistance to it among critics and commentators, who would rather pigeonhole him as the narrator of stories about Glasgow childhood. So maybe that's true, but one can only write about what one can write about [*laughs*]. I suppose if I was to identify the shift that I am aware of in this, it is the shift from the obsession with this idea of will to being more interested in the nature of truth. I suppose for me personally the issue of will is not so important any longer, because I have reached the position that I was struggling towards in those earlier novels, which is of saying, at least theoretically, that the will of the individual is not the ultimate criterion of judgement, that God is the ultimate criterion by which everything must be judged. Therefore I am more interested now in pursuing the question of how the truth of the reality of the universe, the reality of the way things are, both metaphysically and in human society, comes to us, how is it mediated to us, in what ways can we recognise it; emotional truth, psychological truth, theological truth, metaphysical truth, however you define it? So, I suppose that is what I am more interested in now, rather than in the questions which concern the volition of the individual. I think a great deal of my energy, that had gone into my fiction before, began to go into studying religion and trying to work out my position in relation to religion. I also found it difficult to re-align myself as a writer in that way. Jung was an important influence, I think, in helping me to do that, but it took quite a long time, and for a period I felt that the vocation of the novelist and the other "vocation" might not be compatible. During those years I wrote several non-fiction books. I wrote a study of Bob Dylan's lyrics, and then I wrote a spiritual autobiography, which mercifully hasn't been published, and then I wrote my book on the Double. I did write a few short stories, but it was actually fifteen years between the publication of *Pagan's Pilgrimage* and the publication of my next novella, *Imelda*.

MD: Leonard Balmain, the fifty-year old narrator of most of *Ghostwriting*, treats us, at the beginning of his story, to a wise but sad reflection on the chastening effect necessity has on pride: 'Youthful genius would rather sweep the streets than compromise its integrity. Then, one day, someone asks you to write a review. No harm in that, especially if you are fearless and incorruptible, strong-minded and impervious to blandishments. Next thing you know, you are writing a newspaper column which seems at first to be witty and perceptive but after a few months is agreed by everyone to have gone off, to have become bland and anodyne. Then you're asked to edit an anthology of contemporary verse. If things go badly, you could soon be putting together a collection of obscene limericks or copy-editing a fundraising handbook. And if they go really badly, you could eventually find yourself replying to an advertisement for a ghost writer — and telling yourself that that is, after all, a thoroughly postmodern thing to do.' Now, Leonard Balmain is not John Herdman: even the latter's hackwork (which includes, for example, the editorial direction of two volumes of *The Third Statistical Account of Scotland*) has a distinction and durability which, as far as we can tell, Balmain's does not. Balmain's dejection is that of an underachiever: he doesn't *deserve* recognition. But I can't help divining in this passage, however ironised, something peculiarly writerly — what should I call it? — your own disappointment at not receiving the recognition which you think your work *does* merit? Is this fair comment? Did you hope that your writing might have been more widely appreciated than it has by now? If so, how do you explain the neglect? Is it that you have specialised until recently in novellas and short stories, forms which many publishers consider curiously unmarketable? Can it be attributed to your failure to remain in the public eye by producing a regular stream of volumes? Are your themes simply uncongenial in an age like the present? Are you too Scottish for the English but not Scottish enough for the Scottish? Is it just bad luck? Or what?

JH: Well, I think you've put your finger on most of the main reasons there. I think all of these are probably true. The novella is certainly more a European form than a British one. It is very difficult to interest publishers in novellas. For whatever reason, I have never managed to tame a London publisher. When I say that, I would be quite happy to be published or prefer to be published in Scotland if the publishers in Scotland were capable of distributing and promoting the work as it should be, but that's never happened to me anyway. I think the long gap in my productivity certainly had an adverse influence. I think also that the sort of themes I deal with are not the sort which are currently fashionable. I think that I am not the sort of writer that metropolitan publishing wants to see as its image of a Scottish writer at the moment. I don't come from the right background, my preoccupations aren't the right ones, I'm probably a bit too literate, a bit too literary [*laughs*]. I think the obsession with literary prizes and awards is a terrible disease of the present time. Journalists seem to be unable to mention writers at all without adorning their mentions of them with the words 'award winning' or 'who have swept the board of awards' and so forth. This I find profoundly unhelpful. It tends to dismiss all writers who haven't won awards, and writers don't win awards for all kinds of complicated reasons.

MD: What have you produced since *Ghostwriting* and what are we likely to see in the future from John Herdman?

JH: Well, strangely enough, in view of your previous question about the popularity of certain forms, I have in fact written a film script of my novel *Imelda*. There is some slight interest from a small independent producer at the moment. Whether anything will come of it remains to be seen, but I have at least written the script and it's there if anyone is interested in doing it. I have also just written a memoir of Scottish political and literary life in the late sixties and early seventies, which I hope will be out before the Scottish Parliament sits; before, in fact, the elections in May. It has really been written to commemorate some of those interesting characters who would have liked to see that day and are not now going to see it, and who are in danger of being forgotten. In a larger way it's an attempt to memorialise what was quite a vibrant and important period in Scottish cultural life, written from my personal perspective. I am also trying to write a new novel, but it's at the very early stages of development at the moment, so I hope that my fictional career is not yet quite ended.

Novella

Sure
enough
the work was
 finished, complete –

all knew the measure
of having to say / how
thrawn grace is or did they know?

and is knowing as perfect as –
as walking across?
                    OK, listen.
The radio at the till is playing
translations from binary code – Soul – full on.
No, a roiling pulse of rival radiation
and it's Classical, Talk, double on double
switching, twisting, and here's a ballad: John Wesley Herdman.

Richard Price

Robin Fulton Macpherson, Six Poems

Distant Shore

Blackwaterfoot to Drumadoon –
the new waves break into my day
at this far other end of life.

Out of my sight but not far round
the horizon grey warships wait.
High in a blue sky clouds patrol –
they seem to hear and see nothing.

Now and then an Avro Anson
slowly or a Spitfire quickly
drills a hole in the firmament
whose fabric closes in again
as if a lifetime has been lost.

Littoral

The East Sutherland coast
north of the Green Table,
scree giving under me –
frightened and on my own
on my thirteenth birthday.

When father died I watched
the wind caressing grass
along the slopes of Loth
the way a mother might
stroke a child thought lost now found.

September the Fifteenth

The dead go on having birthdays.
Here's father's again.

Our voices carry well across
the dip in the hills between us:

an inch-deep world dense as cities
in shadows beneath cotton-grass,

emptiness to those who can't see,
astonishment to those who can.

Two Islands

The painter borrowed one.
And I borrowed one. His is not mine:
his spiky line of hills
not the one to which I raised my eyes,
his fine-grained ruffled sea
not my lightless pools in narrow burns.

Our islands weigh the same,
including even rhododendrons,
hawthorns and double-daisies.
The same number of oaks grow on them.
When we die each will take
his weightless island away with him.

A Persistent Garden

Torbeg is still Torbeg.
The garden is alive

with soft marigold tips
too razory to touch

comforting cornflower blue
too acid to look at

nasturtium seeds, promise
turning too harsh for lungs.

I am the nobody
still staring back at me.

Local

«Trout from the river, fried in local oats» -
by this time do I need a tourist guide
to find my way to half-forgotten rooms
in unforgettable childhood?
                    Here's one:
not a last supper but a dream supper,
a kitchen table, three generations
safely inside 1947
with the whole weight of Caithness (unperturbed
by the depth of its past) resting lightly
            on evening shadows.

My Friend, John Herdman

David Campbell

Stuart MacGregor, the founder of The Heretics, would greet me in the street with, 'How's your cock, Campbell?'

John Herdman and I, fellow members of The Heretics, enjoyed a less outrageous but nevertheless fun and mischievous exchange in our flytings — the time-honoured tradition of insults exchanged by Scottish poets.

John's respectable outward appearance and demeanour (unless he is riled) do not suggest a lover of fun, mischief and fantasy albeit that his humour is frequently sharp and tart, as evidenced in his witty Clapperton stories and those featuring his Aunt Minnie. This relative he visited as a reluctant family duty but with considerable distaste, particularly as he was compelled to express his affection with a kiss so that 'their moustaches mingled.'

This flyting mode of mutual respect and affections is often totally baffling and mistaken for antagonism by our southern neighbours. In my exchanges with John at their mildest, as expressed in some of our emails, might be such as this: 'I can't say it wasn't a joy to hear your voice, John', and his response: 'You know, my dear friend, there is nothing I wouldn't do for you and nothing would be too much trouble.'

Unfortunately, much of our invaluable correspondence has been lost but here is a sample.

26/5/75

Dear Mr Campbell,
Perhaps you have heard of the Reverend R. J. Slater and his nationwide campaign in the cause of temperance.

Each year, for the past fourteen years he has made a tour of England and Scotland delivering a series of brilliant lectures on the evils of drinking and the danger of alcoholism.

On each tour he has been accompanied by an assistant Norman Fortescue. Norman was a pathetic case — a young man from a good family whose life was ruined by excessive indulgence in alcoholic beverages. Norman would appear with the Reverend Slater at the lectures and sit on the platform slumped in his chair, drooling at the mouth and staring at the audience with bloodshot eyes, while the lecturer would point out this tragic example of what drinking would do.

Unfortunately last summer Norman died.

A mutual friend has forwarded your name and we wonder if you would care to take his place and accompany the Reverend Slater on the winter tour this year?

I am,
Your concerned friend,
Algernon Swinburne
President, League for the Abolition Alcohol

33 Dundas Street
Edinburgh 3
18th June, 1975

Dear John,

I have been invited by Professor Algernon Swinburne to assist the Reverend R. J. Slater in his tour of Scotland. Unfortunately, since my drinking has recently decreased greatly and my health correspondingly increased, I fear I am no longer a suitable or useful candidate for the position.

However, I have marked how your normal bumbling inarticulacy has degenerated into complete incoherence in your own drinking bouts. I have noticed also your ungainly movements, continued salivation and a certain pink puffiness in your features, combining to give the image of someone in the last desperate stages of advanced alcoholism. Consequently, I feel that it would be only fair if you put your otherwise purposeless life to some use and adopted this position for which I am no longer suited.

Please find enclosed a copy of Professor Swinburne's letter.

Kindest regards
David Campbell

The Fork

Peter Burnett

In 2015, in response to Creative Scotland's Literature Sector Report, I wrote a long-form poem in the Doric — a poem called 'Grissy Stibbles'. The poem, very much in the MacDiarmid style, and formed in iambic pentameter, simultaneously offered a criticism on the bureaucratic interference in literature in Scotland — criticism of our many Quasi-Autonomous-Non-Governmental Organisations — which I coupled with personal descriptions of my own journey into and through, what is now rather loftily known as 'the literary sector'.

This personal journey took me back to 1993, which was the year I made a conscious move towards involving myself in Scottish letters. I mean to say, that it was in the spring of that year when I made the decision as a young person, to write a book — the moment in fact when *I decided to become a writer.*

In writing the poem 'Grissy Stibbles', I recalled exactly what I was reading on the day I made up my mind to write. And the four authors on my bedside the day I wrote the first lines of my first book were immortalised in the poem, as follows:

> A late starter I was aged twenty five
> faan I pickit up novels an typitt my first,
> readin Elizabeth Smart, Todd McEwen
> John Herdman and Hesiod. Thon was aa
> it took tae me tae bolt fraily fae the
> village kittie, gang tae wark nae mair and
> become a writer in the big city.
> Like Hesiod, an individual
> wi a role to play, a major source o
> Greek Mythology, ferming techniques and
> economic thocht. Like McEwen a
> humourist o Scots naturality
> an like Smart a prose poet — mysel as
> subject — til which I added Herdman, pooder and

shot. I learnit tae write a published novel
fae ma readin, and drap by drib fae the
cleverality fit spilled o'er the lid o' the crock,
cooncil fae my peers and maistly tenty
weedin.

I first encountered John Herdman weeks before I began to write my novel, but there he was, and he has remained an influence ever since. These were indeed my chiefest influences that day — Smart, Herdman, McEwen and Hesiod.

It has remained a subject of fascination for me that Irvine Welsh's novel *Trainspotting* was also published that year — because it was not Irvine Welsh that inspired me, as he inspired many of my generation — it was John Herdman.

The first time I laid eyes on John Herdman was at a reading of his 1993 novel *Imelda* — although it would not be until around 2012 when I would actually meet and speak to him — and have the great pleasure of telling him what an influence he had been. That year, the Year of the Fork, 1993, I was to read *Imelda, Pagan's Pilgrimage* and *A Truth Lover* — and my favourite of these was the last.

Even then, I could see that 1993 presented the writing community of Scotland with a fork in the road — and as a writer or publisher one could either go the way of Irvine Welsh — as many did — or they could do as I did — and remain in what some might have then called 'the Scottish tradition', which actually reaches from the front doors of Hogg and Stevenson, right until the 1990s and the works of John Herdman — which are in my view, much in that tradition.

And when it came to the philosophical and social aspects of deciding to be a writer it was to the Herdman book *A Truth Lover* that I was drawn. I was in fact in those days, intoxicated by it. This is because even though I had *decided to be a writer*, it was my then job to mask this attempt at a career as a calling, something that *A Truth Lover*'s narrator Duncan Straiton, excels at.

Before I had even joined the literary scene and met my first writer friend, or been to my first poetry reading, I had Duncan Straiton to inform me of what I must do. It is not often, for example, that we tell the bloody awful poets in our midst that their poetry is in fact bloody awful — and this is something that Duncan Straiton does, and is punished for. The first lesson here then, it appeared, was to lie when needed. Instead of lying however — Duncan Straiton, that exemplar of disesteem, is asked what he thinks of a colleague's poetry at one point and he tells the truth — that the poetry is in fact no good at all.

Here we find out why the truth is in fact often not worth the trouble, because the young poet despises Duncan Straiton for his truth-telling — verbally abuses him and is extremely upset. But yet the lie is the sympathy that Duncan Straiton offers. When you tell me my book is good when in fact it stinks — you are doing more than preserving my feelings — you are telling a lie enough to encourage me to continue and maybe write a better book next time. In telling the poet the truth though, Duncan Straiton does not betray the cosmos, but like Shiva, is the standard of invincibility, might and terror. None of these are conditions fair for human life, however, and so as individuals and as a society, we tend to prop up such poor versifiers, if only for their own wellbeing. In fact, it's not Shiva but Jonah that is invoked in the name of truth in *A Truth Lover* — Jonah who was filled with knowledge of the wickedness of the city of Nineveh, 'intact in his own rightness' as John Herdman says, and it was not from love but from truth that he was compelled to warn the inhabitants of the city. 'For Jonah's mode was the mode of truth and not the mode of love,' John Herdman writes, 'and it is possible that it is not given to one soul to be perfect in both truth and in love.'

When Duncan Straiton finally returns to Edinburgh at the close of Part One of *A Truth Lover* he is firm in his resolution to be true, and so refuses a legal call as a witness to a violent crime and is charged with contempt of court and finds himself in prison for three months.

It is curious to find out what the truth might represent in such a story as the violent incident at the head of *A Truth Lover*.

This is where I feel John Herdman may be talking explicitly about the calling of a being a writer. In prison, Duncan Straiton continues reflecting and there are more commentaries on this splendid idea — truth — with much of it prompted by a laying aside of his pride and his reading of the Bible, as exampled in the analysis of the story of Jonah. It looks and feels like self-regard, but the calling to truth that Duncan Straiton feels is exactly as earnest and specious as the calling to become a writer that I — and perhaps even John, in his day, felt.

Duncan Straiton writes: 'Stupidity: how pervasive is that most subtle of moral vices, from which only an exceptionally strong soul can hope to be entirely free. It must be in early childhood that the soul learns to be stupid, learns to protect itself from the truth by refusing to understand — and once that way has been chosen, how useless, how inconceivable to think of going back!'

The truth is a subject that is rarely tackled head on like this, and doubly so within the realms of the postmodern where it is said that truth is entirely subjective. To wit, Harold Pinter:

> There are no hard distinctions between what is real and what is unreal, nor between what is true and what is false. A thing is not necessarily either true or false; it can be both true and false.

One feels, however, that had Duncan Straiton assumed this from the off, he would have had significantly less trouble with the world — but yet I cannot blame him. I can't blame Duncan Straiton for his drilling onward through the bedrock of experience, because his earnest endeavour, while frustrating for himself, is fascinating for the rest of us. A person will never drill through that bedrock and reach a satisfactory point. Maybe the fortunate ones achieve some kind of Heideggerian endpoint where they feel they have become the thing they set out to be — but I doubt it.

A Truth Lover is in this manner something of a road-movie of a novel. The structure is pillar to post, and the narrative a series of encounters with others, broken up by reminiscent anecdote and fable, historical and biblical. There are no recurring characters, with the loose exception of Duncan Straiton's best friend, Alan Bryce, who initially serves as a foil. Even in real life characters recur, but not in the life of Duncan Straiton, who has little to comment on in terms of friends and family.

I think I found *A Truth Lover* so compelling in 1993 because I was also setting out on such an earnest path — it felt earnest at the time, although for many years now, I have just had fun, and treated my work as fun — it's much better that way. But at the start — in 1993 — I was terribly serious, and a little fervid, just like Duncan Straiton. *A Truth Lover* describes such an ardent and diligent journey — a human working on a significant philosophical problem with no other tools than their own brute experience. What Duncan Straiton lacks is that which he commences the novel with — someone to discuss matters with. For it has always been central to the philosophical tradition to which he belongs, that serene or abstract ends are achieved through debate and dialogue.

In considering one of the strangest tales in *A Truth Lover*, that of the habitual liar who works with Duncan Straiton, we hack hard at another facet of truth — the existence of lies, and one person's propensity to tell them, even when it cannot serve them in any way. This man's tale ends in suicide and so it is highly cautionary — and his suicide is a sign that he has fallen away from everything — society, God and himself.

I am looking back on Duncan Straiton now, just as I might my younger self. All that Duncan Straiton seeks is truth, strangely. Not truth about reality, nor the truth of any given situation — but truth in and of itself, almost like he is a philosophical lepidopterist. The objects presented to young Duncan Straiton through his senses do represent some things which are also true, insofar as they exist. But even though I have described Straiton as digging downwards through the bedrock of reality, nihilism seriously damages your health, and he remains incapable of achieving his end.

Thank goodness — and thank John Herdman too — that Duncan Straiton is only fictional and that I have had his recurring example all of these years. I have never regretted not following the pack after The Fork of '93 — and I can even confess to never having read *Trainspotting* — although I've read pretty much of the rest of Irv's oeuvre.

And I don't think I ever will read *Trainspotting*. Having read *A Truth Lover* and my other favourite works by John Herdman, every four or five years since 1993, I have made my move — chosen my path — followed my leader. I know that for many, 1993 was the year during which the best clichés Scotland had to offer were perfected into a braw new set of tropes and similitudes. But back then, I set my sights on being the new John Herdman, as he was the person I chose to aspire to.

Did anyone else join me?

I don't know, but at the same time I don't meet that many Herdman readers who are of my generation. Maybe for me to follow John pointed to something deeper than the acceptance of a literary influencer. The reason that Cartesian acrobatics don't interest Duncan Straiton is tacitly attached to the idea of God. If the world were perhaps only to exist in his mind then he and the world would be one and the same, and the resulting issues would not be changed. In this way, Dr Johnson would rap him on the knuckles and say: 'Thus I refute you!' Like Duncan Straiton, and maybe like John Herdman himself — I have been quite alone, quite content to be alone — and am a truer artist for it.

Méditation sur la pierre et l'eau

Jean Berton

Cher John,

Vous m'avez fait l'honneur, à l'automne 2020, de me confier un texte de poésie en prose pour que je l'insère dans l'anthologie de poésie écossaise du vingt-et-unième siècle, en traduction française, que j'étais en train de composer : « My Stone » / « Ma pierre ». En travaillant sur ce texte, je me suis souvenu que Iain Crichton Smith a écrit dans « Deer on the High Hill » (chant V) : « You must build from the rain and stones ». Aujourd'hui, j'ouvre ma conscience sur un galet du Rhône tenu dans ma main gauche et j'entends cette injonction avec davantage de clarté …

Je suis né et j'ai grandi dans un petit village au pied du Massif central, un petit village souvent inondé (avant 1968) par le Rhône, ce fleuve d'une force impressionnante qui descend des Alpes enneigées jusqu'à la Méditerranée. Ce petit village s'appelle « Glun », dérivé du gaulois « cal », la roche. Ce toponyme a été latinisé par les occupants romains en « cal-dunum » : la roche-fort ou le fort-de-roche … L'explication est limpide comme l'eau de source : sur l'autre rive du fleuve, dans le village-pléonasme de La Roche de Glun, se trouve un rocher que l'eau du fleuve n'a pas pu raboter comme les autres au cours des millénaires.

Le lit du Rhône, à la confluence de l'Isère, s'est élargi puis rétréci au fil des siècles pour devenir un mélange inégal de galets et de limon, immense espace oxymore de pierre et de terre fluide qui m'a généré.

Pour réduire la vitesse de l'eau, mes ancêtres ont fait serpenter le Rhône en construisant des digues de pierres énormes capables de résister à l'irascibilité du fleuve : ainsi, ces rochers séparaient l'eau vive du fleuve des lônes, étangs d'eau trouble et dangereuse, sans interrompre le passage de l'eau du côté vif au côté stagnant. Alliance fascinante de la pierre et de l'eau pour l'enfant que j'étais.

Ma pierre, mon Glun, mon « cal(d)un », a résonné, un jour,

comme un écho de cet autre pays que les Romains ont jadis dénommé « Calédonia », cet autre gigantesque fort-de-roche qu'ils n'ont pas pu envahir et transformer à leur guise, il y a quelque dix-huit siècles … L'eau bondissante descend des montagnes et se renforce de ses affluents généreux : elle se heurte à la roche, jour après jour, dans son voyage vers la mer ; son brame m'impressionne, m'envoûte, me pénètre, me façonne. Son ardeur m'emporte comme un galet.

Un galet chaque jour un peu moins rugueux qu'un enfant curieux ramassera sur la rive pour en observer chaque tache de couleur qui lui fera imaginer les clairs-opaques de ma vie.

En regardant les montagnes à l'est et à l'ouest, l'enfant demandera d'où je viens. Le Mistral lui chantonnera la ballade de mes voyages, la complainte de mes choix, le refrain de mes désirs.

Les énormes remous du fleuve terrifiant lui révèleront mes questions interloquées, mes doutes assourdis, mes silences circonspects, mes fantômes occultés.

Les nuits de Mistral, ce vent qui vient du nord pour escorter le Rhône jusqu'à la mer, je me rêve galet détaché du fort-de-roche que l'eau et le vent font rouler vers le terme de ma vie.

Alors la mer m'absorbera, me fracassera sur les plages de Camargue, me réduira en sable livré à la fougue des vents.

Alors, entre deux vagues poussées par les tempêtes venues d'Afrique, entre deux puissants souffles de Mistral, je regarderai le ciel et je chercherai mon étoile-satellite qui me connectera avec les fragiles « machairs » des îles de l'ouest et les âpres cailloux des rivages de l'est des Hautes-Terres d'Ecosse, mon autre chez-moi.

Doppelgänger, Scottish Poetry Library, Tweeddale Court
(*a true story*)

The event over, the wine flowing freely, our chat had a prickly
start: I was sidling past only for him, newly back in the country,
to accost me with: 'Hey, tell me what you *really* think of my poetry!'

Sotto voce out of the question, given the bardic babble
all round, no option but proffer acclaim as loud as I was able,
each compliment attracting an ever more fierce rebuttal

such as, 'You don't think much of it at *all*, you erse.'
Which naturally I disputed, resorting to chapter and verse
but succeeding at each stage only in making things worse

till at last, glowering like Orson Welles in 'The Third Man'
he drained his glass and said, 'you're talking total *merde*, man —
this lavish praise is just because you think that I'm John Herdman'.

Stewart Conn

JH@80

Alan Spence

I first came across John Herdman back in the mid-'70s, initially through his work. I read his story 'Clapperton' in *Scottish International* and it really did make me laugh out loud. The suppressed rage channelled into surreal comedy was utterly engaging and quite unlike anything else I was reading at the time. This was a unique voice, sharp and witty, hilariously aware of the absurd.

It seems fitting that his early work should have appeared in *Scottish International* as he has always been both. (Scottish *and* International). Like Stevenson he is a master of the short form, the novella, which I think of as particularly European. (He also shares with Stevenson that wonderful elegance of style and a sense of the macabre, a very satisfying black humour).

I must have met John in person not long after I'd read 'Clapperton'. It was probably at a reading, and I took a liking to him straight away. Those qualities I'd seen in the writing were there — the quick intelligence, the good-humoured feistiness. But I also found him affable and kind, sensed a spiritual depth. I found I could talk to him comfortably and openly about my own meditation practice and found him both interested and sympathetic.

In the late 1970s, John and I were both included in an anthology of Scottish writing. We were talking about the book and John had been checking the biographical notes at the back. He pointed out that I was the youngest contributor and he was the second youngest. I mentioned this to David Campbell who laughed and said, 'That's exactly the kind of thing John *would* notice!' (It made me smile because it was the kind of thing I noticed too!)

In the early '80s I was reading with John at the Traverse at a Heretics event. I spoke to John at the interval and was raving to him about Ivor Cutler's album — *Jammy Smears* — which I'd just been listening to. John grinned, said, 'You know Ivor's here tonight?'. It turned out Ivor was indeed in the audience, and John took me over straight away and introduced us, leading to another friendship I cherished.

My friendship with John has been similar in that we might not see each other for years, but when chance arranged a meeting, or one of us had occasion to contact the other, we would just pick up where we had left off, with an easy familiarity. I have always, quite simply, felt good in his company.

I still have a small gift John gave me many years ago, a little solid metal figure of an Indian deity — probably Lakshmi the goddess of prosperity and wealth. He had come across it somewhere and just thought it was something I would like. (He was right). The gift was unerringly thoughtful, as unexpected as it was appreciated.

When my teacher Sri Chinmoy visited Edinburgh in 1996 to give a Peace Concert at Murrayfield Ice Rink, among the 4,000 folk in the audience were a few special guests in the front row. One of them was John — an old friend of his was also a follower of Sri Chinmoy — and again I felt that spiritual depth I had always sensed in him, an attentiveness to what was going on, a respect. I was grateful he was able to be there, to share in what was at the very core of my own life.

If John and I were to be included in a contemporary Scottish anthology anytime soon, he'd likely be the oldest contributor and I'd be the second oldest.

Recently I met up with John, again after far-too-many years, and once more — forty years on — the occasion was a Heretics event at which we were both reading. There was a fellow in the audience who seemed to take exception to John and started haranguing him. The man had already had a go at Tom Hubbard and a woman in the audience and made a point of leaving the room when I started reading. But John seemed to be the main focus of his vitriol. I mailed John after the event, asking what was the story. He replied:

They pursue me wherever I go! I ended that interview by remarking, 'I'm not enjoying this conversation,' whereupon he shot off like a wounded rabbit. He didn't appear to understand the difference between fiction and philosophy.

That reply was pure John, terse and droll, straight to the point, still making me laugh. I'm grateful for his work and his friendship. Long may he continue, a chiel amang us takin notes.

Notes on a Rare Volume Acquired in Lilliesleaf

Stuart Kelly

The late 1990s: bliss it was in that dawn to be alive. Britain had a Labour Government, Scotland had voted for devolution and Twitter did not exist. Tony Blair was still Bambi and Cool Britannia, and his Doctor Jekyll was yet to become the warmonger Bliar Mr Hyde. America had a modicum of sanity, if only vestigial taste. During this period, I started to take contemporary Scottish literature seriously. After years in Oxford, where the Balliol Junior Common Room took neither *The Scotsman* nor *The Herald*, I was woefully under-read in what was new. I had read the work of Muriel Spark, Alasdair Gray, James Kelman and Irvine Welsh, but little else. Applying myself assiduously to knowing the literary production of my own country, I was delighted to discover a body of work that was intellectually vibrant, self-conscious, able to be emotionally engaging while still being acute and ironic. I started to read work by Allan Massie, A. L. Kennedy, Janice Galloway, Andrew Crumey, Frank Kuppner, James Meek, Emma Tennant — and John Herdman. Happier days indeed. It was a time before snarl and whimsy.

It was during this period that I discovered perhaps John Herdman's most capricious and innovative work. I refer, of course, to *The Third Statistical Account of Scotland*, Volume XXVIII, The County of Roxburgh, 'edited' by John Herdman. There is a long tradition of authors impersonating editors for their work; most notably in James Hogg, on whom Herdman has written eloquently, but also, for example *Jane Eyre: An Autobiography* edited by Currer Bell. One can see why, with his interest in doubles, feints and the erosion of the boundary between what is true and what is believed to be true, Herdman would undertake such an ambitious and innovative project. I do not think it an overstatement to call it the postmodern work par excellence by a Scottish writer.

The book presents itself as part of a series, published by the Scottish Academic Press in 1992. The 'editor' never signs any of the pieces, but one can detect a Herdman-esque tone in the fly-leaf's statement that 'the description of the parishes vary in length but all are of absorbing interest, and there is much in these pages to inform and please the general reader'. What follows are accounts of the then twenty-seven parishes, with the information purportedly taken from local ministers and worthies in the 1950s, expanded by updates from the 1980s. There is a classic Herdman sense of nostalgia and wilful ambiguity: take, for example, the entry on Lilliesleaf which asserts 'The village has a past of considerable antiquity; it would appear to have no future'. The same entry says that a local well is dedicated to 'Saint Quentigern', surely a fictive wink at St Kentigern.

Thomas de Quincey, writing about Walladmor, called it 'the most complete hoax that can ever have been perpetrated'. *The Third Statistical Account of Scotland*, Volume XXVIII may well trump the *Opium-Eater's* boast. Reading and rereading it, I am in awe of the detail Herdman has conjured. Partially this is due to the use of real life figures as 'contributors'. There was, in truth, a Rev. Joe Brown who tended the parish of Yetholm, and W. A. MacTaggart CBE (known as Willie) was the treasurer at Lilliesleaf. Herdman captures their distinctive voices in vignette masterpieces of ventriloquism. Who but Joe would have noticed 'there has been a re-appearance of bicycles' (surely a sly nod at the work of Flann O'Brien?) and who but Willy would have thought fit to mention 'in certain places turnips are now being grown on the flat instead of the ridge'?

There are keeks of the kind of jouissance one associates with Herdman, an almost Rabelaisian glee in lists and taxonomies. For example, the village is Bowden, we are informed, has been known as Bothelden, Bouilden, Bowlden, Bolden and Bouden, as well as a misspelling as 'Bothendenam', and stories are told of an 'obscure Celtic monk' called either Bothan or Baithene. An ironic tone is often adopted: 'there are no pigs at all in the parish', 'there is a dearth of shops', 'outbuildings — once a library, formerly a ladies' waiting room, and stabling for seven horses were the property of the church until 1928', 'many of the young people work in Kelso and so have acquired town habits'. The shade of John Galt, and his narrators who reveal more than they realise, clearly animated the entire work. But even here there is a melancholy, as when he writes of Hobkirk: 'At pig-killing times there was feasting — on liver and bacon, potted head, white and black puddings, and roast pork. Events were dated by reference to the pig-killing. They made a white pudding with raisins in it which is never seen now'.

Occasionally, there is a note in the satire more sardonic, especially in relation to Hawick. Hawick, between '1841 and 1988 saw a revolution in housing and a massive fall in the death rate, huge changes in the knitwear industry, a great decline in church-going and a revolution in politics with the introduction of universal suffrage'. Two revolutions in Hawick? Herdman stretches credibility here, but more so when he says 'Great changes, but also great continuity; for Hawick continues to be a male-dominated society ... the (MALE) Cornet still requests his MALE equestrian supporters to accompany him.'

As Herdman has demonstrated in his memoirs of the literary life half a century ago, he has a keen eye for the mutability of things. In this exemplary work, there is much about indoor toilets and whist drives, the forelocks that go not untugged, whether or not one is on the National Grid, the lack of smithies and how the editor of a local newspaper 'drives readers "up the wall" with "bees in his bonnet"'. But as with all of Herdman's work there is a gentleness alongside its gothic inflections.

Were one to doubt that *The Third Statistical Account of Scotland*, Volume XXVIII is a work of very cunning fiction, I would direct readers to page 96, which recounts 'the author of the second or *New Statistical Account* describes at length a practical joke played by Lady Bennet on Thomson [the poet James Thomson, author of *The Seasons* and 'Rule Britannia'], who always stood in extreme fear of the supernatural'. Given that Herdman used the story of the spontaneous combustion of Thomson's father, the minister of Southdean, as part of *My Wife's Lovers* shows how much he drew from the folklore of Roxburgh.

The Third Statistical Account of Scotland, Volume XXVIII is perhaps Herdman's most intriguing work, and it shows his capacity for invention and empathy. Either that, or it's just all true.

Dr Herdman

Richie McCaffery

It's not the most propitious way of starting a contribution to a festschrift for John Herdman's eightieth birthday with talk of tombs and graveyards. But then again, there is a soaring passage in John's second book *A Truth Lover* (1973) where the protagonist Duncan Straiton stands in a remote graveyard to inspect the graves of his ancestors and is almost electrified by their posthumous power on him:

> I have walked in the places where they walked, and sat down in the churches where they worshipped, and have felt that they acknowledged me, and that I understood their lives. I have stood beside their graves in a remote churchyard in late autumn, and my flesh has crept up to the grand words to which their souls thrilled …

Perhaps I was something of a morbid youth, but I've always enjoyed mooching around old graveyards and in Northumberland, where I grew up, there are plenty of small village burial grounds, their head stones weathered, lichened and tilted, the ancient yews muscling in on the memorials to the point of collapse. One such monument, in the grounds of the Church of St Mary in Lesbury, is a grand ashlar vault for the family of 'Doctor Herdman'. Built in 1827, Dr John Herdman had to wait until 1842 to take his place there. He was eighty years old. A gazetteer for Northumberland mentions the sale of his furniture by auction in Lesbury in 1843.

In early 2020, just before Coronavirus brought the world to its knees, I had the pleasure of having lunch with Dr John Herdman in Edinburgh and afterwards Walter Perrie and myself went to his flat for the purposes of interviewing him on his life and work. Straightaway I was struck by the ancestral, antique furniture that had been so tastefully shoehorned into a relatively small space. Perhaps the Herdman clan had been trying for nearly two centuries to buy back the chattels dispersed in that 1843 auction.

I had recently watched the film *Only Lovers Left Alive* (Jim Jarmusch, 2013) — a beautifully offbeat take on the hackneyed vampire story. In it, John Hurt plays Christopher Marlowe who, having become a vampire, faked his own death so he could live forever in hiding in Tangier. With all of John Herdman's engagement with doubleness and the clearly supernatural elements of some of his stories, I did wonder the day I visited him if Dr John Herdman was himself one of the undead. Luckily, my worries were quickly allayed when he told me that the Dr Herdman entombed in Lesbury was one of his more eminent antecedents.

Dr Herdman had been a society doctor, tending to the Duke of Sussex, but he began to care more about the poor. Like John the writer, who lost interest in the legal profession he was being groomed to join, John the medic became disillusioned and entered the clergy instead. Both men are distinguished by their reformist drive, intellectual restlessness, engagement and compassion and between them they have made their unique and enduring marks on the arts, sciences, society and theology.

Dr Herdman is dead, long live Dr Herdman!

Fear without loathing, and John Herdman

Lesley Storm

I.

'Who's the beardie bloke?'
'That's John Herdman.'
GULP
'I'll introduce you.'
'I need another drink. Later. Maybe.'

This was a long a time ago. Ted Heath led the most inept and incompetent UK government, the economy was flat-lining. I was young. Beer was 20p or less per pint, and the days of our youth are the days of our glory, I thought. The spirit of 'mad John Knox of Haddington' was palpable everywhere — pubs shut at ten pm, between two-thirty and five in the afternoon, and opened not at all on Sundays.

I was a poet, I thought, and my life changed that day. I talk too much, I was assured by a medical professional around that time. But I could be frightened into stony silence if certain conditions prevailed. In those days a life-size cardboard cutout of John Herdman might have caused apoplexy and sudden death — luckily for me that never happened. A large photograph might quieten me considerably. That never happened.

I have scoured the medical literature, studied psychology. There is no name for my condition, no cure and no hope of a recovery. The author of the wonderful and strange *A Truth Lover* wasn't someone you could talk to — listen to, or read, but not speak to — not me. I was terrified. I still am in awe of John Herdman, and the years that followed and the lengthening list of admirable publications have done little to assuage my condition, so that *Memoirs of My Aunt Minnie / Clapperton* (1974), *Pagan's Pilgrimage* (1978), *Stories Short and Tall* (1979), *Imelda* (1993), *Ghostwriting* (1995), *Four Tales* (2000), *The Sinister Cabaret* (2001), and *My Wife's Lovers* (2007) — were constant reminders that I am tongue-tied in his presence.

My life changed. Friends and lovers died, became mad or so booze and drug addled that death might be a blessing. I lost my literary ambitions. I became a wage slave, and the possibility of being struck dumb by John Herdman sharing my space receded, the idea became the stuff of nightmares, and I had Thatcherism with which to contend — that most terrifying of nightmares. I worked in public librarianship — each successive Herdman volume passed through my hands at some point. I read them, bought some, and forgot my fear. I had nothing to worry about.

Turn. Turn. Turn. No good thing lasts forever. I began writing again in my mid-fifties, and plucked up courage enough to grab a spot at an open-mic night and read my own work to an audience for the first time in almost forty years. I was hooked. Again.

II.

'You should come to The Heretics sometime,' I was advised.
'The Heretics? Are they no aa deid?'

There was a new group! A new gathering of literary and musical heretics? Indeed! They were not all dead. The irrepressible Dolina MacLennan had survived the ravages of time, Donald Campbell was alive and writing, and the terrifying John Herdman was still with us — older, seemingly taller, grey, still beardie. Others (some older, some far too young) — William Neil and Stuart MacGregor — have found their place in Scotland's literary Valhalla. Time is never kind to literary reputations.

III.

I was startled at first. Is that ... nah ... couldn't be ... nobody can be that old!

It was John Herdman — large as life, sitting quietly at the back of an audience in the Saltire Society HQ in Fountain Close. And I have changed. I am no longer terrified of John Herdman. I can nod now, mumble something and move on, but I'll not stop or try to engage him in conversation. I remain in awe of John Herdman.

One of the great joys of my old age has been in preparing electronic texts of some of John's work for republication by Leamington Books

— scanning paperbacks, processing through OCR and editing the resultant mish-mash into a workable text for Peter Burnett, John's latest publisher and John. I say joy, but working on an awful scan of *Voice Without Restraint* was a nightmare. My wish to insert comments, clarifications and editorial notes (and my antipathy to Dylan) was so overwhelming that I had to work from the back going forward — line-by-line, sometimes.

I survived my ordeal. I have files on my Mac with weird names — 'Herdman's Truth', 'clap end herdman', 'herdmans voice' and 'Herdman's Ghost'; but he is no ghost, and my fear of John Herdman is quite real.

I am an old woman. The weird ensorcellment of *A Truth Lover* has receded somewhat, still I cannot speak to John Herdman. I may speak to him one day — we're neither of us getting any younger.

Fegs

Carl MacDougall

Dear John,

I hope you are well.

You'll mind a week or two back, Lizzie and I were at the Abernethy-Allisoun wedding, when Billy Donaldson, or Uilleam Mac Dhòmhnaill, former politician and self-styled Freeman o' the North, gave me what he called his life's work, his Novel, as yet unfinished.

Lizzie was adamant.

Don't, she said. Don't even look at it. You'll have to give it back, and the only decision you have to make is when you're going to return it.

He'll have a huge strop, stay in the huff, call you for everything, claim you're the reason the work is unfinished, that the rejection was too hard to bear, make a scene of cutting you off in public at every opportunity, then, some time, maybe two or three years down the line, he'll have something he'd like you to see, which will be a few pages of whatever this is you're going to reject, rewritten, with the good bits, such as they are, removed.

It's too late.

And that's just your part of the problem. He'll harass me in the street and send six months to a year's worth of emails beginning: *Dear Limmer.*

Aw, Zakie, no, don't tell me. Why is it too late? What happened?

You'll be wondering what I've been up to, he said, though, of course, the thought had never crossed my mind.

Well, I have it here and I want you to be the first to see it.

The work was conceived and would be realised in three languages, beginning with Scots, *The Hamely Leid.* The second part would be in English, *The Saxon Leid* and the third would be in Gaelic, *The Leid o' the Hert,* a language with which MacDonald was and as far as I am aware still is entirely unfamiliar, but he hopes to find a translator for the final part which he has yet to commence.

Principally, the proposed novel, as yet untitled, covers the social, political and economic life of Scotland from The Flight Through the

Heather to the present day and MacDonald offered our company, The Lobby Press, publishing rights for, he suggests, an advance of at least £25,000 o Saxon siller.

I will, of course, he said, help sales in whatever way I can, television appearances, foreign tours and the like.

The manuscripts were in three Tesco bags.

I suggested an editor?

I'll have a big whisky, he said, the bigger, the better. And no editors. I will not have my manuscript tampered with. Either accept it intact or leave it be.

How many pages are there?

The first part should come in at about somewhere between three and five hundred pages.

Just the first part?

Pairt Yin!

And in single spacing?

Of course.

This was when Lizzie said the dancing was about to start. MacDonald put the bags in my hand, said he would be sure to give me a wee while, no too long though, to read the manuscript and he would be in touch to discuss terms. In the meantime, he set off to find a partner for the Gay Gordons, a dance the announcer called the Happy Highlanders.

Later, things became strangely hazy. As you know, I have in the past suffered a slight memory loss, nothing that a week or two's mild drinking, usually wine and beer rather than absolute abstinence, can't fix, but this time things seem strangely persistent.

I remember we enjoyed reading random passages from the novel aloud to each other and wondered if you have come across the document in any of the three Tesco bags. I must have had it with me when I left the wedding, but what happened between leaving you and arriving home, I have no idea. I thought it would be best to check with you before contacting taxi companies and so on. I imagine they will be used to people leaving bags with them, though perhaps not three Tesco bags filled with sheaves of paper.

This is all I have. I cannot say anything other than it was in my kilt jacket's inside pocket. Can you please let me know if this strikes you as one of Billy Donaldson's pieces:

Dreich.

And wi a wind frae the Forth that wad tak the skin frae yer back.

It's the haar that does for me; the haar and the snell. The Guid alane kens how muckle coal, wid an turf it taks tae heat this draughty chaumer and though the lass is fine enough and redds it up weel, cleans the grate in the morning and biles a kettle for my tea, it's the daurk, they daurk, cauld nichts I cannae thole.

Maybe a year syne, round aboot the Lammas time I was fearin St Anndra's Nicht for yon's the stert o winter here. Frae then till the Pasch time when the bairns roll their eggs doon Calton Hill there's naethin here but haar, haar and a snell, snell blaw that brings a host tae my kist an sounders thro my banes wi sic a shiver that even broth and the bree itsel cannae shift it.

So it was roon aboot the Lammas, or maybe eftir, I asked the lass if she'd like tae keep me warm.

Whit wey would I dae that?' says she.

Lie wi me, says I.

Havers, maister, says she, and awa she runs, comin back the neist morning tae gie me tea and brose wi a guid tate bree.

Did ye sleep weel, maister? says she.

Indeed I did not, says I.

Whit wey, maister, did ye no sleep weel?

For the freezin cauld and chitterin.

Ye micht get a guid sleep the nicht, says she.

An hoo am I tae sleep weel the nicht.

Ye'll shairly sleep if ye were warm.

And what wey'll I be warm?

I'll keep ye warm. I spak wi my mither an she said I'd be a fule no tae dae it. And she said I was tae tell ye it's the sign o a betrothal, that ye should mak guid my wages an gie me noo a promise o marriage signed an sealed wi a lawyer's haun.

An awa she rins, singin in yon oorie wey that wid pit the fear o God intae a stane.

My frien an lawyer, Maister Angus Clerk o Duddingston near pished his breeks when I walked in wi the quine.

Is this your bride? says he, fell sair wi mair lauchin.

So I asked the lass tae lea us in peace tae sort it oot.

No, I willnae, says she. Ye'll hae tae let me read the paper that says we're tae be merrit an I'm tae get your siller gin you dee afore me.

That's whit I'm aboot tae dae wi my guid frere, Angus Clerk o Duddingston. Awa ye gang while we sort this oot. Awa an get yoursel a fairin, I says an gied her whit sma cheenge I had, tho it wasnae muckle.

She cam back in an hour, by whilk time I had agreed wi Angus Clerk o Duddingston that there should be nae paper, that we should mak up a paper that would sound fine eneugh tae the likes o her and when their marks were on it, put the paper in the back o the fire and let the bits gae up the lum.

Weel, back she comes an her mither wi her, the size o a cuddy wi a creasy goon on her that could staun on its ain and licht up a daurk corner.

Richt noo, says the mither. Read awa.

Sae Angus gets stairtet in his best Scots.

This being the year of our Lord whitever it is and in the city of Edinburgh, he stairts. This being the office o Maister Angus Clerk o Duddingston in the Flesher's Close.

Haud on a wee, says the mither, her steys near burstin. How can you be Angus Clerk o Duddingston if this is you here in the Flesher's Close?

Madam, says he. It is merely my office, these premises which are situated in the Flesher's Close. My heart and my soul, my very fibre of life itself, my loved ones and estates are in Duddingston.

Fire awa, she says.

And this here being a solemn contract herewith drawn up before these witnesses present here and now to witness this contract.

What did I tell ye, mither, says the lass. It's fine enough.

We'll see, says the mither, tho a drap o bree would seal the bargain.

And Angus gies her a guid drap in the erse o a tankard, which she finishes in wan swally, belches and wipes her mou an her neb wi a cloot she took frae some place inside the tap o' her goon.

Fire awa, she says.

It is stated here that the first pairty o this solemn contract being the gentleman present in the room wha isnae Angus Clerk o Duddingston, but raither the ither gentleman, Sir Roderick Farquhar Mackenzie of Keppoch Hill, Springburn Bank and the Mosshouse, wha has parks in Possil and lands in divers bits an places, wha is auld and snell but no yet dottert, is tae lie wi the lass cried Morag MacDonald born here in Edinburgh, wi a mither but alas nae faither but is believed tae be descended o guid Heilan stock, for the purpose o keepin auld Mackenzie warm at nicht. In return this is noo a promise o marriage and he'll lea aa his estates an everything tae the lass that maks his bed.

This solemn document is signed afore God an the folk in this room.

Fire awa, says the mither.

We sall return tae this same place the morn's morn says Angus Clerk o

Duddingston when we sall hae a minister of religion tae seal the bargain and tie the knot o luve atween thay twa.

And whit religion wad the meenister be? says the mither. Ye'll shairly no hae my dochter an this auld craitur merrit by some Popish son o' Satan wi a hert as daurk as the lum.

Indeed not, said Angus Clerk o Duddingston. Your dochter and Sir Roderick Farquhar Mackenzie of Keppoch Hill shall be merrit the morn's morn by the Reverend Doctor Thomas Blair o Pinkston.

Whit, says the mither. That auld creepin Jesus wha's kenned the length o Leith for saving lassies tae hissel rather than the kirk an drinkin drams till he could neither speak nor staun.

The Reverend Blair is a respected man of God.

Weel he's no respected here and the same pox as took his whauraboots years ago tak yours, says the mither. An while you're at it ye can ask him if he's got rid o yon itch he had in a gey fearsome place, if his bowels are yet mended an if aa yon scratching and roaring still keeps him awake at nicht and when you've feenished ye can ask if he mind's on me and if he's ony nearer to payin me the fower pounds Scotch he owes me frae yon time when he dookit me in watter and tellt me I was saved.

Maister Angus Clerk o Dudingston was sair afronted.

Madam, he says.

Dinnae you madam me. I'll gie ye madam. If you are tae hae Tam Blair marry my dochter and this puir auld buddy that's near sleepin, let me ask, Can a lassie be merrit by her ain faither?

Beyond this, I have nothing.

I know you will allow this request to lie between us, but how am I to proceed? I could offer him something and say I'll hold on to the manuscript in the meantime with a promise to publish, should it ever reach fruition.

I have few other options, as we know it is only money that will get rid of him, at least for a while.

Any thoughts or advice you can offer would be heartily welcomed. And should you find any part of the missing manuscript, perhaps we could have another reading.

Zak.

And for God's sake, John, please don't lose this. My life depends on it. I think it's called *Fegs*, which I think means cigarettes.

Hamish Whyte, Six Poems

CONSIDERATION

Late home
Lizst often slept
on the stairs
to avoid
disturbing
his mother.

LIBATION

In the course
of their meeting
Beethoven ordered
six coffees
for himself
and twenty three
hot chocolates
for Haydn.

PRESTIDIGITATION

Einstein's party trick
was to remove his shirt
without taking off
his jacket.

COLLABORATION

In the summer of 1917
Mr Pound and Mr Eliot
played tennis together.
Owing to his double hernia
Mr Eliot served underhand.

PRESENTATION

When he was eleven
Louis Zukofsky
read the whole
of Shakespeare
to win the class prize:
The Boy Electrician.

AGAINST THE FLOW

When I worked as a librarian we had to do two or three
evening shifts a week, six till nine. In my first few years at
least, I loved going in. The quiet train to Central Station.
Negotiating my way out through the crowds waiting on
the concourse at half past five. Walking the city streets,
people rushing the opposite way. Queues at the bus stops.
The pleasurable contrariness of going to work at the
same time as others were going home, starting as others
finished.

An Open Letter to John

Douglas Eadie

Dear John,

When Richie McCaffery invited me to contribute to your eightieth birthday festschrift, I immediately said yes. You and I go back a long way, never very close or working together but, as it were, fellow travellers through and on from *Another Country* as the title of your account of the Scottish (largely Edinburgh) literary and political life of the 1960s and early '70s so succinctly and literature-savvily puts it. A rereading of the book in preparation for the festschrift made me realise, somewhat disconcertingly, that we're among a very few survivors from that era. Not that many in the first place, those of us who are left should stick together. That's why I'm adopting this second person approach: a sort of chat rather than an essay or an article. One of two old codgers codging.

Unlike you, I have a pretty patchy and unreliable memory. Nor — again unlike yourself — have I ever kept anything remotely resembling a diary or a journal. So what I am attempting here is based on bubbles of recollection over more than half a century — not a sure foundation for a tribute to a writer and — can I say? — observer for whom I have the greatest respect, admiration and affection. You will forgive the bubbles, noting with your customary accuracy that it's in the nature of bubbles to burst.

So, to start with, your pal Zelda. 'Who?' you ask. Well, back in 1989, Alan Bold, poet and MacDiarmid biographer, got a hand-written note from the then kenspeckle Maurice Lindsay inviting him to contribute to an anthology he and his wife were putting together in celebration of *The Scottish Day*. Alan duly obliged only to receive a type-written response from Lindsay apologising for his earlier scrawl but advising that the intended collection was not in celebration of the Scottish day but rather of *The Scottish Dog*. Nothing daunted, Boldie took up his pen again and wrote and submitted 'Zelda':

... A poet I knew called his goldfish
Ezra, after Pound. But the fish
Caused no commotion
And had no cantos to croon
As it opened and closed
Its golden mouth ...
The filmmaker friend
Who called his Labrador bitch
Zelda
Got nearer the mark.
Like her eccentric namesake
Zelda was a character ...

Alan, however, was by no means Zelda's only brush with the
younger generation of Scottish literati that Edwin Muir famously
characterised as 'men of sorrow and acquainted with Grieve'. Much
earlier and more mutually intimate was her encounter with yourself.

This was in the autumn of 1973. You had been chauffeuring a
trio of Irish poets — including the estimable Pearse Hutchinson —
round the Gaeltacht on the second of a series of annual Irish/Scottish
exchanges organised by The Scottish Arts Council's Trevor Royle
and his Dublin counterpart, Eoghan O'Neill. Having finished the
tour with a reading which must have been either in Stornoway or at
Ullapool's newly flourishing Ceilidh Place, you and the others were
on your way south towards Kinlochewe where Deirdre and I with
young family and even younger Zelda were living in an unplumbed
two-up-two-down cottage. You were and are as meticulous a driver
as in every other activity so I have no doubt you were in the right
of it when your car collided with another. The other (tourist — yes;
English — yes English; fact becoming legend — thought differently
and it took the policeman called to the scene to arbitrate with a
sentence that you, genius mimic that you are and taking on the voice
of Free Presbyterian doom, would that evening pronounce over and
over again: 'There is only one side to a single-track road!'

(Re your mimicry, I can attest that for me it gets in the way
between recollection and reality. Any time I think of Sorley MacLean
or Hamish Henderson, it's your voice being theirs that I hear in my
head. As for poet and activist Willie Neill, whom I scarcely knew,
your imitation has him forever pigeon-holed for me (Phile under

Phake Phanatickery) with your account of how, mildly reproached for racism, he responded with an extended rant in which he professed love for all the world's nations, creeds, races and tribes with just the one exception: 'I hate the fucking English!' Come to think of it, maybe your voice that I hear in my head isn't your real one either: for that we maybe have to listen to the tenor purity of your singing of Stuart MacGregor's 'Coshieville'.)

So, back to Kinlochewe. There you were, rescued and relaxing with the rest of us into the *craic*. You had your shoes off to better enjoy the heat from our open log fire and that other kind of heat from a bottle of Glenmorangie contributed, as I remember, by Pearse. Then, getting up to cross the room to recharge your glass, you found your stocking soles chillingly absorbing a puddle made by the not-yet-fully-house-trained Zelda. Not so much disgusted as discombobulated, your revenge would have to be sweet.

The cottage's facilities were up the garden with night-peeing for males *al fresco*. Freshly re-socked and shod, you waited till your bladder was fully ready before going out to do the business and encouraging Zelda to follow, which the puppy did friskily enough. A minute or two later you came back, your eyes — indeed your whole face — gleaming with glee. Zelda was nowhere to be seen. 'Got her back!' was how you explained it.

The following year, 'Clapperton' was published and I like to think there was at least a trace element of autobiographical recall in your account of how your eponymous hero …

> floundered down the stairs and through the hall, and rigid with rage and vexation began to stride down the garden path; the dog Trixie, who had ventured out to the front door, scuttled before him fouling the pathway in her terror, so that Clapperton was soon stotting gracelessly from foot to foot, sometimes so much misjudging his distance that he landed, with a dull squelch, in that which he sought to avoid …

Thinking back for this open letter to that unsung Wester Ross weekend, I took from the shelf for the first time in years a slim volume that, just before his return to Dublin, Pearse had given to you to pass on to me with apologies for not having had the time to come up with a proper inscription but with the printed dedication to Eoghan O'Neill of his great poem 'Achnasheen' scored out and my name substituted (also Talisker changed to Glenmorangie). It was your trip with Pearse that had inspired the poem with:

The Gaelic names beating their wings madly
Behind the mad cage of English …

Smashing. And I use that Raj-sounding word advisedly here because it was you, John, who told me that it derived from officer-class versioning of Highland squaddies' *Is Math Sinn* — 'very good'.

We both had a go or goes at the Gaelic, yours more sustained than mine. In our time in Kinlochewe, Deirdre and I started a weekly class with the 'incomer' Church of Scotland minister from Torridon, a couple of others and, at the helm, our neighbour Mrs Ross, a native-speaker from Lewis. But these meetings quickly dissolved into local gossip in, of course, English and with Mrs Ross coquettishly teasing 'the meenister'. When we came back south to Edinburgh, we got together with yourself for Gaelic-learning sessions with Dolina MacLennan but these too tended all too easily to revert to English for discussion about the latest in these heady days of *Scottish International*, 'The Cheviot, The Stag and the Black Black Oil' and the build-up to the 1979 devolution referendum, the one that MacDiarmid voted 'no' to by virtue of being dead.

I think the first time I had encountered (a more mutually defensive word than simply 'met') you was in 1970 or maybe '71 when I was unsuitably and briefly employed by the Scottish Arts Council as literature assistant and you were editor of *Catalyst* and also heavily involved with *The Scots Independent*. This was a weekly newspaper promulgating the world view of an SNP then still marginal but, following the 1967 Winnie Ewing Hamilton by-election bombshell regarded by the guardians of the status quo as increasingly and capably disruptive of said status quo. Anyway, you had turned up one day at my basement office in Rothesay Place, Edinburgh, where what most regularly got done was *The Scotsman* crossword five times a week. You wanted to pitch for a grant that would enable *The Scots Independent* to carry a regular literary page with payments made for poetry and other new literary writing.

(Anent paid poetry, back then such a thing wasn't even a gleam in the eye for most though it should be said — unbelievably from today's perspective — that the BBC Scottish Home Service had its own well-established tariff: five guineas for broadcast poems up to twelve lines long, ten guineas for twelve to thirty lines, etc. Robert Garioch used to contend in characteristically mischievous fashion that the reason he specialised in the sonnet form was that fourteen lines a time took you comfortably into the ten-guinea bracket.)

So I'm sure I must have encouraged you though I have no recollection of whether a formal application was actually made nor, if so, whether it was successful or not. What I do vividly remember from that first conversation is your seriousness of purpose, determination to the point of implacability. In any case, Bob Tait's SAC-supported *Scottish International*, in which we both became involved, was coming over the horizon.

In the same period, there flourished in Edinburgh without Arts Council grant a loose grouping called The Heretics. Its meetings were monthly in the West End Hotel (whence of a Sunday another group of mostly Gaels would sally forth on a pub-punctuated procession known as 'Crossing the Minch' to the Hebridean Bar beside Waverley Station) with special Fringe Festival events including on one occasion bringing Billy Connolly all the way from Glasgow. The Heretics was poetry, song and story and your readings from (performances of?) the likes of *Memoirs of My Aunt Minnie* were a regular highlight. It was at a Heretics meeting that I once filmed Sorley MacLean: he was at his sonorous best (please don't imitate, John) and I think — though I can't check this — that you were in the audience. Aly Bain certainly was, front row, somewhat bamboozled.

Another Country indeed. I see from my book shelf that back then I reviewed *A Truth Lover* as 'the most impressive debut by a Scottish novelist for years'. And I meant it though it was also good to be able to give a pal a pat on the back. You went on to more than fulfil that promise. If I had had the talent, let alone the energy and finance required to make a film out of *Imelda* or *The Sinister Cabaret*, I'd have jumped at the chance. There again, such a project might well have turned out to be a disaster in the same way as several attempts (including one by no less than Ingmar Bergman) to film your man Hogg's *Confessions of a Justified Sinner* have all come to nothing. Some literary works are impregnable, untranslatable into other forms; the bond between intention or vision and expression is just too strong.

You have a parallel existence in scholarly and religious commentary of which I know nothing. But I suspect that there as in your fiction your words keep as tight a grip on your thought as your thought does on your words. Not for you either the stream of consciousness or the polysyllabic ponderings of the pointy-heidit. Wodehouse and Flann O'Brien as much as Dostoevsky and Schopenhauer. And not forgetting Bob Dylan.

So, John, in the same year your big Eight-Oh and further hurdles on the road to an independent Scotland cleared? Hmm. In respect of the latter, you've done your bit and we'll know more about what lies ahead by the time your festschrift is published. For the former, a richt guid williewaucht and a — far from the last, I hope — singing by your own good self of Stuart's 'Coshieville' and/or Hamish's 'Freedom Come All Ye'.

Sláinte

Douglas

Ian Spring, Two Poems

Dead Crow

I found the dead crow
in the field lying
as wet as winter,
feathers fraught
like leaves
forsaking the tree.

You never knew death,
gliding gallus on the wing.
Yet the worm was within you,
and a certain grace
leads now to this
sudden cot of grass.

Newhaven Fisher Boy

(based on the Hill and Adamson calotype)

His father's breeks he has girded on
and here he stands proudly with his creel;
the soft collodion features of his face
beneath the borrowed tam o' shanter grim
enough for the long exposure.

Afore the beached bow of the boat his bare
feet caress the cobbles and grains of sand,
half turned to the demanding apparatus,
nervously feeling the impending
release of the clench of his hands.

And what is it we hold here? Only a
sunbeam in manoeuvre, refracted by
the lens of disinterested compassion?
Yet so much seen and unseen, told and untold:
the keening of the fish wives, the girls

gossiping gutting fish, the Kirk's demanding
bell, the hard darg of the day's work,
bloated ghosts of the recovered drowned.
A father lost, a boy sinking into
the raiments of a forgotten life.

For this moment, your imagined story
haunts my present as I gaze rapt
upon your resuscitated image of long ago.
And your life unfolds into the future of the
past, devouring the rest of the light.

Ian Spring

John Macmillan Herdman

Nicholas Blyth

I count it a privilege to be able to participate in this celebration of a fine writer, whose work merits a reputation outside his native Scotland far greater than that which it has so far been accorded.

This is a crying shame and at least as much a loss to the literary world as to the author himself.

It speaks volumes, however, for both the tenacity and the integrity of the writer in question that he has pursued with unabated vigour the direction in which he knew his major strengths lay. That he is now, at eighty years old (and still vigorous), a 'seasoned' writer, accredited and praised by an ever-expanding circle of critically astute admirers, is a major triumph.

I first encountered John in 1960. We were undergraduates — thrown together, so to speak — at Magdalene College, Cambridge. A close friendship that had its somewhat haphazard birth in those days has been strengthened over more than half a century and holds good to this day.

Reflecting, as best I can, on the evidence of some sixty years between then and now, I detect a process in which the fusion of several distinct elements has given us the person whose achievements we celebrate today.

At the core of this success is a character of formidable determination. I'm speaking here of something much more (and much 'other') than mere stubbornness, which is as likely to lead an aspirant to disaster as to glory; I mean someone who, in his early attempts at authorship, trod a pain-stricken and lonely path of self-searching and solitary ambition before arriving, bloodied and bruised, at an unshakeable conclusion: that his strength (and maybe his salvation!) lay in satire of a particularly venomous kind; and this he has brought to a rare perfection over the years.

From the time I knew him, there was something of Jonathan Swift in his ability to detect eccentricity and then to highlight it in ways that provoked a mixture of absolute horror and vicious amusement. He evinced a natural spontaneity in this direction: he could take an instance of weakness or greed, of ugliness or cruelty or crass stupidity, and explore/develop it to its 'logical' conclusion, advancing it in rapid stages through exaggeration and distortion (think Swift's *A Modest Proposal*) until its conclusive manifestation became something so grossly awful or degraded or disgusting as to be almost literally unbearable ... yet conceivable, for all that, because presented '*in all seriousness*'.

At first sight this may seem to be distasteful: humour of a decidedly reprehensible nature, based on cruelty, distortion and absurdity, but there is far more to the picture than this. It is often such satire that can actually determine positives by the assertion of negatives and by the shock people experience when they find themselves party to it. For all John's supposed dislike of human beings ('*I hate not people in general but only most people in particular* ...' (from *A Truth Lover*), the animosity that expresses itself in his earliest works is directed almost as much inward as outward: occasional bouts of self-loathing which, needing to vent themselves somewhere, must bear the brunt of their own fury.

John emerged / progressed from all this — gradually but not slowly — developing a style in which not he alone, but he with his 'helpers', his 'troupes', his 'middle-men', confronted the world in a much more penetrative way. Narrative became an act, a dance, a show. The fierce satire was not diluted, but contained within a context of elaborately contrived events, encounters and strange beings — treated seriously but, clearly, either crazed or demonic or serving strange deities; acting out charades, providing (in one obvious case) a surreal 'dark' cabaret and offering opportunities for the mysterious ringmaster (or puppeteer) to demonstrate his art(s).

The effect was essentially different from that of the early writings, from which, quite often, bile, resentment and acerbity had merely gushed. Yes — anger, disgust and a marked degree of malevolence were still present, but now they were effectively 'stylised', controlled; not, of course, suppressed but 'managed', 'presented' — even enhanced.

I sense also (though I know John will correct me if I'm wrong) that, along with this important progression, the author's general (if not comprehensive) loathing of humankind underwent a change; one whereby — although not, of course, abjured, it had been incorporated into something more ... something bigger: something more broadly and legitimately judgemental; something to which dilution had actually imparted a stronger, more stimulating taste.

This was a change whereby — by means of 'technique' — a distance was created between writer and audience: the written word delivered with immaculate precision, not from a single, easily-identified protagonist, but through the medium of such a chorus as might recall that of the troupe assembled at the asylum of Charenton in Weiss's Marat/Sade.

John has learnt to live in — and to profit from — this *demi-monde*, as at-home in it now as was Samuel Beckett for whom John and I shared a comparable admiration. (And this was back in the day before Beckett — to his acute dismay — became broadly fashionable and when people were still walking out of his plays at the first interval!).

It would be surprising if a writer as sharply critical as John could ever be said to be content with his performance. Is perfection a myth? The very notion of it a recipe for madness? I suspect he does not ask himself that question (and maybe never did). He is a craftsman. He writes quite slowly, I know. He 'fashions' his work fastidiously and has developed an acute awareness not only of the possibilities of language to excite and inform, but also of its dangers when carelessly or irresponsibly treated. He writes with sustained precision — each word having its proper place in any given sentence — and never wastes a word or chooses a weak one ... even when faced with a range of (so-called) 'synonyms'. His commitment to using words according to their exact meaning is so scrupulous as to be almost fanatical.

People of his calibre are not merely highly skilled practitioners of language but should be seen (and valued) as its responsible custodians on behalf of a public more and more committed to the deeply debased jargon of the email and the SMS. It is by the strenuous demands they impose on themselves that others can see just what 'good writing' means. While we still have such responsible users there will always be standards, but I fear that their masterpieces will fall into neglect ... become regarded as less and less 'accessible' to today's 'readers'. The stifling dictates of rampant 'inclusivism' (a word I loathe) will eventually specify that all books must be able to be read, marked and inwardly digested within two hours (maximum) and that vocabulary smacking of 'elitism' or of a good education must be banned by law!

As is, I hope, evident, I deal here more with John as a writer than with the body of his published work, all of which I have been privileged to read, and which cannot be effectively dealt with in so brief a commendation. Bearing this in mind, I must make a statement concerning the man behind the books, reflecting the qualities of character that have made his success possible.

John Herdman is, first and foremost, a man of impeccable and courageous honesty and has been so — manifestly — since the beginning of his 'life's work' as a writer. In those early days he submitted to the exigencies of pitiless self-examination and frank disclosure — tinged with underlying tones of anger and defiance; and these experiments eventuated in 'statements', which were almost, at times, *manifestos*. They were a young man's declarations, the beginnings of a 'thesis': prerequisites of what was later to become the mature and brilliantly crafted style of the subsequent works.

To wrestle with truth can be a debilitating, sometimes terrifying, experience. That John sometimes found it so is beyond doubt. Why would he not? Possessed of a demandingly inquisitive mind and a first-rate brain, he was never going to settle for half-truths, illusions or comfortable placebos. The struggles evident in *A Truth Lover* are at times deeply painful to read, but they invite enormous admiration — as well as compassion. The chronicler of this fierce and prolonged exercise in self-definition stubbornly refuses to accept unresolved conclusions. With dogged determination he continues to explore every hypothesis and, even when driven to a conclusion, is still reluctant to accept it, for fear that his very relief might provoke a further disintegration.

The courage (and, indeed, the confidence) to wrestle in this way in the relentless pursuit of truth has delivered for him a rich and fully deserved reward; and this comes not as a temptation to complacency but as an assurance that what was so grimly worked and suffered for was not in vain.

A writer needs these qualities of character: courage, self-belief, integrity, patience, persistence, honesty and an unwillingness to compromise. He must also have something to say. John Herdman qualifies on all these scores.

In his resolve to be a writer he chose a tough, a lonely, life. It was a courageous choice. From the moment he introduced himself to a reading public he persisted in that bleak pursuit. His was the 'the lidless eye that loves the sun' and when things were tough he never prostituted his art, by lowering his standards; 'never made a poorer song / That (he) might have a heavier purse …'

When we are no longer susceptible to development, our life is effectively over; we resign — actually abandon — ourselves to that barren stasis which produces only repetition — and that laboriously. I hope and pray (and, indeed, expect) that John will never come into that category (in fact, that he will never come into any particular 'category').

Tennyson's *Ulysses* says it all: 'How dull it is to pause, to make an end!'

The survivor of Troy, nearing, at last, after twenty years of battle and adventure, his hometown of Ithaca, discovers within himself a perverse reluctance to settle for relative inaction and a life of humdrum domesticity. A force deeply entrenched within him cries out against it, condemns it as a craven and premature concession to the passage of time. He will never succumb to it: this shameful temptation to 'rust unburnish'd' rather than 'shine in use'! As though to breathe were life!' The very prospect appals him.

He makes his defiant statement, his 'boast', so to speak, assuring himself (and us) that it is possible for every hour to be saved

> From that eternal silence, something more,
> A bringer of new things ...
>
> And this grey spirit yearning in desire
> To follow knowledge like a sinking star
> Beyond the utmost bound of human thought ...

John is essentially restless, as all true artists must be. Writing — and the exacting challenges that accompany it — are for him an interminable preoccupation: a way of life, a means of thinking, a road to understanding ... and this, I think (presumptuously), is how it should be.

I reflect with delight that he has never allowed himself to be imprisoned in a 'bubble'. In a most attractive book, *Another Country*, he employs his unique talents — his powers of observation, of critical judgement and of witty, perceptive comment — to enliven a subject that on the surface may have seemed of only moderate or parochial interest. I read the book, actually, with excitement! In his scholarly work on the lyrics of Bob Dylan (*Voice Without Restraint*) he demonstrates, once again, his concern for meaning, interpretation and the potentialities of language, especially when explored through music and performance; his enthusiasm not only for Dylan's recordings of the songs, but for the depths of their content and for the ingenious ways in which Dylan explores their ambiguities and subtleties.

These books are, of course, very different from the novellas, but the mastery is the same.

I genuinely look forward to what John Herdman will write next.

Satiric Capri From A Hibernian Perspective

Michael Hollington

PREFATORY NOTE

John Herdman has been, and is, of considerable significance in my life. This could never have been foreseen when we first met in October 1960 as fellow students of English Literature at Magdalene College, Cambridge — to some extent rivals, though John, with his elephantine memory and other formidable intellectual powers, was undoubtedly *il miglior fabbro*. In fact, it has come about as a result of three noteworthy strokes of fortune, one entirely serendipitous and positive, the other two the exact reverse. Mixing in different circles, we were cordial acquaintances rather than friends at Magdalene, although both of us developed separately then an affectionate relationship to our teacher Arthur Sale that lasted for the rest of his life, until 1999, and that would also perhaps in the course of time have brought us together by another route. Instead, our friendship proper began in the summer of 1968, five years after we had graduated, when by sheer coincidence I happened to be in Edinburgh working as a tour guide for European visitors, and bumped into John on The Mound on a warm sunny day off.

From that moment the relationship grew apace. In the autumn of that year, I began nine years as a lecturer at the University of East Anglia, and so as a consequence was not back in Scotland for a while. But we kept in constant touch, often through correspondence. John regularly sending me his work as it appeared, and I writing appreciative comments in reply after reading it. I also remember him visiting me once or twice during my time in Norwich, and later in France. But my own return visits to Scotland were infrequent, especially between 1987 and 2002, when I held a chair in Sydney, Australia, and only became more regular when I had permanently returned to Europe in 2002.

It became apparent early on after 1968, as we got to know each other better, that we had shared similar impressions of Magdalene, where Prince William of Gloucester (and later his brother) entered the college at the same time as we did. We were both very much outsiders to what we saw as the dominant ethos there, that of the prince and his entourage, whom a similar American friend of the time dubbed 'turkeys' — John as a Scotsman, I as a class outsider from north London. People like ourselves, which included such as John Simpson or Bamber Gascoigne, who later became luminaries at the BBC (and who might well, the latter especially, have joined the 'turkeys' had they wished to), tended to gravitate towards the alternative college ambiance of the ex-centric Arthur Sale and his wife Nell, both from D. H. Lawrence's birthplace, Eastwood in Nottinghamshire, and to bond with each other.

1 thus followed John's significant involvement in SNP cultural politics with vicarious interest and pleasure. Neither of us would have thought it at all likely, however, that I might at some point in a measure 'turn Scottish,' until the momentous vote south of the border to leave the European Union in 2016. With John, and a substantial majority of Scots, I saw this decision as catastrophic, not only for Scotland; having only recently returned, resettling in Kent in 2013 as an Honorary Fellow of 'Britain's European University' on the understanding that we belonged politically and culturally in Europe, I at first intended to leave altogether.

But then I thought of Scotland, and started to write to John about retaining a base there. He offered much-needed encouragement and support, and so it came about that I began in April 2017 to rent a house in Ayrshire, to be closer this time to Arran, Argyle and the Western Isles, which I knew much less well than the eastern side of Scotland.

Still, until 2020 it did indeed serve principally as a base, to return to from time to time after the latest bout of (in Brecht's phrase) 'wechselnd die Länder öfter als die Schuhe' (changing countries more often than shoes) that had become a habit as part of my lifestyle. But then in 2020 came the third 'hammer-blow of fate': Covid, when I happened to be here rather than elsewhere. For me, along with many undesirable consequences, a year plus of staying put on my own in Scotland resulted, permitting me to grow closer to the kind and friendly people around me, and to the aspiration towards independence for Scotland they all seem to share — all those I know at least. I voted with them, for them and for myself, in May.

All this began essentially with John, and the modest piece of writing that follows also owes much to him. At some point since 2017 he has expressed the hope that I might turn the focus of my literary attentions to a greater extent than hitherto to Scotland. Apart from a stray essay on *Waverley*, the consequence of that novel's appearance on the Agregation syllabus in France one year in the last quarter-century, I don't think I have attempted anything on Scottish writing before now.

In dedicating it to John, I hope to underline what I see as the profoundly Scottish essence of his work by emphasising, not so much its Gothic features — his debt to writers like Hogg and Stevenson, the treatment in his fiction of the significant theme of the double, with its links to German Romanticism (on which he has also published a significant critical monograph), and his achievement in keeping their influence alive by reinventing them in contemporary Scotland, is obvious enough — as his perhaps equally important contribution to the long and vigorous tradition of Scottish humour and satire, stretching back through Mackenzie and Douglas through Smollett to the Middle Ages, and even beyond, perhaps. It is a robust, at times savage and even cruel version of satiric writing, of which the vigorous representation and castigation of 'wicked' sexual deeds is one speciality. It is reinvented in John's work in a playful, postmodern manner, in which the Calvinist element that had a part to play in its development is no longer evident. The two Scottish writers discussed here, Compton Mackenzie and Norman Douglas, seem to look forward to it in this respect, though their novels are specifically satiric *romans à clef*, and John's not, though I could be wrong here ... Compton Mackenzie has a particular relevance to him, for at Merchiston Castle School in Edinburgh in 1959 John received a prize from his hands, and took to heart what the distinguished guest had to say in his public address. His advice was that if we weren't sure what we wanted to do with our lives, the best thing was to be sure about what we didn't want to do. John has subsequently lived by this rather Beckettian precept.

But the piece that follows is very much a tentative first step. I hope to have a few more years above ground in which to read or reread some of the Scottish books John has given me in the past, and perhaps write about them — George Douglas Brown, Lewis Grassic Gibbon, or Sorley Mclean, and even to learn Gaelic to read the latter in the original. And of course, to reread John's own work! But if I hope this for myself, I hope even more that John himself will live to a great age, and perhaps in the course of it take up writing again, if not of fiction, then of critical writing about Scottish writers, outdoing me once again as he did at Cambridge sixty years ago. In Australian English: go for it, mate.

The focus of this essay is two writers of Scottish descent, Norman Douglas and Compton Mackenzie, who wrote brilliant satires on what may be thought of as fairly typical behaviour at the ongoing party that took place in Italy on the island of Capri in the early twentieth century. Neither of them can be described, in Australian English, as dinky-di Scots: though he merits an entry in the *Collins Encyclopaedia of Scotland*, above all as one of the founders of the Scottish Nationalist Party, Compton Mackenzie was born in England to theatrical parents — an English father and American mother — and only settled in Scotland in his forties. Norman Douglas, by contrast, was three-quarters Scottish, and of impeccable descent, his paternal grandfather being 14th Laird of Tilquhillie in Aberdeenshire, where Douglas spent much of his childhood, his maternal grandfather General James Ochoncar Forbes, 17th Lord Forbes, also of Aberdeenshire. But Douglas went the other way, despising nationalism, and spending most of his adult life on the continent of Europe, often on the run after a series of sexual misdemeanours, chiefly in Italy. He does not figure in the *Collins Encyclopaedia of Scotland.*

These two were members of a distinguished company of expatriates on an island which, by 1917, when Douglas's groundbreaking novel *South Wind*, had become a byword for libertarian political, intellectual and sexual freedoms. Writers like D. H. Lawrence and Vernon Lee, revolutionaries like Gorky and Lenin, and a richly varied assortment of male and female homosexual and other sexual minorities, found their home there from time to time, invariably overlapping at some point with Douglas and Compton Mackenzie.

First, some very general contextualising. It is a commonplace that the seemingly endless agonies of the years 1914–18 gave way after the armistice to a period of unrestrained hedonism in the 1920s. But Capri very much anticipated this trend — the party had been going on there since at least the 1890s, and continued throughout much of the Great War. *South Wind* is important for its role in establishing the genre I shall explore here — the satiric *roman à clef*, a particular speciality of the 1920s, represented not only by the two books by Compton Mackenzie I discuss but also by such better-known works as D. H. Lawrence's *Women in Love* and Aldous Huxley's *Chrome Yellow* and *Point Counterpoint*. It became an immediate bestseller, for fairly obvious reasons, because it offered readers some form of escape from the continuing horrors of slaughter at the front. The cover of a recent edition, which depicts Miss

Wilberforce in the novel, regularly drinking herself silly at parties and then proceeding to take her gear off, gives a fair idea of the general tone. Five years before James Joyce's *Ulysses*, it depicts a *nostos* to Britain, the return of an Anglican bishop after a tour of duty in colonial Africa. But there is a crucial difference: instead of plotting a prudent course through the trials and temptations of his journey, like Leopold Bloom in Joyce's masterpiece, this particular homecoming hero, as we shall see, simply succumbs to the compelling siren power of the south wind.

But Capri had gained its dubious reputation long before 1917. It stems in fact from almost two thousand years ago, when the emperor Tiberius retired there in 26 AD 'An old goat arrives on goat island (Capri)' was the joke at the Atellanean farces of the time. During the early part of his reign Tiberius had been both an effective ruler and accomplished military leader, but in later life he is reputed to have gone to the dogs at the villa Jovis that he built for himself on top of the second highest peak on the island. Tacitus describes him as abandoning his previous absorption in state affairs and giving himself up to a life of seclusion and 'occultiores in luxus et malum otium', which Michael Grant translates as 'secret orgies, or idle malevolent thoughts.' (Tacitus 190) Suetonius goes much further, providing explicit details of the deviant sexual preferences he began to indulge in: 'on retiring to Capri he made himself a private sporting-house, where sexual extravagances were practised for his secret pleasure. Bevies of young girls and young men, whom he had collected from all over the Empire as adepts in unnatural practices, and known as *spintriae*, would perform before him in groups of three, to excite his waning passions.' (Suetonius 139). He also cites multiple expressions of a sadistic impulse that took full advantage of the vertiginous cliff geography of the island. Writing a century after the horrors he describes, Suetonius declares that 'in Capri they still show the place at the cliff top where Tiberius used to watch his victims being thrown into the sea after prolonged and exquisite tortures.' (140–41)

It doesn't really matter for my purposes here in illuminating a vein of Celtic humour that a number of modern historians express reservations about the veracity of these sensational accounts. The point is that in the period studied, from the later nineteenth century onwards, Capri's ancient reputation was a draw card for a variety of sexual misfits, many of them schooled in the classics, in particular from Northern European countries with more puritanical attitudes and stricter laws against homosexuality. Some of these, as we shall see, had a vague desire to follow in the footsteps of Tiberius. 'I have an ambition to live near the villa of Tiberius,' proclaims Bob Marsac in Compton Mackenzie's *Vestal Fire* (VF 57).

Thus, from Britain, in the years following the Oscar Wilde verdict, came a trio consisting of Somerset Maugham, E.F. Benson the son of the future Archbishop of Canterbury, and John Ellingham Brooks, who remained on the island until 1929. Lord Alfred Douglas himself, together with another of Wilde's lovers, Robert Ross, spend two months on Capri in 1896, while Wilde himself languished in prison. Famous names from Germany who helped establish the prevailing tone included most conspicuously that of Friedrich Alfred Krupp, the head of the armaments family, who came to Capri four years running between 1898 and 1901 on his oddly named yacht *Puritan*. His version of emulating Tiberius seems to have consisted in part in the sacrilegious desecration of a holy place — the historian William Manchester describes his purchase of two caves, the Grotta di Fra' Felice ('Brother Felix' being a hermit who had made them his home) and their transformation into parodic religious retreats, where male guests would arrive in monastic garb and then disrobe, entering 'a kind of terraced, scented Sodom ... a kind of Krupp fun-club ... [where] they submitted to sophisticated caresses from him, while three violinists played. An orgasm was celebrated by sky-rockets.' (Money 67) These proceedings were sometimes photographed, which led to Krupp's expulsion from Capri, and presumed suicide in 1902, Kaiser Wilhelm attending his funeral.

But such attempts by immigrants from elsewhere to keep up the Tiberius tradition on Capri seem regularly to founder on a fundamental obstacle. The totalitarian emperor had obviously set the bar of depravity impossibly high, especially in the torture and cliff-throwing department. Naturally, then, the Hibernian satiric writing we shall examine here often employs a mock-heroic mode that exploits the gap between limited contemporary debauchery and the apparent, if imaginary limitlessness of Tiberius's orgies.

Yet if you were to imagine that the satiric impulse in the three novels I shall briefly explore is simply driven by some Calvinist-inspired *saeva indignatio* against sexual deviancy you would be entirely wrong. Norman Douglas was an unashamed paedophile who established himself on Capri in order to be able to practice his lifestyle with minimal interference. He had many followers and admirers in this, but also plenty of detractors: Raymond Mortimer, reviewing his autobiography *Looking Back*, remarks sardonically that 'he coolly admits to odious conduct that anyone else would try to forget,' and even his biographer Mark Holloway has to include 'many anecdotes — most not in print — that illustrate (if true) the casual nastiness of which Douglas was occasionally capable, and the imbecile admiration which such acts could arouse amongst his more fatuous and sycophantic followers.' (Holloway 255, 315) As far as I know, Compton Mackenzie was by contrast largely heterosexual, but thoroughly promiscuous. He insisted on fashioning an open marriage with his wife Faith, who, herself, enjoyed both male and female lovers. Although Compton left Capri in the course of the '20s for other islands — Herm, Jéthou, Barra: he is the subject of D. H. Lawrence's story *The Man Who Loved Islands* — Faith stayed on a good deal longer. Both of them, with Douglas, can be counted as quintessential Capri insiders, thoroughly representative of the often dissolute mores of the expatriate community of the time.

Thus, for fairly obvious reasons, including the fact that many of its targets were still alive and might easily recognise portraits of themselves in thin disguise, the satire of these books is for the most part light-hearted. There is one significant exception, perhaps — the portrait of Baron Jacques d'Adelswärd-Fersen, who had committed suicide in 1923, as Count Bob Marsac in Compton Mackenzie's 1927 novel *Vestal Fire*. Fersen can be classed as a Franco-Swedish equivalent of Krupp, his family as rich as Croesus, the owners of steel foundries at Longwy on the border between France and Luxemburg. And like Krupp, he too built himself a Capri pleasure-dome, also high up, situated as he wished not far beneath the ruins of Tiberius's Villa Jovis, whom he too wished to emulate in depravity.

The house, called the Villa Lysis, has been restored and is open to members of the public as one of the tourist attractions of present-day Capri. I visited it with friends a few years ago, and have to report some misgivings about the fact that despite its marvellous location and sensational views of the Amalfi peninsula, the house is essentially organised around an airless, windowless underground opium den, in which Fersen, who was an addict, spent much of his time with his young boys from Capri and Naples. It seems likely that Mackenzie felt some kind of revulsion towards this individual, for his depiction of Marsac on Capri (renamed Sirene by him, and Nepenthe by Douglas) is often fierce in tone. Here is one early example where the narrator seems to speak *in propria persona*, guiding our assessment of Bob, if we have any doubts on the matter: 'Carlyle once said that Herbert Spencer was the most unending ass in Christendom. He had not met the Count.' (VF 47) This is to be followed later by other interventions in the same voice, for instance to convey to us in obviously obscene metaphor the thoroughly detumescent quality of the 'grand manner of courtesy' with which he receives an absurdly sentimental poem by two American lesbians claiming to be sisters expressing their infatuated passion for him, 'which, alas, like a toy balloon, popped under his inflation and evaporated in a puff of pomposity leaving behind nothing but a horrid little dribble of damp membrane.' (138). The balloon image in fact recurs at regular intervals, for instance to describe the only number ever to have appeared of a review to be edited by him, in the preface to which he imagines 'that his soul was storming against the empyrean, but when in reality it was just bobbing against the ceiling of a room like a toy pink balloon.' (232)

Indeed, Mackenzie is obviously thinking of that opium den in the Villa Lysis when he has his narrator remark, late on in the novel: 'Marsac, becoming all the time more and more dependent on cocaine, continued to live his futile existence at the Villa Hylas. There is little interest in following the psychological progress of a drug-taker whose mental symptoms reproduce with a cloying monotony the symptoms of all those who have taken drugs before them.' (397) He even has, of all people, the character Duncan Maxwell, based on Norman Douglas, declare that 'Marsac is a most horrible bore and prison is much the best place for him' (222) — imprisonment, that is, for much the same activities as Douglas himself indulged in, but practised by Marsac in the eyes of Mackenzie and others, with infinitely less stylishness and élan.

But Marsac, whenever he speaks, is genuinely amusing. Compton Mackenzie clearly inherited a theatrical funny bone from his father, a very successful theatrical impresario who toured the country with a company specialising in restoration and eighteenth-century comedy. Best known to non-specialists nowadays, perhaps for his authorship of the Ealing comedy *Whisky Galore!*, Mackenzie, in these two less well-known 1920s Capri comedies, can again make you laugh out loud. Marsac speaks a Franglais which Miles Kingston would have had no difficulty in incorporating into any of his books — 'many thanks for your gentleness' is a random example taken from page 58, surrounded by any number of specimens of a stock-in-trade taken from Sheridan's

The Rivals, the malapropism: 'I have an intention to take a furnished villa as soon as I can fit myself with one;' 'I shall make my *dessein* and invite a fabricator to say his price;' 'I shall be very happy to offer you a perch, monsieur' (a church porch.) Or, to sample his daft pseuds-corner nonsense at slightly greater length: 'What I demand for myself and what even my *poésie* has not satisfyingly responded is the *but* of life. There are moments, I assure you, when I have demanded for myself the *courage* to find in death the answer to the eternal enema of life.'(55)

Marsac is but one of a goodly number of comic turns in *Vestal Fire*, however. The prim and proper, onomastically named Mrs. Rosebotham, is just as funny as the debauchees she denounces with recognisably Scottish ferocity: 'Mrs. Rosebotham was sure that it was the absence of golf, more than anything else, which made Sirene so bad for people's morals.' 'I'm told that the orgies in the villa Partenope last Winter were unspeakable,' she thunders, 'Are we living in the time of Tiberius, or are we living in the time of Edward VII?' *Plus ça change*, one must retort. The American lesbian 'sisters,' who worship Marsac and give the book its title by building in their garden a replica of the Temple of Vesta in Rome, draw attention to the essential mock-heroic tone of the book in their folksy, kitschy exclamations of touristic delight: 'did you ever see a cuter little temple anywhere? Why, it doesn't look like a temple, Mamie. It looks more like a cunning little tea-house. If that isn't just the loveliest little temple … what does it tell us about it in the guidebook?' (29) And that Mackenzie was a devotee of Dickens, modelling his panoply of eccentric expatriates on Dickensian comic practice by differentiating their speech patterns, can be shown in the character of Maud Ambrogio (in real life, the Welsh woman Gwen Wickham), who is clearly a female equivalent of Mr. Jingle in *Pickwick Papers*, contradicting her own claim of professional discretion in a torrent of indiscretions: 'Mustn't talk if you marry a lawyer. Used to talk a lot before I married dear old Peter. Never talk now. Bad for his business. Weren't you chatting to Mrs. Neave just now? Dear woman! Had an affair with Duncan Maxwell last year. Only repeat what other people tell me. Hate scandal. You walked down with Nigel Dawson. Such a dear boy! One of those. But what does it matter? Why shouldn't he be? Don't care what anybody is. Love everybody.' (40) This applies equally to the numerous walk-on parts, each done swiftly with a Dickensian phrase, like Mrs. Wills, 'shrivelling up inside her stays like a stranded winkle in its shell.' (126)

As we turn to *Extraordinary Women*, Mckenzie's parallel satire on the lesbian community of Capri, we may note first that the central figure is modelled in part on 'a rich Australian of the family Edersham, whose marriage had broken up,' according to James Money (Money 149): Mrs. Francesca Lloyd, known as Checca. In the novel her background is signalled by giving her the name Aurora Fremantle. She is easily the most sympathetic member of her tribe, and the book centres around her sufferings at the hands of a collection of lesbian *femmes fatales*. Seen from an ex-centric perspective, she is the colonial *ingénue* utterly at sea in the company of perverse continental European sophisticates whose chief pleasure lies in inflicting pain.

For me, *Extraordinary Women* is not quite as successful as *Vestal Fire* in finding and nailing its target. Aurora, or Rory, as she of course becomes, attracts our sympathies because of the sufferings she endures at the hands of her lovers, but is herself often presented in caricatured fashion. She is a pseudo-poet and intellectual, like Bob Marsac, having 'begun as a symbolist and was now an imagist,' publishing her work in Paris under the pseudonym *Demonassa*. But in addition to her literary activities she also breeds bulldogs ('she was not beautiful, having herself a considerable likeness to the bulldogs she loved'), uses her money to train quantities of female featherweights ('she had done more than anyone to promote the sport of boxing among women') and smokes large phallic cigars. (EW 46) Sprightly enough at first, this kind of writing is perhaps made to do rather over-extended service in the course of the book.

Until the inspired Mozartian finale, that is, where all Mackenzie's talents as a satirist and caricaturist in the Hibernian tradition are on display. Attempting to lure back her favourite Rosalba, or indeed any other of the women who have attracted her attention, Rory throws a party on the night of the September full moon, to which everyone on the island is invited: 'It was intended to be a Sirenian night of nights. And it was.' (282)

McKenzie's main device for making it so is a time-honoured ploy of comic writers — to throw a fresh comic character on the fire, a young gay Norwegian male named Hjalmar Krog: 'but as he did not look in the least like a person called Hjalmar Krog, we may as well forget that and with everybody else call him Daffodil.' (288) Though his English is far superior, Daffodil talks in the same camp way as Marsac, sprinkling his discourse with Gallicisms: 'I always lay down for two hours before a party. If I don't, my eyes get so *cernés*. And it makes me look *so* naughty ... ' (283) But the difference is huge: Rory at last finds someone who is kind and supportive, if of course uninterested in her sexually. Daffodil is that Pickwickian rarity — a comic good person.

Of course, there are other comic turns at Rory's moon-crazed, orgiastic bash. This time it is not a woman who takes her clothes off, but a man, as Daffodil announces to his new-found friend: 'Oh. Rory … do come! Mr Hewetson simply insists on doing a classical dance, and he's got nothing on but a pink silk handkerchief and a paper rose.' (304) But funnier still is Captain Wheeler, convinced as he is that lesbianism is merely a wartime consequence of the shortage of males, and that he is just the man to provide Rosalba and co. with what they really want. He makes a desperately crude beeline for Rory's beloved: 'I say, you have got a topping figure … you'd make old Venus look like a Sunday-School teacher. What!' (298) He follows her back to her hotel, but just as he thinks he is about to score — 'here I am, my darling' — he collapses on the floor dead drunk. (338) The novel becomes a fast-moving bedroom farce, both gay and heterosexual: Captain Wheeler is doubled by a handsome young local Italian, Carmine, who has a little more success than he ('I am not at all too much drunk. I can do big loves. I am quite strong all over myself.' — 336), and Rosalba's jilting of Rory is doubled by her own jilting by Olimpia and Bébé Buonagrazia, who ride off on white donkeys. (325) At the very end Rory discovers that what she really wants is not Amer Pichon [sic] with Rosalba, but a nice Australian cup of tea with Daffodil. 'Oh, my dear, tea! How divine!', he gushes. (392)

It would be instructive to compare the satire of *South Wind* with that of Mackenzie in the books just examined. Both writers were accomplished classicists, and the pages of *Vestal Fire* and *Extraordinary Women* are sprinkled throughout with quotations from Latin and Greek — Sappho in particular, of course, in the latter novel. Both thus also belong in the Hibernian and European tradition of learned satire, as represented outside of Scotland by Rabelais and Sterne amongst others. Douglas is motivated to no small extent by the intellectual ambition of fostering classical pagan values and beliefs, whereas Mackenzie, in these books at least, belongs with more popular comic traditions in the theatre, even if they perhaps descend ultimately from Atellanean farce. But, that broader context must be pursued elsewhere — here I shall conclude with a very brief consideration of the contribution Douglas's novel makes to Modernist writing. Again, there is contrast: Mackenzie, in these books at least, is producing entirely conventional comic potboilers employing a variety of standard humorous plot devices and characters, whereas Douglas goes much further in the direction of making something strange and new.

I have already suggested a connection with James Joyce's *Ulysses*, and one could easily expand on this, particularly in meditating on the famous tendency to plotlessness in *South Wind*, commented on by a number of contemporary reviewers. 'My brother came to consider a well-ordered plot a meretricious literary interest, like the story in a *tableau de genre*,' wrote Stanislaus Joyce in *My Brother's Keeper*.' (Stanislaus Joyce 106) Another Modernist classic of 1924, published only two years after *Ulysses*, Thomas Mann's *Der Zauberberg* (*The Magic Mountain*), is also relevant here, for it too concerns a visit to a cousin which ends up with the magic of the place asserting itself, inducing lotus-eating and finally bringing about profound alteration in the hero's outlook on things. *South Wind*'s 'plotlessness,' which is perhaps not really that, thus brings it into alignment with a number of Modernist texts that explore a period of hibernation as a necessary precondition of real, lasting change.

But in another way, *South Wind* looks forward to a later Modernist development, exemplified in Faulkner's *Sanctuary* or Robbe-Grillet's *Le Voyeur*, that is to say, the novel with a hole in the middle of its plot. In this sense I agree with Jan Morris, who regards its plot as leading very subtly to its climax, the 'murder' of Muhlen or Retlow by Heard's cousin Mrs. Meadows — if it is that, for Morris is right to emphasise that we conclude the novel with a sense of mystery. One moment the bishop sees Mrs Meadows walking with Muhlen on Nepenthe near the cliff's edge, and remembers 'that sensation of giddiness, of gulping terror, with which he had watched the falcon swaying crazily over the abyss,' (SW372) the next moment Muhlen is no longer in the picture. The bishop concludes that he is 'face to face with an atrocious and carefully planned murder,' but, such is the influence of the south wind on Nepenthe, does nothing about it.

One remembers Tiberius at this point of course, and his habit of throwing his victims over the cliffs of Capri. Over and over again he returns in these books — in the figure of Ernesto Jones in *Vestal Fire*, for instance, who is fiercely jealous of Marsac and his villa: 'Were he Tiberius he would have the whole lot of these degenerates flung headlong from the *salto* into the dark sea a thousand feet below there to be clubbed to death by the oars of waiting mariners.' (VF 119) Leaving the question entirely open whether Mrs. Meadows — another female pugilist perhaps? — is a true Tiberius who stages a real repeat of antiquity, or whether the supposition that she is and does is merely a projection that reflects the bishop's descent into degeneracy, or whether, indeed, the whole issue exists entirely inside readers' own heads, Douglas creates a truly Modernist version of the matter of Capri.

BIBLIOGRAPHY

Beachy, Robert. *Gay Berlin: Birthplace of a Modern Identity*. New York, NY: Vintage, 2015.

Douglas, Norman. *Old Calabria*. Harmondsworth: Penguin Books, 1962 [1915].

—*Siren Land*. West Dayton: Penguin Books, 1948 [1911].

—*South Wind*. London: Capuchin Classics, 2009 [1917]. (SW)

—*Together*. Harmondsworth: Penguin Books, 1945 [1923].

Hazzard, Shirley. *Greene on Capri: A Memoir*. London: Virago, 2000.

Holloway, Mark. *Norman Douglas: A Biography*. London: Secker and Warburg, 1976. (Holloway)

Joyce, Stanislaus. *My Brother's Keeper*. Boston MA: da Capo Press, 2009 [1958]. (Stanislaus Joyce)

Linklater, Andro. *Compton Mackenzie: A Life*. London: Chatto and Windus, 1987.

Mackenzie, Compton. *Extraordinary Women*. London: Hogarth Press, 1986 [1928]. (EW)

—*My Life and Times: Octave Five 1915–23*. London: Chatto and Windus, 1966.

—*Vestal Fire*. Hogarth Press. London: 1985 [1927]. (VF)

Money, James. *Capri: Island of Pleasure*. London: Hamish Hamilton, 1986. (Money)

Suetonius (Gaius Suetonius Tranquillus). *The Twelve Caesars*, trans. Robert Graves. Harmondsworth: Penguin Books, 1957. (Suetonius)

Tacitus, Publius Cornelius. *The Annals of Imperial Rome*, trans. Michael Grant. London: Penguin Books, 1996 [1956]. (Tacitus)

The Watcher by the Threshold:
John Herdman and the Scottish Literary Tradition

Trevor Royle

The title of this essay is taken from John Buchan who used it both for a short story published in *Blackwood's Magazine* and *Atlantic Monthly* in December 1900 and for the title of a short story collection in 1902 which also contained 'The Far Islands', 'Fountainblue', 'No Man's Land', and 'The Outgoing of the Tide'. All are set in Scotland and four contain a supernatural element, but it is the title story that links Buchan directly to John Herdman. It is also a very un-Buchan kind of story which owes much to Robert Louis Stevenson and contains elements of the biography of the Byzantine emperor Justinian as found in the writings of Procopius, particularly in his *Anecdota* or *Secret History*. As for the origin of the title itself, in a short prefatory note to the 1902 edition Buchan quoted mischievously from the writings of a fictional Donisarius, Monk of Padua who, he said, flourished in 1310: 'Among idle men there be some who tarry in the outer courts, speeding the days joyfully with dance and song. But the other sort dwell near the portals of the House, and are ever anxious and ill at ease that they may see something of the Shadows which come and go. Wherefore night and day they are found watching by the threshold, in fearfulness and joy, not without tears.' This is a literary device which Buchan had already used in his earlier story 'A Captain of Salvation' in 1896 but whatever its exegesis 'The Watcher by the Threshold' is a story about a case of demoniac possession and the need to exorcise evil in an otherwise blameless character who has been caught up in events not of his making, yet is intensely aware of the shadowy figure tormenting him.

In his own writing career Herdman produced a highly-regarded history of the double in nineteenth century fiction and employed the conceit of duality in the creation of some of his own literary characters. I shall return to 'The Watcher by the Threshold' later in this essay, but by way of introduction here is some biographical scene-setting. I met

John Herdman in the spring of 1971 not long after I had been employed by the Scottish Arts Council to work in its Literature and Drama Department as assistant to Alistair Skinner, a brilliant but troubled administrator who really wanted to be a dramatist, which he did indeed become a couple of years later. At the time of my appointment, the council's director was the mercurial Ronald 'Bingo' Mavor, another administrator with literary ambitions who seemed to be weighed down by the responsibility of being the son of the great dramatist James Bridie (O. H. Mavor) and who eventually carved out his own reputation as a dramatist with several successful stage plays including the production of a West End success *A Private Matter* in 1972. Working with colleagues like Skinner and Mavor was an exhilarating experience and from the outset the latter had made it clear to me that the eventual aim was to split the department's twin responsibilities and to evolve Literature as a separate entity — there already was a separate Literature Committee which was chaired by the novelist and Oscar-winning screen writer Neil Paterson, who was equally ambitious for this transformation to take place. In an unpublished memoir Mavor claimed that 'the job of the [Scottish] Arts Council was, essentially, to listen to what Scotland's creative artists wanted to do and, whenever possible, help them do it.'[1] With that in mind I was encouraged to meet as many writers as possible and to listen to their views about what could be done to improve matters or about existing schemes which were not working, or which were downright unpopular; the two faults being frequently related. My appointment diary for that year suggests that I might have met John Herdman on Thursday 1 April when I attended a meeting of The Heretics (an innovative poetry and music society) in the Glencairn Hotel in Edinburgh but even if my memory is playing me false — it was after all fifty years ago — he had swum into my ken long before that date.

At the time one of my closest friends was John Armstrong Black whom I had met while playing tennis in St Andrews. His younger brother David Macleod Black published poetry under the name D. M. Black and had several slim volumes to his credit including two much admired collections *With Decorum* (1967) and *The Educators* (1969). He was one of the rising stars of the younger generation of poets, having been included in Penguin's *British Modern Poets* series in 1968, and I took a keen and almost proprietorial interest in his progress. From John I knew that he had been at New Park preparatory

---

1 Ronald Mavor, obituary, *The Times*, 14 September 2007.

school in St Andrews where his brother had formed a close friendship with John Herdman based on shared literary and cultural interests and it was to last a lifetime. Although they parted when D. M. Black was sent to Trinity College Glenalmond in Perthshire, while John Herdman proceeded to Merchiston Castle School in Edinburgh, their friendship continued through a lengthy literary correspondence in which they explored and debated matters of mutual interest. One further matter of biographical interest intruded once I got to know John Herdman: it transpired that one of his cousins, Andy McKerrrow, had been our family doctor in St Andrews.

But even without those connections it would have been unusual had I not met and formed a friendship with John Herdman. By the beginning of the 1970s he had already emerged as one of the more prominent enablers in the Scottish literary scene, was a recognised performer of his own work, did not disguise his political beliefs and had a well-deserved literary reputation. He was born on 20 July 1941 in Edinburgh, the son of Willie Herdman, a wealthy grain importer with a wide range of social contacts in the city's legal and literary worlds and who possessed an uncanny ability to mix 'freely and quite without condescension with people from every social background'.[2] From private schooling in Scotland, Herdman proceeded to Magdalene College Cambridge where he graduated with first class honours in English and more importantly found out more about himself, later admitting that 'it was, ironically, at Cambridge that I discovered my own Scottishness, became aware of myself as a Scot'.[3] He also came to an understanding that he wanted to be a writer to the exclusion of all else and returned to Edinburgh in the summer of 1967 to throw himself into the fray.

It was a period pregnant with possibilities, not least on the political front. The Scottish National Party (SNP) had come into being in 1934 as a result of the amalgamation of the existing Scottish Party and the National Party of Scotland and it had enjoyed mixed fortunes in the polls, winning only one short-lived parliamentary seat (Motherwell) in 1945. At the start of the 1960s, party membership stood at around two thousand and the party's influence in Scottish politics was negligible. All that was to change as the decade unfolded; by its end the SNP had become an established party and was no longer considered a joke

2 John Herdman, *Another Country*, Thirsty Books, Edinburgh, p.18.
3 John Herdman, *Conversations with Scottish Writers*, No. 8. Fras Publications, Dunning, 2020, p.15.

or a haven for idealists. There were several reasons for this upturn. The first was an internal reorganisation of the party's structure which resulted in a growing membership, funds were raised, and activists worked long and hard to get the message across to doubting voters who responded by taking the SNP seriously, regarding it as a viable alternative to the existing larger parties. The second change was the emergence of a new leadership with Ian Macdonald as the first fulltime national organiser and William (Billy) Wolfe, a committed and thoroughly decent man, who stood for West Lothian in a by-election in 1962 when he came a creditable second to the Labour candidate Tam Dalyell, an Old Etonian socialist whose ancestral home, the House of Binns, was in the constituency and whose ancestor, also Tam Dalyell, had founded the Royal Scots Greys cavalry regiment (later Royal Scots Dragoon Guards) in 1678.

Although Wolfe was not elected as an MP, he had come to prominence and this led to him being chosen as vice-chairman and essentially deputy leader and then chairman in 1969. Not only did Wolfe institute a top-to-bottom review of the party structure but he was instrumental in moving it to the left and embracing radical policies such as land nationalisation and nuclear disarmament — it helped that Wolfe was a member of the Scottish Campaign for Nuclear Disarmament (CND) and later served as its treasurer. All this appealed to a younger generation of voters who were disenchanted with Labour and the Conservatives, were opposed to the presence of the US Navy's Polaris submarine base at Holy Loch which had arrived in 1961 and disliked the tacit British support for the war in Vietnam. In 1963 the SNP adopted its thistle-looped logo which soon became as recognisable as the equally ubiquitous CND peace symbol based on the semaphore symbols for 'N' (two flags held 45 degrees down on both sides) and 'D' (two flags, one above the head and one at the feet, forming the vertical line) for 'Nuclear Disarmament' within a circle. The electorate responded well. At the 1966 general election the SNP contested twenty-three seats and although none was won the nationalists' profile had been raised. A year later the party contested Glasgow Pollok in a by-election and won 28 per cent of the vote allowing the Conservatives to win; unthinkable in a seat that was once solidly Labour. That same year in the local elections the party won 200,000 votes and gained sixty-nine seats. It was clear that momentum was growing.

All this was a prelude to the SNP breakthrough at Hamilton in a by-election held on Thursday 2 November 1967 when Winnie Ewing, a lawyer by training and a nationalist by conviction, won the seat with a handsome majority — 46 per cent of the vote — and in so doing put Labour in second place. Echoing a popular musical of the day, *Stop the World, I Want to Get Off*, her first words passed into legend — 'stop the world Scotland wants to get on' — and it is not stretching the facts to claim that her victory caused a sensation not just in Scotland but across the UK. Not only was it the beginning of a new era in nationalist politics but it also marked the end of the SNP's time in the doldrums. After Hamilton anything seemed possible and even though Ewing failed to hold the seat in the 1970 general election when the sole SNP seat was won in the Western Isles by Donald Stewart, the party had arrived as a formidable force in Scottish politics. The pinnacle was reached in the general election of October 1974 when the SNP polled almost a third of all votes in Scotland and returned eleven MPs to the Westminster parliament.

At the same time there was a renewal of cultural nationalism which, while not related in any direct way to party politics, was centred on the status and wellbeing of the country's artistic life. By the beginning of the 1960s other changes were affecting the cultural scene. not least as a result of the success of the Edinburgh Festival, founded in 1947, and its impact on the city. Chief amongst these, because it was pivotal to so many other innovations, was the establishment in 1959 of the Paperback Bookshop in Charles Street off George Square in the heart of the university campus where the present informatics building now stands. Its creator was Jim Haynes, an American airman from Louisiana who had been based at nearby Kirknewton, a former wartime RAF base which housed the US Air Force's 6952nd Security Group and was also host to the Cold War 'hot line', a secure teletype communications link between Washington and Moscow designed to lessen the threat of an accidental nuclear war. (This top-secret link was established in 1963 and ran across the Atlantic from Washington to Oban. From there it proceeded across Scotland through Kirknewton towards Moscow by way of Denmark, Sweden and Finland.)

Haynes arrived at Kirknewton in 1956 having requested a posting to 'the smallest possible military base, near a major city and university'. Haynes fell in love with Edinburgh and stayed on after being demobbed to set up business in an old junk shop selling only paperbacks and quickly established himself as a major influence in the city's culture scene. Not only was the Paperback a bookshop, it was also a coffee shop, gallery, salon and theatre space. The venue was also known for being part of the counter-culture movement, stocking books by American Beat authors such as Allen Ginsberg, William Burroughs and Jack Kerouac. Perhaps its most memorable artefact, and the one by which it is best remembered, was the stuffed head of a rhinoceros which hung outside the door and which Haynes had retrieved from the clearance of the New Club in Princes Street. In the following year Haynes and his bookshop made front page news when a female customer (rumoured to have been a missionary) came into the shop to order a copy of D. H. Lawrence's controversial novel *Lady Chatterley's Lover*, which had just been republished by Penguin Books. When she returned to collect it, she carried the book outside with tongs and set fire to it, a scene which was captured by the photographer and filmmaker Alan Daiches (son of Professor David Daiches, a great critic and cultural enabler) who was also integral to the city's growing counter-culture and who covered other significant events in Edinburgh including the International Writers' Conference of 1962.

The book burning was very much a sign of the times as the novel had just been published in an unexpurgated version and Penguin was about to be prosecuted under the recently introduced Obscene Publications Act; not only did this cause a sensation but the 'not guilty' verdict resulted in a far greater degree of freedom for publishing sexually explicit material in the UK. Haynes and Alan Daiches played a role in a process which enhanced the mood of greater liberalism throughout the 1960s. Both, too, were involved in the creation of the Traverse Theatre which opened its doors on the night of 2 January 1963 in James Court in the Lawnmarket in a tenement building known as 'Kelly's Paradise, a crumbling former doss-house and brothel barely a stone's throw from the Castle'.[4] The plays were a double bill — *Huis Clos* by Jean Paul Sartre and *Orisons* by Fernando Arrabal — and within four years the tiny theatre club had announced its presence as a formidable and exciting force in world theatre. From the outset the Traverse had the status of a private theatre club both to raise capital and to evade the censoring activities of the Lord Chamberlain's office, an important consideration in a period when any play wishing to be licensed for public performance could be censored by this department of the Royal Household — the restriction ended in September 1968 with the passing of the Theatres Act. Being a club gave the Traverse a certain cachet and its appearance in

4 Joyce Macmillan, *The Traverse Theatre Story 1963–1988*, London, Methuen, 1988, p.9

Edinburgh seemed to open up all kinds of possibilities; the James Court theatre being considered 'sexy, exciting, electrifying'. Although the story of the early Traverse quickly became mythologised and although it was to experience many ups and downs, including three changes of venue, it succeeded in its aim of keeping the spirit of the Festival alive throughout the year and quickly built a formidable reputation for pioneering new work by the best contemporary dramatists from across the world. These included Arrabal, Sartre, Genet, Jarry, Ionescu, Christian Dietrich-Grabbe, William Snyder, Yukio Mishima, Ugo Betti and Edinburgh-based Stanley Eveling.

Amongst its founders were Haynes, who had already used the basement of the Paperback as a theatre;, Tom Mitchell, a Cumbrian designer and property developer and Richard (Ricky) Demarco, an artist and teacher with Italian antecedents and another great cultural activist and visionary who left the Traverse to found his first gallery in Edinburgh's Melville Crescent in 1966. A notable impresario, Demarco quickly forged close links with eastern European artists and travelled several times to the Soviet Union, establishing dialogues and laying the foundation for cultural collaborations. It is also fair to say that these cultural innovations were very much part of a group effort which included the publisher John Calder (who was already running the Ledlanet Nights seasons of opera, music, drama and exhibitions at his estate in Kinross), television producer Sheila Colvin who later became Associate Director of the Edinburgh Festival and the graphic designer John Martin who, with Douglas Soeder, established Forth Studios which was to give the Traverse Theatre and the Richard Demarco Gallery their graphic identities. Others involved with both the Traverse and the Demarco Gallery included lawyer Andrew Elliott, accountant Jim Walker and Andy Muir, Calder's Scottish agent.

The literary scene was also twitching into life. In 1967 the magazine *Scottish International* was founded under the editorship of Robert Tait with a policy of embracing political as well as cultural matters and providing a platform for debate. That same year also saw the arrival of the nationalist magazine *Catalyst* which aimed to 'stimulate discussion in the question of an independent Scotland' and in which, as we shall see, John Herdman came to be involved as editor. Then, four years later, the literary magazine *Lines Review* gave over its summer 1971 issue to the publication of a polemical essay by the poet Alan Jackson entitled 'The Knitted Claymore: An Essay on Culture and Nationalism' which became the subject of heated argument and prompted a long-running and equally impassioned correspondence in the pages of *The Scotsman*. (Mention should also be made of four other magazines which promoted contemporary Scottish literature, mainly poetry: *Akros* founded by Duncan Glen in 1965, Joy Hendry and Walter Perrie's *Chapman* first published in 1970, the long-established Gaelic magazine *Gairm* and David Morrison's *Scotia Review*.)

Other manifestations included the production of the play *The Cheviot, the Stag and the Black, Black Oil* by the radical 7:84 Theatre Company which cast a leery eye at Highland history, from the Clearances to the more recent exploitation of oil in the North Sea and which was first performed at the 'What Kind of Scotland?' conference organised by Tait in 1973. It too provoked a huge amount of questioning of Scotland's role and the need for change. The discovery of oil had also played a role in stimulating that national conversation. The SNP adopted the slogan 'It's Scotland's Oil' and a debate was sparked about the revenues and their ownership, the implication being that these should be purely for the benefit of the Scots. At a time of mounting unemployment, particularly in the declining heavy industries, arguments of that kind carried popular resonance.

Herdman threw himself into that febrile background decisively and purposefully by quickly becoming a paid-up member of the SNP and vice-chairman of one of the party's Edinburgh branches. As an activist he did not shirk from the mundane duties of canvassing and fund-raising, but he was also aware of the necessity of harnessing the growing cultural outpouring to what was happening in the world of politics. Two initiatives caught his fancy, and both achieved wildly different results. The first was his involvement in the founding of 'The Heretics', an informal cultural grouping which came into being in the spring of 1970 with the express purpose of giving a convivial platform to poets and musical artists and in so doing to promote the 'poetry and music of Scotland's living tradition'. Amongst its founders were two writers and performers from quite different backgrounds who were united in their ambition to create something lasting and ambitious which also reflected the national mood — the poet Willie Neill who wrote in Scots, English and Gaelic and Stuart MacGregor a young medical doctor with extensive interests in folk music and the author of the novel *The Myrtle and the Ivy* (1967). The founders also included the Gaelic singer Dolina MacLennan and her husband George Brown as well as Sylvia Frazer who worked as a cartographer in the Scottish Office. The opening meeting was held on 7 May 1970 in the New Town Hotel. Subsequent meetings took place on the first Thursday of every month and amongst early and regular performers were younger poets Donald Campbell, Liz Lochhead and Rory Watson, as well as established figures including Norman MacCaig and Robert Garioch. Musical contributions came from performers such as folk singer Billy Connolly and fiddler Aly Bain who would go on to enjoy stellar careers as popular entertainers. In short, The Heretics were of their time and a boisterous manifestation of the evolution of a national culture. As I was to discover, those monthly sessions were not only innovatory but also great fun.

It was perhaps only natural that John Herdman would gravitate towards an involvement with them not just as an enabler but also a performer in his own right, with spirited renditions of extracts from his novel *A Truth Lover* (1973) and his extremely amusing short story 'Clapperton' which he read to clearly captivated audiences. However, the arrival of The Heretics and its undoubted success were to lead him into uncharted territory because at his own admission 'nationalism still seemed to be the preserve of literary intellectuals, folk singers and fiery students' yet as he also noted the emergence of the SNP also attracted its fair share of fanatics anxious to peddle their own agendas.[5] Prominent amongst these was the 1320 Club which came into being in 1967 and took its name from the year of the signing of the Declaration of Arbroath and numbered a handful of well-known literary nationalists amongst its founders, including Hugh MacDiarmid, the classicist Douglas Young and the artist and writer Wendy Wood (Gwendoline Emily Meacham). It was hoped that the presence of these luminaries would give the 1320 Club a superior tone but at the same time it embraced 'conspiratorial and authoritarian tendencies' which put it at odds with its wider cultural ambitions and from the outset it attracted the opprobrium of the SNP leadership.

In fact, that embattled position seemed to suit those who ran the 1320 Club. It had been founded in part to oppose what seemed to be the SNP's moderation and its preoccupation with 'bread-and-butter' issues, such as economics and the business of government; as a ginger group it wanted to stir things up and to adopt a broader-based and more radical approach to the business of achieving independence. Unfortunately, this well-meaning philosophy allowed it to be hijacked by activists pursuing their own agendas and by the late 1960s the 1320

---

5 John Herdman, *Another* Country, pp.21 and 27.

Club had gained a reputation as being right-wing and extremist largely because it had fallen under the baleful influence of Major Frederick Alexander Colquhoun Boothby, a former army officer and cousin of the colourful Conservative MP Robert Boothby. Under F. A. C. Boothby's guidance — he adopted the title of 'Organiser' — the 1320 Club became increasingly secretive in its dealings and as it did so, it created further disquiet in nationalist circles. As the row grew so did it begin to occupy space in the correspondence columns of *The Scotsman*, especially after the Club was disowned by Winnie Ewing MP. Early in the following year the distinguished folklorist and man of letters Hamish Henderson entered the fray when he contributed a hard-hitting letter apostrophising Boothby's grouping as the '1320 dead-enders' or 'self-elected Elect' who had 'done much to make Scottish self-government a subject of mockery not only South of the border but amongst broad masses of the Scottish people as well.'[6]

Needless to say, Boothby responded in kind and the correspondence widened to include a misjudged contribution from MacDiarmid, who was already at odds with Henderson over the contribution made by the folk tradition to Scottish culture and earlier the two men had engaged in a lengthy literary 'flyting' over the subject. Into these troubled waters Herdman entered a cautious toe in the early winter of 1969 when he allowed Willie Neill to put his name forward as his successor as editor of *Catalyst*. By then Neill was completing a degree in Gaelic at Edinburgh University after having been crowned Bard at the National Mòd and could find neither the time nor the energy to complete his studies as well as editing the magazine and dealing with Boothby. As he already knew Herdman as a contributor and clearly trusted his literary judgement it was only natural that he would nominate him as the next editor. Under most circumstances this would have been a sound move but with the 1320 Club being in the news for all the wrong reasons the times were out of joint and Herdman was to experience a difficult stint in the editorial chair with constant interference from Boothby and his sinister sidekick Ronald Macdonald Douglas, variously described as an author and journalist, former diplomat, and perfervid Scottish patriot.

Fortunately, in his literary memoir *Another Country*, Herdman left an astute record of his dealings with the club, the magazine and the main personalities involved and from it emerges a sorry story as he was swallowed up in what the journalist Arnold Kemp described as a

6 Hamish Henderson, letter to *The Scotsman*, 21 February 1968.

'bibulous and disputatious demi-monde of mad poets and paranoic activists, whose taste for vicious infighting was out of all proportion to their political importance at the time.'[7] Herdman edited only two numbers of *Catalyst* and in the autumn of 1970 he resigned, leaving Macdonald Douglas to achieve his ambition of running the magazine which quickly degenerated into an undignified rag. Herdman had never been a member of the 1320 Club but that he was right to escape its founder's malign influence became clear in 1975 when Boothby, as leader of the self-styled Scottish Liberation Army, was arrested and convicted after a bungled bank robbery and received a relatively lenient sentence of three years in prison, of which he only served eighteen months, thereby giving rise to never disproved rumours that he was a police stooge. By then it had also become clear that in the 1950s, prior to returning to Scotland, Boothby had been implicated in a scandal in the Home Counties featuring Satanic rituals with teenage boys and girls.

All this mattered not a lot to Herdman, who seems to have emerged from those bizarre events a wiser and more experienced person, having had to stand up for his beliefs in the face of attempted coercion or what would be called in a later age management bullying. In his first issue he published a short piece entitled 'Self-Determination' by a writer called Tom Anderson which received Boothby's fulsome praise, only for it to be revealed that the author was Herdman himself. While sophistical japes of that kind had a certain appeal to the creator of *Clapperton*, they could not disguise the fact that Herdman was emerging as a solid writer in his own right whose work could stand comparison with authors of the stature of James Hogg, Robert Louis Stevenson and, as I hope to show, John Buchan. His work as an enabler with The Heretics also attracted attention. Not only did it bring him into contact with other writers, many of them establishment figures, but he was gradually becoming recognised as a substantial literary figure himself. His progress was both organic and, in hindsight, structured. Having decided that writing was his destiny he immersed himself in the work of (in no particular order) Bertolt Brecht, Arthur Rimbaud, James Joyce, Fyodor Dostoevsky and Rainer Maria Rilke, all of whom influenced his future literary style and part of the period of 1958–59 was spent travelling in Europe and the Near East, providing experiences that were to find their way into his first novel *The Truth Lover*.

7 Arnold Kemp, *Confusion to Our Enemies: Selected Journalism of Arnold Kemp 1939–2002*, edited by J. A. Kemp, Glasgow, Neil Wilson Publishing, 2012, p.113.

While Herdman had already published a slim volume of fictional prose in *Descent* (1968) this was a breakthrough novel and was justly praised by the critics, in particular by the Anglo-Irish novelist and poet P. J. Kavanagh who declared in a review in *The Guardian* that *The Truth Lover* had been 'written as though it had been very well translated from the nineteenth century Russian'.[8] This was perhaps a nod in the direction of the so-called nineteenth century Golden Age of Russian literature and prominent writers such as Dostoevsky, Mikhail Lermontov, Ivan Turgenev and Nikolai Gogol. The latter was an early practitioner of the literature of surrealism and the grotesque whom Herdman admired for his creation of two stories 'The Nose' and 'The Overcoat' for 'the inimitable mixture of social satire, fantastic humour and aberrant psychology which characterises his writing [and] was a rich spawning ground of dualistic obsession'.[9] Both stories clearly influenced Herdman's later work with the 'nose' and 'the overcoat' of Gogol's titles assuming the identity of 'rudimentary doubles' but closer examination reveals that Kavanagh, who died in 2015, may also have found a link between Duncan Straiton, Herdman's truth lover, and Rodion Raskolnikov, the protagonist of Dostoyevsky's novel *Crime and Punishment.* A volatile and excitable former student living in St Petersburg, Raskolnikov possesses a dual personality, being apathetic and anti-social yet also revealing himself to be kind and compassionate.

The opening passage of *A Truth Lover* finds Straiton walking the streets of Edinburgh in the company of his friend and alter ego Alan Bryce, with whom he is discussing the nature and validity of belief. Accused by Bryce of being fanatical about his integrity Straiton responds heatedly: 'Certainly I rely upon anything which comes to me with the conviction of truth … you can't claim a monopoly of conviction … nor, I think, of truth either.'[10] To this Bryce retorts that his friend's belief stems from the violence of his spiritual pride and at that the two men part in some rancour with Bryce playing no further role in the narrative. Their philosophical disagreement had been sparked by an incident in which an elderly woman blocked the pavement, prompting Bryce to suggest pushing her into the gutter; in turn this initiates a discussion between the two men on the desirability of killing off all elderly people aged over seventy. This is the first point of comparison between Straiton and Raskolnikov who kills indiscriminately an elderly

---

8 Quoted on the jacket of *Pagan's Pilgrimage* (1978).
9 John Herdman, *The Double in Nineteenth Century Fiction*, Palgrave Macmillan, London, p.99.
10 John Herdman, *A Truth Lover,* Akros Publications, Preston, 1973, p.9.

female pawnbroker and her sister and feels neither regret nor guilt. In a crucial passage in which he is quizzed by the investigator Porfiry Petrovich, who suspects that he is the murderer, Raskolnikov posits the theory that in certain circumstances a superior man has the right to consider himself above social and moral laws.

> I simply hinted that an 'extraordinary' man has the right ... that is not an official right, but an inner right to decide in his own conscience to overstep ... certain obstacles, and only in case it is essential for the practical fulfilment of his idea (sometimes, perhaps, of benefit to the whole of humanity).[11]

However, having committed the crime of murder Raskolnikov does not manage to find an equilibrium. Intense anguish and an overwhelming feeling of guilt slowly catch up with him, to the point where he is forced to confess, in order to be relieved of the torment that has been inflicted on him by his own conscience. At the end of the novel, having been imprisoned in Siberia, he falls victim to what he has been struggling to distance himself from; namely his own emotions and is forced to embrace his human condition. Likewise, having attempted to come to terms with his delusional beliefs Straiton escapes from Edinburgh after witnessing a violent episode in a pub and travels in Europe to avoid giving evidence before returning to face a short jail sentence for contempt of court. Like Raskolnikov he too finds an absolution, likening his preoccupation with the 'clear love of truth' to a 'burrowing beast' which has taken possession of him and has to be driven out or immured. That realisation comes to him while he is undertaking menial work in a hotel in the Scottish Highlands and it leads him to understand that his will has been both diverted and perverted. In search of redemption, he decides to walk up the Lairig Ghru to the Pools of Dee, a high and challenging mountain pass through the Cairngorms which leads him to his own personal catharsis.

> A feeling of solidity and serenity had slowly been gathering strength within me as I came down: I knew I would be able to enter life again, however painfully. I thought of the grim spiritual journey which I had been making for a year or more,

11 Fyodor Dostoevsky, *Crime and Punishment*, translated by Constance Garnett, Macmillan Collectors Library, London, 2003, p.267.

driven by my will towards a goal which I perceived only dimly and whose nature I might never understand. I had reached only a grey, arid death of the spirit, in which for a time I had thought with grim relish to rest content.[12]

Herdman's next novel *Pagan's Pilgrimage* (1978) takes this insight a stage further by creating a Raskolnikovian character who conceives a plan to commit an actual murder, in much the same way that Dostoevsky's creation murders his victims secure in the knowledge that he is doing the right thing and will not face any consequences. The action is described by Horatio Pagan, both central character and narrator, who is burdened by an alter ego called Raith who, mysteriously, looks like him and encourages him in his opinions. Although Pagan is a hopeless disappointment in his private and professional life, having failed at university and turned his back on a legal career, even his relationships with women are disastrous, he clings obstinately to the belief that he has been marked out for greatness: 'Clearly I was intended for some great destiny quite out of the common range, and I waited with great impatience for this to reveal itself.'[13] Eventually realisation comes to him through the shadowy intervention of Raith who persuades him that he can only achieve that destiny through a monstrous act of assassination. In the final section of the novel Pagan plans to murder Lord Gadarene, an absentee landlord who is hitherto unknown to him, but he fails woefully in the attempt and returns to be reunited with and absolved by his dying estranged father. The novel introduces several more Scottish themes — Pagan's overbearing father is created in a similar mould to the monstrous father John Gourlay in George Douglas Brown's novel *The House with the Green Shutters* (1901), Brieston is the same grim west coast village in which John Macdougall Hay set his novel *Gillespie* (1914), and Gaderene's factor is called Sellar, the same name as the Duke of Sutherland's factor who gained notoriety during the nineteenth century Highland Clearances. However, Herdman is not merely paying obeisance to familiar Scottish tropes; rather he is intent on improving them and adapting them to his own account of one man's struggle to repossess his soul.

As a result, critics were divided in their response to *Pagan's Pilgrimage* and its genesis in Hogg's novel on which it was clearly based. Was

---

12 Herdman, *A Truth Lover*, p.82.
13 John Herdman, *Pagan's Pilgrimage*, Akros Publications, Preston, 1978, p.18.

Herdman writing homage or pastiche? Or was he indulging in parody to the detriment of his literary intention? In his review of the fiction of 1978, Professor Douglas Gifford was in no two minds that there had been a failure of nerve. Although he remained an admirer of Herdman's talent he felt that the stylistic approach detracted from the seriousness of intent. 'Herdman has tried to fuse his own vein of Clapperton-short-story humour with his Truth Lover seriousness, and the result is an interesting, sometimes very funny, failure.'[14] As a seasoned Hogg scholar Gifford could have been accused of pursuing his own agenda but he was right to find a link between the comic world inhabited by the hypochondriac Clapperton and the deadly seriousness of the moral predicament facing Duncan Straiton. In his study of modern Scottish literature Alan Bold takes a similar tack, seeing the central characters as deliberate caricatures so that 'the substance of Horatio Pagan's pilgrimage is his hilarious struggle with himself.'[15] Bold also recognised with grim satisfaction that Herdman's central character came from a long line of instantly recognisable Scottish failures who were none the less convinced of their own innate superiority and ability to turn the course of history.

None of this detracts from the fact that Herdman was addressing the issue of duality from two different backgrounds — the double as propounded by Dostoevsky and Gogol in the Russian literary tradition and its equivalent in Scotland as by exemplified Hogg in *The Private Memoirs and Confession of a Justified Sinner*, a complex work of diabolical possession , theological satire and local legend, in which evil is portrayed as inherent not in the sublimation of the will but in the corruption of religious doctrine. The story, which is set in the period just after the Act of Union of 1707 is told in three parts — the 'Editor's Narrative', 'The Private Memoirs and Confessions' and the 'Editor's Comments'.

The first part introduces two brothers — George Colwan, the son of the Laird of Dalcastle and Balgrennan and Robert, the supposed son of his mother's spiritual adviser the Revd Robert Wringhim who according to the boy's narrative 'took pity on me, admitting me not only into that [church visible], but into the bosom of his own household and ministry also, and to him am I indebted under heaven, for the high conceptions and glorious discernment between good and evil, right and

---

14 Douglas Gifford, 'Scottish Fiction 1978', *Studies in Scottish Literature 1978*, vol. 15, p.246.
15 Alan Bold, *Modern Scottish Literature*, Longman, Harlow, 1983, p.260.

wrong, which I attained at an early age.'[16] The brothers, who grow up apart, are constantly in conflict and are polar opposites in character, personality and beliefs. Their mutual antagonism culminates in George being murdered by an unknown assassin and when Robert is accused of fratricide he disappears and is 'lost once and for ever'. In the second part, the same story is told from Robert's point of view and emphasises the antinomian obsession that sins committed by an 'elect and justified' person cannot imperil the hope of salvation. Robert has reached this conclusion through the narrow Calvinistic teachings of his father aided and abetted by the promptings of Gil-Martin, a shadowy figure who is the Devil personified and he commits a number of crimes including the murder of his brother. At the end of this second part of the novel, still believing himself to be justified in his actions and haunted and taunted by Gil-Martin, he commits suicide, taking his memoir with him into the grave. Finally, in a short final section, the 'Editor' explains how he came into possession of the manuscript and ruminates on the circumstances of Robert's demise.

Before leaving Hogg's novel it is worth contemplating the figure of Gil-Martin who exists on two levels. First, he is the living incarnation of the Devil and therefore a figure to be feared; secondly, he is also an agent of evil capable of taking possession of young Robert's mind and causing him to turn to wickedness. He also possesses the chameleon-like ability to appear in the likeness of others, notably at different times in the forms of both brothers. This dualism between inner and outer reality leads Robert to believe himself to be two people, making the concept of a split personality the dominant theme of the novel. As the critic Kurt Wittig suggested in his study of the Scottish tradition in literature, this theme was taken up by another novelist Robert Louis Stevenson in his seminal work *The Strange Case of Dr Jekyll and Mr Hyde* (1866).[17] The central character, Dr Henry Jekyll is haunted by the consciousness of a dual identity within himself and experiments with a drug that will separate his personality into good and evil. The evil aspect, which is intended to absorb all his wicked instincts, is a hideous manifestation he calls Mr Edward Hyde and, in that guise, he begins to commit a number of crimes culminating in murder. Increasingly unable to control his metamorphoses, Jekyll finds Hyde becoming the

16 James Hogg, *The Private Memoirs and Confessions of a Justified Sinner*, with an introduction by Andre Gide, London, Cresset Press, 1965, p.90.
17 Kurt Wittig, *The Scottish Tradition in Literature*, Oliver & Boyd, Edinburgh and London, 1958, pp.249–250.

dominant character and to save himself from public exposure is forced to take his own life. The inspiration for Stevenson's use of the divided personality is supposed to have come from the true story of William Brodie, an eighteenth-century Edinburgh deacon who was a robber by night and an upright citizen by day.

Although Kurt Wittig did not mention it, the concept of the divided self was also adopted by John Buchan, who followed in Stevenson's footsteps, revealing a rare capacity to tell a historical story at a smart pace and with the minimum of what Stevenson called 'tushery' (affectedly archaic language). Stevenson died in 1894 just as Buchan was making his way in the world and carving a career as a writer while a postgraduate student at Oxford. Having to live off his pen he was extremely prolific and while he told his friend Charlie Dick that he was 'not going to write any more Scotch stories' his output proved otherwise and one result was the publication of *The Watcher by the Threshold*, a collection of five stories which he dedicated to Sandy Stair Gillon, an Oxford friend from Edinburgh, telling him that 'it is of the back-world of Scotland that I write, the land behind the mist and over the seven bens, a place hard of access for the foot-passenger but easy for the maker of stories.' The title story had already appeared *in Blackwood's Magazine* and although Buchan thought it 'horrible' he also told the publisher that it was an attempt 'to fit a sort of gruesome comedy to a particular type of Scotch moor'.[18]

In that guise many familiar Buchan motifs are present — the central character and narrator is Henry Grey, a successful London barrister equally at home on a Scottish sporting estate like the House of More where 'the shooting was good', the host Robert Ladlaw is 'a cheery, good-humoured fellow, a great sportsman, a justice of the peace and deputy-lieutenant' married to Henry's cousin Sybil — but beyond those familiar literary themes all is not what it seems. Henry has been invited to the House of More by Sybil who is worried by her husband's poor mental and physical health. From the outset Henry is appalled and worried by what he finds as Robert is a shadow of his former self and is clearly in low spirits. His condition is a reflection of the grim surroundings of his estate which Buchan describes in appalled detail: 'Framed in dank mysterious woods, and a country of coal and ironstone … it was a sullen relic of a lost barbarism.'[19] The exact location is never explained although Buchan hints that it is east of Perth which would

18 Quoted in Janet Adam Smith, *John Buchan*, London, 1965, p.102.
19 John Buchan, *The Watcher by the Threshold*, William Blackwood, Edinburgh and London, 1902, p.143.

take it into Angus or north Fife, neither of which seems likely from the description of the topography; in light of what transpires, the most probable setting is the county of Clackmannanshire which takes its name from Gaelic *chlach Mhannainn* 'stone of Manau' — Manau being the Brythonic name for the people inhabiting a province straddling the Forth, including much of modern Clackmannanshire. This is a far cry from the rolling hills of Galloway or the grandeur of Highland glens which form the backdrop to most of Buchan's fiction and the reason becomes partly clear at dinner when Robert explains his predicament as Henry takes stock of the changed surroundings within the house, once an untidy but companionable shooting lodge given over to field sports but now a mausoleum devoted to obscure classical studies and busts of Justinian who was also haunted by an evil being. But it is Robert's physical and mental state that cannot be ignored. Questioned by Henry, he is convinced that he is being haunted by an indistinct and voiceless spirit which clings to the left-hand side of his body and is connected in some untold way to the prehistoric Mannan or Manau people on whose land the House of More is built. Robert is a rational educated man, but he believes that 'some devilish occult force, lingering through the ages, had come to life after a long sleep.'[20]

Henry is uncomfortably aware of the danger facing his friend but the following day he is called back to a consultation in London and before leaving enlists the help of the local minister Bruce Oliphant, a sceptic who finds his faith threatened by the dilemma facing Robert Ladlaw. During Henry's brief absence matters move swiftly to a conclusion as Ladlaw takes flight across the moorland; with the help of estate workers Oliphant pursues him and finds the strength to cast out the spirit, setting Ladlaw free with the words, 'Lord, take the thing away! Get thee behind me, Satan!'

> And then something happened which was the crowning marvel of the business. It was a still sharp day; but suddenly there came a wind, hot and harsh, and like nothing they had ever known. It stung them like nettles, played for a moment in their midst, and then in a kind of visible cloud passed away from them over the bog in the direction of the Red Loch. And with the wind went the Thing which had so long played havoc in the place …[21]

---

20 Ibid, p.165.
21 Ibid, p.201.

This is not the Devil of folk literature, far less the bagpiping bogle of Robert Burns's 'Tam O'Shanter', but, as Ladlaw tells Henry, this is the 'visible, personal Devil in whom our fathers believed'.[22] Its presence on the Scottish moor is enough to shake Henry and Oliphant out of their earlier complacency and both are changed ineradicably by the experience. Like Gil-Martin it also has a physical presence — one of the attendant gamekeepers is aware of a creature with a huge arm which 'flew out like a steam-hammer' bowling him over and knocking out teeth — but the real evil lies in this Devil's ability to subvert and control Ladlaw, just as Wringhim was subverted and controlled by Gil-Martin. And returning to Stevenson, just as Jekyll was subverted and controlled by Hyde. Equally significant is the fact that Ladlaw's Devil infiltrates the left-hand side of his body, just as Herdman's Duncan Straiton likens his obsession to a 'burrowing beast'.

In that respect John Herdman stands firmly in the tradition of Scottish literature's fixation with the duality of man's nature and the origins of the nature of evil. Not only has he investigated the process in his study of the nineteenth century example, but he has also contributed to it in his own fiction, thereby emerging as one of the most significant Scottish writers of his generation.

---

22 Ibid, p.160.

Walter Perrie, Two Poems

Winter Walk

See, now the wintering birds are here, waxwing, fieldfare,
snipe, vociferous geese, they promise we are halfway to
spring when, summoned by light, they will disappear
north to pair, feed, breed in their unshattered blue
as they sang, bred, fed before our foolish sapiens was here.

Too swift and southing soon our cuckoo summers go:
the hardy stay, berry-full robin and wren prepare
for hard times. We too can squirrel our winters away,
harvesting memory, line a storm-spared mossy store
with stories, affections, snug spaces to hang-up a rainbow.

For John Herdman

May bright holy days delight you
moons incite you
stars invite you
dark affright nor illness blight you
devils bite you
slander slight you
                 as you play.

Let no enmities detain you
rage arraign you
fears enchain you
pride nor avarice entrain you
sloth restrain you
envy gain you
                 day by day.

May the Host of Saints defend you
friends attend you
Heaven send you
tears and laughter to extend you
fortune friend you
angels mend you
                 on the way.

Walter Perrie

The Faces

John Herdman

I was distraught. I had not slept for two nights — I believe almost not at all.

On the third night, soon after I had closed my eyes, faces began to appear. They were small, clear-cut like cameos, very exact. They emerged from a generalised dark and cloudy background, and I was aware that a large number were simultaneously present, although I could focus on only one at a time. When I did so it persisted for only a few seconds, to be replaced instantly by another. This was frustrating because I wanted to take a good look at each one of them, to see if any were recognisable. They were fully individualised faces, not stylised, not caricatures. They looked like real people who might walk on earth. Their features reflected powerful passions, good and ill, but these were not connected to myself. Their multiplicity astonished me. They were old and young, male and female, dark and fair; all retained their unique individuality for those few seconds of their persistence, and all were preternaturally vivid; yet I could hold on to none of them.

As soon as I opened my eyes, although the room was dark, the astonishing parade vanished; I felt entirely normal although I was exhausted: my thoughts and senses functioned as they should. As soon as I closed my eyes once more, the faces returned as before. These sharply-etched features were most unusually full of character, as if they lived more intensely than others. No two were the same, yet the images replaced each other with unfailing rapidity and resource. From what inexhaustible reservoir were they drawn, what superhuman artist fashioned them? Did they arise from within the unfathomable matter of my own brain, or were they received by my mind from some unknowable, unsounded fount of creation?

For a long time this odd peep-show continued to reproduce itself. But at last I fell asleep.

John Herdman: Bibliography

- *Descent* (Fiery Star Press, Edinburgh, 1968).
- *A Truth Lover* (Akros Publications, Preston, 1973).
- *Memoirs of my Aunt Minnie / Clapperton* (Rainbow Books, Aberdeen, 1974).
- *Pagan's Pilgrimage* (Akros Publications, Preston, 1978).
- *Stories Short and Tall* (Caithness Books, Thurso, 1979).
- *Voice Without Restraint: Bob Dylan's Lyrics and their Background* (Paul Harris Publishing, Edinburgh, 1982; Delilah Books, New York, 1982; (Japanese translation) CBS/Sony Publishing, Tokyo, 1983).
- *Three Novellas* (Polygon Books, Edinburgh, 1987).
- *The Double in Nineteenth-Century Fiction* (The Macmillan Press, London, 1990; St Martin's Press, New York, 1991).
- *Imelda and Other Stories* (Polygon, Edinburgh, 1993).
- *Ghostwriting* (Polygon, Edinburgh, 1996).
- *Cruising: A Play in Two Acts* (diehard publishers, Edinburgh, 1997).
- *Poets, Pubs, Polls and Pillar Boxes* (Akros Publications, Kirkcaldy, 1999).
- *Four Tales*, with an introduction by Macdonald Daly (Zoilus Press, London, 2000).
- *The Sinister Cabaret* (Black Ace Books, Forfar, 2001).
- *Triptych: Three Tales* (Fras Publications, Blair Atholl, 2004).
- *Imelda*, trans. into French with a postface by Maïca Sanconie (Quidam Editeur, Paris, 2006).
- *My Wife's Lovers: Ten Tales* (Black Ace Books, Perth, 2007).
- *Some Renaissance Culture Wars* (Fras Publications, Blair Atholl, 2010).
- *Another Country* (Thirsty Books, Edinburgh, 2013).
- *Imelda*, trans. into Italian by Valentina Poggi (*Scritture d'Oltremanica* 13) (Aracne editrice, Canterano, 2017).
- *La Confession*, translation into French by Maïca Sanconie of *Ghostwriting* with a postface by Jean Berton (Quidam Editeur, Paris, 2018).
- *Imelda* (Leamington Books [Gothic World Literature

Editions], Edinburgh, 2020).

- *Clapperton*, with *The Devil and Dr Tuberose* (Leamington Books [Gothic World Literature Editions], Edinburgh, 2020).
- *Ghostwriting* (Leamington Books [Gothic World Literature Editions], Edinburgh, 2021).
- *Voice Without Restraint: Bob Dylan's Lyrics 1961–1979* (Leamington Books [The Magic Road], Edinburgh, 2021).

Edited:

- *Third Statistical Account of Scotland*:
  Vol. XXIII, The County of Berwick (Scottish Academic Press, Edinburgh, 1992).
  Vol. XXVIII, The County of Roxburgh (Scottish Academic Press, Edinburgh, 1992).
- *Move Up, John*, by Fionn MacColla (Canongate, Edinburgh, 1994).

Articles, essays, reviews and contributions to journals (excluding letters to the press):

- 'Rat's Progress' (short story), *Plain Words*, Cambridge, June 1961.
- 'Using the Enemy's Weapons' (article), *Catalyst*, Spring 1969.
- 'Literature and National Self-Confidence' (article), *Catalyst*, Autumn 1969.
- 'Hugh MacDiarmid as Essayist' (review article), *Akros* 14, April 1970.
- Editorial Comment, *Catalyst*, Spring 1970.
- 'Self-Determination?' (article), under pseudonym 'Tom Anderson', *Catalyst*, Spring 1970.
- Review of *The Serpent*, Neil M. Gunn, *Catalyst*, Spring 1970.
- 'Snawed Up' (poem), *Scotia* 5, May 1970.
- 'The Death of the Anglo-Saxon Idea' (article), in *The Celt in the Seventies*, Annual Volume of the Celtic League for 1970.
- Editorial Comment, *Catalyst*, Summer 1970.
- 'Centah of the Empah' (verse), under pseudonym 'Tom Anderson', *Catalyst*, Summer 1970.
- Review of *The Scottish Insurrection of 1820*, P. Beresford Ellis

and Seumas Mac a' Ghobhainn, *Catalyst*, Summer 1970.

- Review of *The Penguin Book of Scottish Verse*, ed. Tom Scott, *Catalyst*, Summer 1970.
- 'Scottish Poetry, 1959–1969' (review article), *Akros* 15, August 1970. 'A Fever Image' (prose poem), *Scotia* 11, Nov. 1970.
- 'The World of D. M. Black' (article), *Scottish International* 13, Feb. 1971.
- 'Against Comfort' (article), *Knowe* 2, Feb. 1971.
- 'Towards New Jerusalem: The Poetry of Tom Scott' (article), *Akros* 16, April 1971.
- 'The Condition of Prose' (article), *Knowe* 3, April 1971.
- 'James Hogg and his Reputation' (article), *Scotia* 16, April 1971.
- Letter to the Editor, *Akros* 17, July 1971.
- Review of *Scottish Short Stories 1800–1900*, ed. Douglas Gifford, *Scottish International*, August 1971.
- 'Politics III' (essay), in *Whither Scotland?*, ed. Duncan Glen, Gollancz, London, August 1971.
- Letter on Alan Jackson's 'The Knitted Claymore', supplement to *Lines Review* 38, Sept. 1971.
- 'Gaucho Verse' (article), *Scotia* 21, Sept. 1971.
- 'Tearan Raip' (poem), *Scotia* 23, Nov. 1971.
- 'Sharp's Trilogy So Far' (article), *Scottish International*, Jan. 1972.
- Review of *Collected Poems*, Helen B. Cruickshank, *Agenda*, Autumn/Winter 1971/72.
- Review of *The Albannach*, Fionn Mac Colla, *Lines Review* 41, July 1972.
- 'Addict' (prose piece), *Scotia Review* 1, August 1972.
- 'Clapperton: A Day in His Existence' (short story), *Scottish International*, Nov. 1972.
- Review of three books by George Mackay Brown, *Lines Review* 42/43, Sept./Feb. 1972/73.
- 'The Progress of Scots' (article), *Akros* 20, December 1972.
- 'Twenty Numbers of *Akros*' (article), *Akros* 21, April 1973.
- 'An Aspect of Fionn Mac Colla as Novelist' (essay), in *Essays on Fionn Mac Colla*, ed. David Morrison, Caithness Books, Thurso, May 1973.
- 'A View of the Conference' (article), *Scottish International*,

May/July 1973.

- 'The Sugar Plum Revelation' (short story), *Scotia Review* 3, June 1973.
- 'A Paragon of Falsehood' (extract from *A Truth Lover*), *Scotia Review* 3, June 1973.
- Obituary of Stuart MacGregor (unsigned), *Scotia Review* 3, June 1973.
- Review of *The Three Perils of Man*, James Hogg, ed. D. Gifford, *Lines Review* 45, June 1973.
- Review of *Neil M. Gunn: The Man and the Writer*, ed. D. Gifford and A. Scott, *Lines Review* 45, June 1973.
- 'Stobs Camp' (prose piece), *Scottish International*, Nov. 1973.
- 'Doomwatch' (prose piece), *Scotia Review* 6, April 1974.
- 'John Davidson in Full' (review article), *Akros* 25, August 1974.
- Notice of *A Cled Score*, Duncan Glen, *Scots Independent*, July 1974.
- 'Watchdog Speaks Out' (prose piece), *Scotia Review* 7, August 1974.
- 'Three Tribes' (short story), *Akros* 26, Dec. 1974.
- Review of *Poems by Allan Ramsay and Robert Fergusson*, ed. A. Kinghorn and A. Law, *Akros* 26, Dec. 1974.
- 'Silage' (short story), *Scotia Review* 8, Dec. 1974.
- 'Scene in a Department Store' (short story), *Scotia Review* 8 Dec. 1974.
- Review of *Mercier and Camier*, Samuel Beckett, *Calgacus* 1, Winter 1974.
- 'Time Pieces' (prose piece), *Scotia Review* 10, August 1975.
- 'Fionn Mac Colla's Last Book' (review article), *Scotia Review* 10, August 1975.
- 'Scenario for a Dog-Fight' (prose piece), *Scotia Review* 11, Dec. 1975.
- 'A True Story' (prose piece), *Scotia Review* 11, Dec. 1975.
- 'The Decline and Folly of Inspector Banal' (short story), *Scotia Review* 11, Dec. 1975.
- Article in 'Writers and Education' series, *Scottish Educational Journal*, 16 Jan. 1976.
- Review of *Kafka in Context*, John Hibberd, *Calgacus* 3, Spring 1976.

- Three Short Notices, *Calgacus* 3, Spring 1976.
- 'Attitudes to Bob Dylan' (article), *Akros* 30, April 1976.
- 'Aesthetics and a Sense of Proportion' (essay), *Chapman*, Vol. 4, No. 3, June 1976.
- Review of four 'Parklands Poets' pamphlets, *Akros* 31, August 1976.
- 'Diary of an Unrepentant Goose' (prose piece), *Ferment* 1, Sept. 1976.
- 'Tom Scott's translations from the French' (article), *Scotia Review* 13/14, Aug./Nov. 1976.
- Extract from *Risk* (unpublished novel), *Akros* 32, Dec. 1976.
- Review of *A Book of Men*, Catherine Lucy Czerkawska, *Akros* 32, Dec. 1976.
- Extract from a novel (i.e. *Pagan's Pilgrimage*), *Chapman* 17, Dec. 1976.
- Review of *Modern Scottish Poetry*, ed. Maurice Lindsay, *Akros* 33, April 1977.
- 'The Previously Unpublished Novels of David Lindsay' (review article), *Scottish Literary Journal*, Suppl. No. 3, Winter 1976.
- 'Scots to the Backbone' (essay), in *Jock Tamson's Bairns*, ed. Trevor Royle, Hamish Hamilton, London, 23 June 1977.
- 'Sorley MacLean: A Non-Gael's View' (essay), *Lines Review* 61, June 1977.
- 'Hugh MacDiarmid's *To Circumjack Cencrastus*' (essay), *Akros* 34/35, August 1977.
- 'A Basket of Baby Frogs' (short story), *Words* 3, Summer 1977.
- 'I am a Failure' (short story), *Scotia Review* 17, Summer 1977.
- 'Fionn Mac Colla: The Unpublished Work' (article), *Brunton's Miscellany*, Vol. 1, No. 1, Autumn 1977.
- 'Childhood and Youth' (abridged extract from *Pagan's Pilgrimage*), *The Sou'Wester* No. 1, March 1978.
- 'Fates' (prose piece), in *Our Duncan Who Art in Trent*, Harris Press, Preston, April 1978.
- 'Comedian' (prose piece), *Gallimaufry* No. 5, Spring 1978.
- 'The Emperor Bolingbroke III' (short story), *Words* 5, Spring 1978.
- Review of *The Socialist Poems of Hugh MacDiarmid*, ed. T.S. Law and Thurso Berwick, *New Edinburgh Review*, Autumn 1978.

- 'The Trouble with that Fellow' (prose piece), *A.M.F.* No. 2, March 1979.
- 'The Novelist in Scotland' (article), *Akros* 41, August 1979.
- Review of *The Ministers*, Fionn Mac Colla, *Akros* 41, August 1979.
- 'The Tweak' (short story), *Words* 8, Autumn 1979.
- 'Day at the Zoo' (prose piece), *Story & Stanza* 9, Autumn 1979.
- Review of *Gravitations*, David Black, *Chapman* 25, Autumn 1979.
- Review of *Going Blind*, Jonathan Penner, *University of Edinburgh Journal*, Vol. XXIX, No. 2, Dec. 1979.
- 'Dealing with a Bore' (short story), *Words* 9, Winter 1979–80.
- 'How I Ruined my Career' (short story), *A.M.F.* 4, Spring 1980.
- 'A Practical Joke' (short story), *Chapman* 26, Spring 1980.
- Review of *The South American Sketches of R.B. Cunninghame Graham*, ed. J. Walker, *Scottish Literary Journal* Suppl. No. 12, Spring/Summer 1980.
- Review of *Snobs' Island*, Henrik Tikkanen, *Cencrastus* 4, Winter 1980–81.
- Review of *Scottish Short Stories 1980*, *Words* 11/12 (Review Supplement), May 1981.
- Review of *Lamb*, Bernard MacLaverty, *Words* 11/12 (Review Supplement), May 1981.
- 'Original Sin' (short story), *Chapman* 31, Winter 1981–82.
- Review of *The Life and Works of David Lindsay*, Bernard Sellin, *Cencrastus* 8, Spring 1982.
- 'So It Was' (prose piece), in *Ambages Pulcerrime*, Stourton Press, London, August 1982.
- Review of *Chronicle of a Death Foretold*, Gabriel García Márquez, *Cencrastus* 11, Jan. 1983.
- 'Fionn Mac Colla: Art and Ideas' (article), *Cencrastus* 13, Summer 1983.
- 'Muir, Scotland, Drink and Free-Will' (review article), *Chapman* 35/36, July 1983.
- Note on Sorley MacLean's 'Calbharaigh', *Akros* 51, Oct. 1983.
- Review of *The Terrible Crystal*, Alan Bold, *Lines Review* 87, Dec. 1983.

- 'Volcanic' (review of *The Thistle Rises*, H. MacDiarmid, ed. A. Bold etc.), *New Statesman*, 15 June 1984.
- 'Battle Stations' (review of *The Letters of Hugh MacDiarmid*, ed. A. Bold), *New Statesman*, 5 Oct. 1984.
- 'Five Meditations' (prose poems), *Scotia Rampant* 1, Feb. 1985.
- 'The Truth in the Missing File' (article on Bob Dylan), *The Telegraph* No. 22, Winter 1985.
- 'Metaphor and Mortality' (review article on Norman MacCaig), *Scotia Rampant* 5, Feb. 1986.
- Extract from 'The Previously Unpublished Novels of David Lindsay' (review article), reprinted in *Twentieth Century Literary Criticism*, Vol. XV, Gale Research Co., Detroit, 1985 or 1986.
- 'The Ghost Seen by the Soul' (essay), in *Sorley MacLean: Critical Essays*, ed. Raymond J. Ross and Joy Hendry, Scottish Academic Press, Edinburgh, Oct. 1986.
- 'The Atholl Country Collection' (article), *Scottish Home and Country*, June 1987.
- 'It Ain't Him, Babe' (article on Bob Dylan), *Glasgow Herald*, 10 Oct. 1987.
- 'Acquainted with Grief' (short story), *Glasgow Herald*, 21 May 1988.
- Review of *Hugh MacDiarmid: A Critical Biography*, Alan Bold, *Chapman* 55–56, Spring 1989.
- 'Clapperton', in *The Devil and the Giro: Two Centuries of Scottish Stories*, ed. Carl MacDougall, Canongate, Edinburgh, 15 June 1989.
- 'The Devil and Dr Tuberose' (short story), *Chapman* 58, Autumn 1989.
- 'The Devil and Dr Tuberose', *Beloit Fiction Journal* (Wisconsin), Vol. 5, No. 1 (Scottish Writers), Fall 1989.
- 'Too Much and Too Many' (article), *Glasgow Herald*, 11 August 1990.
- *The Day I Met the Queen Mother* (short story), as title story of *New Writing Scotland* 8, ASLS, Oct. 1990.
- 'A Few Spoonfuls of Pap to Help the Sugar Go Down' (article), *Glasgow Herald*, 24 Oct. 1990.
- Review of *Vladimir Nabokov: The Russian Years*, Brian Boyd,

and The Russian Chronicles, *Scotland on Sunday*, 18 Nov. 1990.

- 'Old Magicians and a Romance of the Dour' (reviews of R. Jenkins, G. Mackay Brown, T. McEwen), *Cencrastus* 38, Winter 1990–91.

- *The Devil and Dr Tuberose*, as title story of *Scottish Short Stories 1991*, HarperCollins, London, August 1991.

- Review of *Vladimir Nabokov: the American Years*, Brian Boyd, *Scotland on Sunday*, 12 Jan. 1992.

- 'Thistles that Have to be Grasped' (article), *Glasgow Herald*, 11 April 1992.

- Review of *Selected Poems*, Duncan Glen, *Lines Review* 121, June 1992.

- Review of *Devolving English Literature*, Robert Crawford, *Lines Review* 122, Sept. 1992.

- Open letter, *Chapman* 69–70 (MacDiarmid Centenary Issue), Autumn 1992.

- Review of *Mirror and Marble*, Carol Gow, *Lines Review* 124, March 1993.

- 'A Time to Restore Our Disrupted Unity' (article), *The Herald*, 19 June 1993.

- 'The Disappearance of Ludmill Johnson' (short story), *Northwords* 3, June 1993.

- Review of *The Great Shadow House*, J. B. Pick, and *Places of the Mind*, Tom Leonard, *Chapman* 74–75, Autumn/Winter 1993.

- 'The Trials of Fionn' (article), *Weekend Scotsman*, 12 March 1994.

- Review of *The Oxford Companion to Twentieth-Century Poetry*, ed. Ian Hamilton, *Lines Review* 129, June 1994.

- Extract from *The Double in Nineteenth-Century Fiction*, reprinted in *Nineteenth Century Literature Criticism*, Vol. 40, Gale Research Co., Detroit, 1993.

- Introduction to *And the Cock Crew*, Fionn MacColla, Canongate Classics, Edinburgh, April 1995.

- Review of *Scotland – the Brand*, David McCrone, etc., *The Herald*, 20 May 1995.

- Review of *Fool's Pardon*, Harry Smart, *Lines Review* 133, July 1995.

- 'Scenario for a Dog-Fight', reprinted in *Norman MacCaig: A Celebration*, Chapman Publishing, Nov. 1995.

- Review of *The Poetry of Scotland*, ed. Roderick Watson, *Lines Review* 135, Dec. 1995.
- 'Memories of Tom Scott' (note), *Scotia Rampant* 21, Winter 1995–96.
- Extract from *Cruising* (play), *Scotia Rampant* 21, Winter 1995–96.
- 'The Life of Torquil Tod' (extract from *Ghostwriting*), *Scotsman Weekend*, 20 April 1996.
- Review of *The Hurt World*, ed. M. Parker, and Voices from a Far Country, Hugh Carr, *Edinburgh Review* 95, July 1996.
- 'The Evil that Men Write' (article), *The Herald*, 16 Nov. 1996.
- Review of *Sing Frae the Hert: the Literary Criticism of Alexander Scott*, ed. Neil R. MacCallum, *Scots Independent*, Dec. 1996.
- 'Horses' (prose poem), *Scotia Review* 22, Spring 1997.
- Review of *Melodrama*, Alan Mason, *The Herald*, 19 April 1997.
- 'Original Sin', reprinted in *The Picador Book of Contemporary Scottish Fiction*, ed. Peter Kravitz, Picador, London, August 1997.
- Review of *The Summer is Ended*, Kenneth C. Steven, *The Herald*, 26 February 1998.
- 'Novelist's Labyrinth' (review article on *Succeeding at Sex and Scotland*, Hunter Steele), *Scottish Book Collector*, Vol. 6, No. 1, Summer 1998.
- Review of *The Summer is Ended*, Kenneth C. Steven, reprinted in *The Month*, July 1998.
- Introduction to *Selected Scottish and Other Essays*, Duncan Glen, Akros Publications, Kirkcaldy, March 1999.
- 'Sic Transit Gloria' (short story), in *The Keekin-Gless: An Anthology from Perth and Kinross*, ed. Robert Alan Jamieson and Carl MacDougall, Perth and Kinross Libraries, 31 March 1999.
- Review of, *The Raucle Tongue: Hitherto Uncollected Prose*, Vol. III, Hugh MacDiarmid, ed. A. Calder, G. Murray and A. Riach, *Zed 2 O* No. 12, Autumn 1999.
- *Sic Transit Gloria* (short story), as pamphlet, Scotia Review Publications, Wick, Feb. 2000.
- Extract from *Imelda*, in *Figures of Speech: An Anthology of Magdalene Writers*, ed. M. E. J. Hughes, John Mole and Nick

Seddon, Magdalene College, Cambridge, November 2000.
- 'Well Pressed' (review article on *Caryddwen's Cauldron*, Paul Hilton, and *Unbelievable Things*, Ellis Sharp), *Scottish Book Collector* 6:11, Winter 2000–01.
- 'William Neill: Cultural Freedom Fighter' (article), *Scotia Review* 24, Summer 2001.
- 'The Decline and Folly of Inspector Banal', reprinted in *Labyrinths* 3, July 2001.
- 'Entering Other Worlds' (article), *Scottish Book Collector* 7:3, Spring 2002.
- 'The Incalculable' (short story), *Chapman* 100–101, Summer 2002.
- 'Ben Despair Lodge' (extract from *The Sinister Cabaret*), in *The Lie of the Land*, ed. Brian McCabe et al., Perth and Kinross Libraries, August 2004.
- Article on Thomas Douglas MacDonald ('Fionn Mac Colla'), in *Oxford Dictionary of National Biography*, ed. Colin Matthew and Brian Harrison, Oxford University Press, Oxford, 23 Sept. 2004.
- Introduction to *Decagon*, Walter Perrie, Fras Publications, Blair Atholl, Oct. 2004.
- 'The Day I Met the Queen Mother', reprinted in *Bringing Back Some Brightness: 20 Years of New Writing Scotland* (*New Writing Scotland* 22), ed. Valerie Thornton and Hamish Whyte, ASLS, December 2004.
- Review of *Grounding a World: Essays on the Work of Kenneth White*, ed. G. Bowd, C.Forsdick, N. Bissell, *Markings* 19, July 2005.
- 'My Wife's Lovers' (short story), *Fras* 3, Autumn 2005.
- 'The Monkey' (short story), *The London Magazine*, December 2005 / January 2006.
- 'The Russian Double' (extract from *The Double in Nineteenth-Century Fiction*), reprinted in *Short Story Criticism*, Vol. 44, Thomson Gale, Michigan, 2005–06.
- Interview with John Herdman, in *Scottish Writers Talking* 3, ed. Isobel Murray, John Donald, Edinburgh, May 2006.
- 'Cambridge Education and a Scottish Writer' (article), *Cambridge* No. 59, New Year 2007.
- Note on Fras Publications, *Sphinx* No. 6, Spring 2007.

- 'Vindolanda' (prose piece), *Fras* 6, Spring 2007.
- 'Ewes Too: The Legacy of James Hogg' (review article on *James Hogg: A Life* by Gillian Hughes), *Scottish Review of Books*, Vol. 3, No. 4, 18th November 2007.
- 'Duncan Glen as Fiction Publisher', in *A Festschrift for Duncan Glen at Seventy-five*, ed. T. Hubbard and P. Pacey, Craigarter Press, Kirkcaldy, 2008.
- 'The Double in Decline' (extract from *The Double in Nineteenth-Century Fiction*), reprinted in *Nineteenth Century Literature Criticism*, Vol. 192, Gale, Cengage Learning, 2008.
- 'The Challenge of Limitation: William Soutar's Diaries of a Dying Man' (article), *Fras* 9, Autumn 2008.
- Introduction to *Johnny Aathin* by William Hershaw, Windfall Books, Kelty, August 2009.
- 'On the Water' (translation of 'Sur l'Eau' by Guy de Maupassant), *Fras* 12, Spring 2010.
- 'Some Other Kinds of Poems' (chapter from *Voice Without Restraint*), reprinted in *The Mammoth Book of Bob Dylan*, ed. Sean Egan, Robinson, London, May 2011.
- 'Zeep: A Master of Language' (prose piece), *One O' Clock Gun* No.20, March 2014.
- 'Self-Interest and Self-Determination' (essay), *Fras* 20, May 2014.
- 'The Devil and Dr Tuberose', reprinted in *The Uncanny Reader: Stories from the Shadows*, ed. Marjorie Sandor, St Martin's Press, New York, February 2015.
- 'The Bed' (translation of 'Le Lit' by Guy de Maupassant), *Fras* 24, January 2016.
- 'The Auld Fellae' (short story), *One O' Clock Gun* No. 22, January 2016.
- 'Mad?' (translation of 'Fou?' by Guy de Maupassant), *Fras* 25, May 2016.
- Review of *Determination*, Robin McAlpine, *Bella Caledonia* (online), 22 September 2016.
- 'The Chink Between the Shutters' (prose piece), *One O' Clock Gun* No. 23, November 2016.
- 'The Heretics: A Documentary Record' (article), *One O' Clock Gun* No. 24, August 2017.
- Note on Stuart MacGregor, *One O' Clock Gun* No. 24, August 2017.

- Review of *Hamilton 1967*, James Mitchell, *Bella Caledonia* (online), 15 January 2018.
- Foreword to *Literary Corstorphine*, Raymond MacKean Bell, the Author, Edinburgh, 2017.
- 'Donald Campbell: An Appreciation', *One O' Clock Gun* No. 26, April 2019.
- 'The Log' (translation of 'La Bûche' by Guy de Maupassant), *Fras* 32, August 2019.
- 'My Stone' (prose poem), *Fras* 34, October 2020.
- 'The Skein' (prose poem), *Fras* 34, October 2020.
- 'The Real Thing: Donald Campbell' (essay), *Fras* 34, October 2020.
- 'Mag Memories' (article), published as an online blog by Scottish Magazines Network, Stirling University, June 2021.

Acknowledgements

Special thanks to Jennie Renton for helping us collate and arrange this varied and wonderful selection of items, for typesetting and providing the book with its finish. Thanks also go to Ambrose Kelly and Josh Andrew for their editorial input, and to photographers Ryan McGoverne, Robin Gillanders and Gordon Wright.

Previously Published ...

James Aitchison — 'Mossmen' first published in *Edges* (Mica Press, 2020).

Margaret Bennett — 'Being Scottish ...' A version was first published in *BEING SCOTTISH: Personal Reflections on Scottish Identity Today* eds. Tom Devine and Paddy Logue, Edinburgh, EUP & Polygon, 2002.

Ron Butlin — 'Beethoven and the Hanging Gardens of Neglect' first published in *Vivaldi & the Number 3* (Serpent's Tail, 2003).

Regi Claire — 'When Our Lives Begin' was first published in *Litro Online*, #FlashFriday, 27 April 2018 and subsequently republished in *The Middle of a Sentence*, The Common Breath, 2020.

Macdonald Daly — a version of this interview first appeared in *Southfields*, six point one, 1999 (pp.85–101).

John Herdman — 'My Stone' and 'The Skein' first appeared online at *The Lyrical Aye* (May 2020) and then published in print in *Fras Magazine* (2020).

Angus Martin — 'In Each Secret Place' first appeared in *The Silent Hollow* (published by the author, 2005).

Jonathan Penner – 'Joseph's Feet' was first published in *Colorado Review* (Fall, 1995) and subsequently included in the author's story collection *This Is My Voice* (Eastern Washington University Press, 2003).